Dr. Nazir Khan

For every child
in Gaza whose smile
was stolen by the cruelty
of oppressors. For every person of
conscience who yearns for a just future.
May Allah guide us all upon the straight path.

The Straight Path: How *Sūrah al-Fātiḥah* addresses modern ideologies

First published in England by
Kube Publishing Ltd
Markfield Conference Centre
Ratby Lane, Markfield
Leicestershire, LE67 9SY
United Kingdom
Tel: +44 (0) 1530 249230
Website: www.kubepublishing.com
Email: info@kubepublishing.com

 Cataloguing-in-Publication Data is available from the British Library.

ISBN 978-1-83592-021-3 Casebound
Proofreading and editing: Yaqeen Institute
Design, typesetting and Arabic calligraphy: Jannah Haque
Printed by: IMAK Ofset, Turkey.

Contents

Author biography

Dr. Nazir Khan MD FRCPC is a medical doctor, clinical neuroscientist, Islamic theologian, and specialist in Qur'anic sciences. He is an assistant professor at McMaster University and a doctoral candidate in Islamic theology at the University of Nottingham. He memorised the Qur'an during his youth, has certifications (*ijāzāt*) in all ten readings of the Qur'an through both major and minor routes of transmission, and has also received certifications in the six books of Hadith as well as numerous works of Islamic theology. He has served as a volunteer imam for many years. He is also a consultant for the Manitoba Islamic Association Fiqh Committee. Following medical school at McMaster University, he completed his residency in Diagnostic Radiology at the University of Manitoba and his fellowship in Neuroradiology at the University of Calgary with dual-board certification. His expertise in both medical sciences and Islamic theology uniquely positions him to address challenging contemporary questions regarding faith, reason, and science. He is a Senior Fellow at Yaqeen Institute and served as the founding President of Yaqeen Institute in Canada.

Author's acknowledgements

In preparing this book for publication, I am indebted to the wonderful team at Yaqeen Institute for their tireless work and support. I would particularly like to thank Dr. Ovamir Anjum, Shaykh Ismail Kamdar, Dr. Julio Rivera, Dr. Nameera Akhtar, and Jannah Haque. I have also benefited from the meticulous feedback of several peer reviewers, including Shaykh Yousef Wahb, Imam Tom Facchine, Dr. Carl Sharif El-Tobgui, Dr. Tallal Zeni, Dr. Zohair Abdul-Rahman, Dr. Ammar Khatib, and Shaykh Suleiman Hani.

Last but not least, this project would not have been possible without the unwavering support of my dear family. Thank you to my parents, Dr. Aliya Aziz Khan and Dr. Viqar Khan, for your love and guidance, and for being my greatest inspiration. Thank you to my wife, Amal, for all your encouragement, patience, and dedication.

أعوذ بالله من الشيطان الرجيم

al-Istiʿādhah

I seek refuge in Allah from Satan, the expelled

Foreword

By Imam Tom Facchine

Dr. Nazir Khan's timely book *The Straight Path* proceeds from the bold and astute observation that the solutions to the current crises facing Muslims and the entire world will not be found in obscure theories or future inventions, but rather in the Divine Scripture most Muslims recite without a second thought. The existential threats to our material and spiritual existence, rooted in ideological deviance, can be dismantled brick by brick with the same simple chapter of the Qur'an that children learn in their earliest years and that Muslims recite at least 17 times each day, *Sūrah al-Fātiḥah*.

Taking this proposition in earnest, the same analysis can be applied to the phrase with which we begin every recitation of the Qur'an: *Aʿūdhu bi-llāhi min al-shayṭāni al-rajīm* ("I seek refuge in Allah from Satan, the expelled," a phrase referred to as the *istiʿādhah* (seeking refuge). The basis for this practice is Allah's statement, "So when you recite the Qur'an, seek refuge in Allah from Satan, the expelled" (Qur'an 16:98).

Before reciting the Qur'an every Muslim is commanded by Allah to first seek refuge in Him. The comprehensiveness of Islam is on display here, leaving no stone unturned. Allah not only gives us a Qur'an to recite and ponder upon, He also gives us instructions for how to read it appropriately within the Qur'an itself. In order to benefit from the Qur'an's guidance, we need to deliberately seek Allah's protection from the satanic forces of evil that aim to divert us from this guidance. Part of embracing the Islamic worldview is to seek to protect our beliefs from ideological misguidance.

The *"fa"* with which verse 16:98 begins indicates a connection to the previous verse in which Allah says, "Whoever does righteousness, whether male or female, while he is a believer—We will surely cause him to live a good life, and We will surely give them their reward [in the Hereafter] according to the best of what they used to do" (Qur'an 16:97).

The implication here is that reciting the Qur'an is not only an act of righteousness; it is also one of the best things a believer can do.

By saying "when you recite" and not "if you recite," Allah alludes to the fact that the recitation of the Qur'an is an essential practice of Islam, one diagnostically constitutive of a believer. In our age, which is dominated by identitarian affiliations bereft of substance, Allah provides us with a way to make good on our claim to Islam. It is not enough that we identify as Muslims; reciting the Qur'an and actualizing its message in our lives makes us identifiable as such.

But the sacred, essential act of reciting the Qur'an can still be corrupted by pride or ill intentions. The external practice is not sound, acceptable, or virtuous without the proper inward demeanor and reverence, necessitating our internal purification. Is this in our power? Can we achieve the necessary inner state through sheer willpower alone? Never; through the *isti'ādhah* we recognise and confess Allah's unique ability to protect us inwardly and outwardly. We put ourselves in the position of Prophet Sulayman, who was grateful for Allah's bounty, yet recognised that even that gratitude was a favour of Allah's endless grace (Qur'an 27:19).

The nemesis we seek Allah's protection from is the accursed Devil, a recognition of the ontological and cosmological fact of evil and evil forces. And yet we are implicitly reminded in this act of *istiʿādhah* that Allah's protection is impregnable and unassailable. Evil is no match for Allah whatsoever. This implication is rendered explicit in the verse, "Indeed, there is no authority for him over those who have believed and rely upon their Lord. His authority is only over those who take him as an ally and those who, through him, associate others with Allah" (Qur'an 16:99–100).

Here we have an immediate reminder as to the actual scope and power of evil. It is not an overpowering force that rivals the Divine, it is merely a suggestive and alluring trap to which our lower proclivities occasionally succumb. This places Islam squarely between materialism on the one hand, which is oblivious to the realities and dangers of evil, and those religions that exaggerate the powers of evil, on the other.

This type of reading is essential for the needs of today. At Yaqeen Institute, the department on Islam and Society focuses on how the Islamic worldview is relevant in answering questions that arise in contemporary thought. I hope that with *The Straight Path* we see not just a new work, but a new genre teasing out the conceptual implications of Allah's perfect guidance to all mankind.

Tom Facchine
Director of Islam and Society
Yaqeen Institute for Islamic Research

بسم الله الرحمن الرحيم

al-Basmalah
In the Name of Allah,
the All-Merciful,
the Ever-Merciful

Foreword

By Shaykh Yousef Wahb

The renowned *tābiʿī* al-Ḥasan al-Baṣrī (d. 110/728) was reported to have remarked, "God has embedded the knowledge of all previous scriptures in the Qur'an, and then placed the knowledge of the Qur'an in *al-Fātiḥah*. Thus, one who comprehends its interpretation is akin to one who grasps the meaning of all revealed texts."[i] In the literature of *ʿUlūm al-Qurʾān,* it is commonly noted that the essence of *al-Fātiḥah* is contained within the *Basmalah,* and the essence of the *Basmalah* is encapsulated in its initial prepositional letter, *"bā."*[ii] This letter, appearing at the beginning of the phrase *Bismillāh al-Raḥmān al-Raḥīm* ("In the Name of God, the Most Compassionate, the Most Merciful"), has been a critical focus of grammatical analysis in traditional Islamic scholarship. Its syntactic function is connected to its semantic role and the lesson it imparts. It ensures that we begin reading the Qur'an with the correct mindset of seeking to be guided by God. The *bā* symbolises

i Aḥmad ibn Ḥusayn al-Bayhaqī, *Shuʿab al-īmān,* ed. ʿAbd al-ʿAlī Ḥāmid, 4 vols., (Riyadh: Maktabat al-Rushd lil-Nashr wal-Tawzīʿ, 2003), 4:44. [report no. #2155].

ii Jalāl al-Dīn al-Suyūṭī, *al-Itqān fī ʿulūm al-Qurʾān,* ed. Markaz al-Dirāsāt al-Qurʾāniyya, 7 vols. (Medina: Mujammaʿ al-Malik Fahd li-Ṭibāʿat al-Muṣḥaf al-Sharīf, 2005), 6:2158.

attachment (*ilṣāq*), a concept central to understanding the relationship between the servant and the Divine. It suggests that the ultimate aim of all knowledge is to draw the servant closer to God. Thus, the seemingly simple *bā* becomes a symbol of rational enquiry guided by spiritual connection, highlighting the ultimate objective of all scholarly and devotional pursuits.

In its verbal structure, the *bā* is intricately linked to the verb "begin," as in "In the Name of God, I commence." The omission of the verb serves to simplify and emphasise that the servant's journey from the very beginning is characterised by ease, lightness, and leniency. It is as though God has chosen the initial word of His Book to be a testament to His tolerance and kindness. But what, then, does one commence with the *Basmalah*? Every pursuit, every endeavour, every act of obedience.

To distinguish between obedience and disobedience, or to discern good from evil, one must seek a complete and coherent worldview. The phrase "In the Name of God" in the *Basmalah* encapsulates such a worldview, mirroring the first command given to the Prophet Muḥammad by Jibrīl: "Recite in the Name of your Lord" (Qur'an 96:1). This directive was not merely an instruction to read from a written text or to vocalise words; rather, it signified a transformative approach to life. It was a call to perceive, think, and act with the consciousness of God's presence, and in accordance with His divine guidance. Implicit in this command is a caution against approaching any aspect of life in the name of anyone or anything other than God. It is in diverting from this divine focus that one becomes susceptible to various forms of misguidance.

This theocentric vision is vividly manifested in *Sūrah al-Fātiḥah*. The foundational principles articulated in these seven oft-repeated verses, known as the Mother of the Qur'an, serve as essential keys for confronting ideological misguidance and offering an ethical alternative. This is the central aim of this work, *The Straight Path*. Dr. Nazir Khan adeptly employs the verses of *Sūrah al-Fātiḥah* as a framework to address the ideological confusion prevalent in modern society, engaging with issues such as atheism, materialism, deism, polytheism, naturalism, relativism, liberalism, and postmodernism.

The Qur'anic studies department at Yaqeen Institute is dedicated to developing resources that enhance our understanding of the Qur'an and reconnect us with its timeless guidance. While many have attempted to address Islam in the context of modern ideologies, the distinctiveness of this work lies in its Qur'an-centred discourse, drawing lessons from each verse of the opening chapter to address the various ideologies discussed. Moreover, readers with an interest in Qur'anic studies will appreciate the extensive array of exegetical works the author has consulted, offering insights into the pearls of wisdom that can be gleaned from *Sūrah al-Fātiḥah*. Interspersed throughout the critique of the moral and philosophical shortcomings of secular ideologies are profound reflections on Islamic theology, Qur'anic eloquence, and the nuances of Arabic grammar, rhetoric, and semantics. This work is poised to serve as a crucial manual for the modern Muslim reader, equipping them with the intellectual and spiritual tools necessary to effectively respond to contemporary ideologies. It will also be a valuable resource for understanding and appreciating the continued relevance of the Qur'anic message in our time, presented in an accessible manner that engages with the dominant ideologies of modernity.

Yousef Aly Wahb
Director of Qur'anic Studies
Yaqeen Institute for Islamic Research

Author's introduction

Sūrah al-Fātiḥah is the most frequently recited chapter of the Qur'an, repeated in each unit of prayer.[1] It contains a supplication to God for guidance and is thus perfectly positioned as the first chapter of the Qur'an. It expresses "the covenant made between human beings and God upon which the mission and task of humankind in this world has been founded."[2] In spite of its brevity (only seven short verses), scholars of Islam have long dedicated extensive commentaries to explaining the profound lessons that can be derived from each verse. At the same time, its guidance is inexhaustible; pondering over its meanings never ceases to unveil new pearls of wisdom that can solve the challenges facing individuals and communities in every epoch. Professor Ahmad Zaki Hammad, a contemporary scholar and translator of the Qur'an, eloquently describes the scope of lessons imparted by the opening chapter of the Qur'an:

> *Al-Fātiḥah* is a guiding star in the expansive universe of the Qur'an. It affirms the covenant with the Lord of All People. It states the believer's mission; it reminds one to consider deeply the state of his or her soul; and it reawakens a person to his or her relationship with the rest of humanity—the righteous, the wrongdoing, and the indifferent—and with all things in this worshiping universe. Thus, *al-Fātiḥah* is more than an ordinary prayer in the movement of good against evil. It is a promise to uphold the higher truths and to honor the earlier proponents and communities of righteousness,

1 The Prophet ﷺ said, "The prayer is not valid for the one who does not recite the *Fātiḥah* (opening chapter) of the Book." *Ṣaḥīḥ Muslim*, no. 394a.

2 Muḥammad al-Ghazālī, A Thematic Commentary on the Qur'an, trans. Ashur Shamis, ed. Zaynab Alawiye, (Herndon: IIIT, 2000), 1.

> seeking, in a way, their company, by learning from their triumphs and tribulations in this life and aspiring to their real success in the Hereafter.[3]

The chapter calls upon us to live ethically according to the divinely revealed guidance of Islam. This way of life is described as 'the straight path' (*al-ṣirāṭ al-mustaqīm*). The guidance one may derive from this chapter is timeless and the aim of the ensuing reflection is to examine the ways in which *Sūrah al-Fātiḥah* speaks to the realities confronting us today. In particular, the final verse of the chapter reminds us that a genuine concern for guidance entails being wary of various forms of misguidance. Attending to the path towards good requires that we remain vigilant of potential routes to evil. At the time of this writing, the contest between good and evil has become strikingly lucid in humanity's collective conscience as people around the world raise their voices to protest the ongoing genocide taking place in Gaza. It is with this backdrop that many of the discussions and reflections in this book have been framed, because it has afforded a unique degree of clarity regarding the nature of evil and injustice. Some civil rights activists have referred to Palestine as a "moral litmus test for the world," and this has never been more evident than the present time.[4] As the world has witnessed a civilian population of mostly children massacred, maimed, burned alive, and starved to death in Gaza with the full support of the most powerful nations in Western civilisation, many have asked how such profound moral depravity could arise in the modern era.

---

3 Ahmad Zaki Hammad, *The Opening to the Qur'an* (Bridgeview: Qur'anic Literary Institute, 1996), 11–12.

4 Angela Davis, "Palestine Is a Moral Litmus Test for the World," Al Jazeera, October 27, 2023, https://www.aljazeera.com/program/upfront/2023/10/27/angela-davis-palestine-is-a-moral-litmus-test-for-the-world.

Human rights expert Craig Mokhiber[5] writes:

> The genocide in Palestine has opened the eyes of millions of people in the US, UK & other western countries to the fact that their leaders are not the civilized descendants of the Enlightenment, but rather cold-blooded murderers & the willing servants of corrupt power.[6]

It is not merely the corrupt leadership that is symptomatic of a moral decline but the apathetic populace that continues to lend them support. People have been conditioned by certain worldviews to abdicate their ethical responsibilities and adopt indifference towards the carnage and oppression meted out by their ruling class. They have been indoctrinated with thought structures that have degraded their sense of humanity and debilitated their moral faculties. Diagnosing these pernicious thought structures and their ethical harms is therefore an utmost priority. Political scientist Ermin Sinanović implicates a number of the ideologies behind the violence of Western imperialism, for instance:

> The post-9/11 anti-Islam industry that presented Islam as uniquely violent was made up to hide the fact that the biggest purveyor of violence in modern history is the West and the ideologies it spawned: nationalism, fascism, communism, and liberalism.[7]

---

5 Mokhiber resigned from his role as the director of the New York office of the UN High Commissioner for Human Rights due to its failure to stop the genocide in Gaza. Ed Pilkington, "Top UN Official in New York Steps Down Citing 'Genocide' of Palestinian Civilians," *Guardian* (US), October 31, 2023, https://www.theguardian.com/world/2023/oct/31/un-official-resigns-israel-hamas-war-palestine-new-york.

6 Craig Mokhiber (@CraigMokhiber), X, March 20, 2024, https://x.com/CraigMokhiber/status/1770444139638739224?s=20.

7 Ermin Sinanović (@SinanovicErmin), X, March 9, 2024, https://twitter.com/sinanovicermin/status/1766431531881341248?s=46.

Psychoepistemic disorder
A morally problematic worldview; a dysfunctional way of thinking and understanding reality.

Resistance against Western imperialism and colonial occupation must include resistance against oppressive systems of thought and unethical modes of being. The decolonization of knowledge has become an important aim of academic scholarship with the realization that the pernicious effects of colonialism extend to the destruction of indigenous systems of knowledge, thought, and values, including those of Islamic epistemology.[8] Indeed, the genocidal quality of colonialism is ultimately tied to its underlying thought structure.[9] Genocides and colonialisms are an inherent structural feature of what Professor Wael Hallaq has aptly described as a *psychoepistemic disorder,* a dysfunctional worldview comprising the ideologies of secular modernity.[10] The Malaysian Muslim philosopher Syed Naquib al-Attas explains that there is no challenge more serious and destructive than the worldview infused into the knowledge disseminated by Western civilisation which has "brought about chaos in man's life instead of, and rather than, peace and justice."[11] This makes the task of dismantling such thought structures a matter of dire necessity not only for Muslims but for all morally concerned human beings.[12] The Peruvian sociologist and decolonial thinker Aníbal Quijano explains that Western imperialism and European colonialism impose a mystified image of their own patterns of thinking while engagings in systemic repression of indigenous modes of

8 Joseph Lumbard, "Islam and the Challenge of Epistemic Sovereignty," *Religions* 15, no. 4 (2024): 406.

9 Wael B. Hallaq, *Restating Orientalism* (New York: Columbia University Press, 2018), 223. See also 136.

10 Hallaq, *Restating Orientalism*, vii, 4–5.

11 Syed Muhammad Naquib al-Attas, *Prolegomena to the Metaphysics of Islam: An Exposition of the Fundamental Elements of the Worldview of Islam* (Kuala Lumpur: ISTAC, 1995), 84–85.

12 Hallaq writes, "Subjecting modernity to a restructuring moral critique is the most essential requirement not only for the rise of Islamic governance but also for our material and spiritual survival." Wael B. Hallaq, *The Impossible State* (NY: Columbia University Press, 2012), 170.

knowledge production and thinking.[13] If the world is presently suffering under a malaise of the mind, then it is only appropriate for Muslims to turn to the Qur'anic chapter frequently referred to as *al-Shifāʾ* (the Cure), one of the names of *Sūrah al-Fātiḥah.*[14]

The guidance of *Sūrah al-Fātiḥah* is relevant in protecting humanity today from a relentless onslaught of man-made ideologies that have precipitated profound ethical failures. In this book, we examine ten major ideologies addressed by implication through the guidance of *Sūrah al-Fātiḥah*: atheism, materialism, deism, secularism, polytheism, naturalism, relativism, progressivism, liberalism, and postmodernism, in addition to various subsidiary ideologies. The Qur'anic verses establish the conceptual foundations that provide us with the tools to dismantle these ideologies by exposing their incoherence and morally unconscionable ramifications. These ideologies were selected for discussion on the basis of their hegemonic influence and current relevance. It is important to recognise how these ideologies undermine or disregard man's moral cultivation and detach man from his sacred covenant with his Creator, unleashing novel forms of tyranny upon the world. Most communities have been ideologically assimilated and subordinated to these doctrines, and despotic dictators have been installed in Muslim-majority nations to ensure their compliance with the interests of the secular world order. Muslims are being heavily pressured to capitulate to these modern forms of misguidance and abandon one Islamic teaching after another until they remain Muslim only in name. Many Muslims have already "self-secularised," adopting the paradigms of secular

13 Aníbal Quijano, "Coloniality And Modernity/Rationality," *Cultural Studies* 21, no. 2 (2007): 168–78.

14 There is a hadith that says, "The opening chapter of the Qur'an contains the cure to every ailment," reported by al-Dārimī and al-Bayhaqī, although its chain of transmission back to the Prophet ﷺ is not authentic; cf. *Mishkāt al-maṣābīḥ*, no. 2170. However, the connection between *al-Fātiḥah* and healing is established in another authentic narration in *Ṣaḥīḥ al-Bukhārī*, no. 5007 and 5736. Munīrah al-Dawsirī explains that Qur'anic exegetes derived this name from this property of the chapter. See Munīrah al-Dawsirī, *Asmāʾ suwar al-Qurʾān wa faḍāʾiluhā* (Dammam: Dār Ibn Jawzī, 1426 AH), 132–33.

ideologies and relegating their own faith to a mere cultural label with no bearing on their moral choices or how they live their lives. They are unaware of the battle for hearts and minds as it does not take the familiar shape of a contest between two opposing religions. The new "religions" of Western imperialism are disseminated throughout culture, entertainment, and academia and are implicit in every sector of society. Popular television shows and movies either explicitly portray religion as irrational and backwards or highlight skepticism towards its doctrines in subtler ways. They incessantly repeat the mantras of liberalism until their viewers are reliably programmed to regurgitate its rhetoric.

It may surprise some to hear that *Sūrah al-Fātiḥah* addresses not one but dozens of these ideological challenges at their conceptual roots, illustrating their flaws and guiding us to the ethically sound alternative. Recognising the guidance in *al-Fātiḥah* as a formidable tool in tackling ideological confusion is not a new idea, of course. In the opening of his work *Madārij al-Sālikīn*, the Islamic theologian Imam Ibn al-Qayyim (d. 751 AH) commented that this chapter "most perfectly and comprehensively contains the foundations of all lofty pursuits" and "includes rebuttals of all the various kinds of heresy and error."[15] The keys to answering numerous forms of ideological misguidance can be confidently linked back to the foundational principles established in the seven oft-repeated verses. The fact that *al-Fātiḥah* encompasses the guidance found throughout the Qur'an is indicated by several of the names of this chapter. This includes prescribed names mentioned by the Prophet Muhammad such as *Umm al-Qur'ān* (Mother of the Qur'an), *Umm al-Kitāb* (Mother of the Book), and *al-Ṣalāh* (the prayer), as well as described names derived through scholarly reflection including *al-Asās* (the foundation), *al-Wāfiyah*

15 Ibn al-Qayyim, *Ranks of the Divine Seekers*, trans. Ovamir Anjum (Leiden: Brill, 2020), 1:82. The full Arabic title of the work is *Madārij al-sālikīn bayna manāzil iyyāka naʿbudu wa iyyāka nastaʿīn*.

(the comprehensive), *al-Kāfiyah* (the sufficient), and *al-Kanz* (the treasure).[16] In fact, one of the prescribed names given to this chapter is "the Magnificent Qur'an" (*al-Qur'ān al-Aẓīm*):

> The Prophet said, "Shall I not teach you the greatest chapter in the Qur'an? ...*Alḥamdulillāhi Rabb al-ʿālamīn* [i.e., *Sūrah al-Fātiḥah*]. It is *al-sabʿ al-mathānī* (the seven oft-recited verses) and *al-Qur'ān al-Aẓīm* (the Magnificent Qur'an) which was given to me."[17]

The Andalusian Qur'anic commentator Imam al-Qurṭubī (d. 671 AH) explained this title as follows:

> It was named so because it encompasses all the categories of knowledge in the Qur'an. This is because it includes praising Allah Almighty with descriptions of His perfection and majesty, and it encompasses the instruction to perform all acts of worship and maintain sincerity in them, while also acknowledging the inability to perform any of it except with His assistance. And it encompasses supplicating to Him for guidance to the straight path, addressing the conditions of those who break their covenants with God, and clarifying the consequences for the deniers.[18]

The current work draws upon the Qur'an's opening chapter and the principles of guidance contained therein to mount a thorough Islamic critique of the principal moral and philosophical failures of contemporary secular ideologies. In explaining any verse from

16 See al-Dawsirī, *Asmā' suwar al-Qur'ān*, 98–147 and Ibn Kathīr, *Tafsīr al-Qur'ān al-ʿAẓīm* (Riyadh: Dār al-Ṭaybah, 1999), 1:101.

17 *Ṣaḥīḥ al-Bukhārī*, no. 4474 and 5006.

18 Al-Qurṭubī, *al-Jāmiʿ li-aḥkām al-Qur'ān* (Cairo: Dar al-Kutub al-Misriyya, 1964), 1:112. Al-Fīrūzābādī (d. 817 AH) says, "Whoever learns its commentary (*tafsīr*) will be as though he has learned the commentary of all the divinely revealed books." See al-Fīrūzābādī, *Baṣā'ir dhawī at-tamyīz fī laṭā'if al-Kitāb al-ʿAzīz* (Cairo: al-Majlis al-Aʿlā li-Shu'ūn al-Islāmiyya, Lajnat Iḥyā' at-Turāth al-Islāmī, 1416/1996), 1:131.

the Qur'an, one must first endeavour to ensure that the verse has been correctly interpreted on the basis of what the Messenger of God ﷺ taught his companions.[19] One's interpretation should not contradict the understanding of the early Muslim community nor the principles of the Arabic language. Once the meaning of the verse has been clarified, one may reflect on the numerous implications and lessons that can be extracted. In this analysis, reference will be made to many classical works of *tafsīr* (Qur'anic commentary) and Islamic scholarship to explicate the meaning of the verses under reflection. While one might aspire to leave no stone unturned, the sheer vastness of the *tafsīr* literature makes it impossible to accomplish this in a single lifetime, given the existence of more than 2,700 extant classical and post-classical Arabic works.[20] There is also a vast number of works published in the modern era that contain important reflections related to contemporary challenges. The geographic and chronological breadth of Muslim scholars consulted in this work further underscores the timeless nature of the Qur'anic worldview. The present discussion includes a variety of illuminating insights from various recent Muslim thinkers who have grappled with the ideologies of secular modernity. This analysis aims to provide a robust understanding of the Islamic worldview as a remedy to the malaise of the prevailing "psychoepistemic disorder."

As with any reflections on the Qur'an, this discussion is not exhaustive and numerous additional connections can always be drawn. In many cases, several verses from *Sūrah al-Fātiḥah* will provide relevant answers to countering a particular ideological falsehood. However, for the sake of brevity, repeating ideologies

19 See Ibn Jarīr al-Ṭabarī, *The Comprehensive Exposition of the Interpretation of the Verses of the Qur'an*, trans. Scott Lucas (Cambridge: The Royal Aal al-Bayt Institute for Islamic Thought and the Islamic Texts Society, 2017), 1:61–65 and 72–73.

20 The vast majority of these remain in manuscript form, while approximately three hundred of these works have been published. See Samuel Ross, "What Were the Most Popular Tafsīrs in Islamic History? Part 1: An Assessment of the Manuscript Record and the State of Tafsīr Studies," *Journal of Qur'anic Studies* 25, no. 3 (2023): 1–54.

between verses has been avoided and left to the astute reader to notice additional connections. Moreover, an Islamic critique of any one of these ideologies could be the subject of an entire book. Here, one must suffice oneself with brief pointers (*ishārāt*). It is the aim of this reflection to open new avenues of reflection for people to challenge the oppressive thought structures of the age in the pursuit of ethical outcomes. It is also the aim to set the stage for Muslims to engage more deeply with Qur'anic guidance in their intellectual responses to various ideological challenges.

These ideologies are the idols of our age, and they must be broken if we are to be free. What follows is a fresh perspective examining how each phrase or verse in *Sūrah al-Fātiḥah* contains within it the answer to each ideology.

The content in this book initially took the form of several classes and lectures I delivered on the subject of the Islamic worldview and modern ideologies. In the course of my conversations, the ideologies discussed in this book were frequently identified as topics of interest to students, scholars, academics, and community members. I found that centring the discussion on *Sūrah al-Fātiḥah* provided a comprehensive framework and a uniquely Qur'anic paradigm for evaluating these ideologies. As the moral failures of the existing thought structures become manifest during the genocide in Gaza, this project acquired a heightened sense of urgency.

I pray that Allah makes this work of benefit to the reader, forgives the author for his shortcomings, and rewards all those who contributed to its publication. *Amīn.*

Dr. Nazir Khan
Yaqeen Institute for Islamic Research
Rabīʿ ath-Thānī 1446/October 2024

If the world is presently suffering under a malaise of the mind, then it is only appropriate for Muslims to turn to the Qur'anic chapter frequently referred to as *al-Shifā'* (the Cure), one of the names of *Sūrah al-Fātiḥah.*

Overview: *Sūrah al-Fātiḥah* and modern ideologies

Verse

ٱلْحَمْدُ لِلَّهِ

Alḥamdulillāh
All praise belongs to Allah

رَبِّ ٱلْعَٰلَمِينَ

Rabb al-ʿālamīn
Lord of the Worlds

ٱلرَّحْمَٰنِ ٱلرَّحِيمِ

al-Raḥmān al-Raḥīm
The All-Merciful, the Ever-Merciful

مَٰلِكِ يَوْمِ ٱلدِّينِ

Māliki yawm al-dīn
Sovereign of the Day of Judgement

إِيَّاكَ نَعْبُدُ

Iyyāka naʿbudu
You alone do we worship

وَإِيَّاكَ نَسْتَعِينُ

Wa iyyāka nastaʿīn
And You alone do we ask for help

ٱهْدِنَا ٱلصِّرَٰطَ ٱلْمُسْتَقِيمَ

Ihdinā al-ṣirāṭ al-mustaqīm
Guide us on the straight path

صِرَٰطَ ٱلَّذِينَ أَنْعَمْتَ عَلَيْهِمْ

Ṣirāṭ alladhīna anʿamta ʿalayhim
The path of those whom You have favoured

غَيْرِ ٱلْمَغْضُوبِ عَلَيْهِمْ

Ghayri al-maghḍūbi ʿalayhim
Not (the path) of those who have incurred anger

وَلَا ٱلضَّآلِّينَ

Wa-lā al-ḍāllīn
Nor (the path) of those who have gone astray

Ideology dismantled	Explanation
Atheism	If you recognise something as a blessing, you must recognise the Benefactor.
Materialism	We have a Lord who nurtures us so we can fulfil our moral purpose, we are not mere collections of particles.
Deism	The most merciful Creator would never abandon His creation without guidance.
Secularism	All human authority is illusory and fleeting and will ultimately vanish in front of the true Sovereign.
Polytheism	We worship God alone rather than the idols of man's making.
Naturalism	We use natural means but ultimately place our trust, hope, and reliance in the Creator.
Relativism	The truth is singular, and the correct path of guidance to God is the one that He has revealed.
Progressivism	We take our moral instruction from the way of the prophets and righteous exemplars of the past.
Liberalism	We do not follow the way of those who claim to pursue the truth but disregard justice.
Postmodernism	Nor do we follow the way of those who claim to pursue justice but disregard truth.

Alḥamdulillāh
All praise belongs to Allah

Atheism dismantled

The short chapter opens with the declaration: "All praise belongs to Allah."[21] The name "Allah" is the Arabic word for God, the sole Creator and Sustainer of the universe. In Islam, God is described with all attributes of perfection; He transcends all deficiencies. The word *al-ḥamd* (praise) implies the ultimate expression of love and gratitude. The Prophet ﷺ said, "Love Allah (*aḥibbū Allāh*) for what He nourishes you with of His Blessings."[22] Ibn ʿAbbās said, "*alḥamdulillāh* is a statement of *shukr* (gratitude), and when a servant says it, Allah responds, 'My servant has thanked Me.'"[23] While the expression "*alḥamdulillāh*" encompasses *shukr*, it also goes beyond it,

21 Note that there is a scholarly difference of opinion over whether the *basmalah* is a verse of *al-Fātiḥah* or not. For discussions among the exegetes in support of the latter view, see al-Ṭabarī, *Comprehensive Exposition*, 119 and 87n1; Ibn ʿAṭiyyah, *al-Muḥarrar al-wajīz* (Beirut: DKI, 2001), 60–61; and Muṣāʿid al-Ṭayyār, *Mawsūʿat al-tafsīr al-maʾthūr* (Beirut: Dar Ibn Ḥazm, 2017), 2:14. For the former, see Fakhr al-Dīn al-Rāzī, *The Great Exegesis*, trans. Sohaib Saeed (Cambridge: The Royal Aal al-Bayt Institute for Islamic Thought and Islamic Texts Society, 2018), 307–17. The master of *qirāʾāt* Ibn al-Jazarī held that both views are in fact correct, just as there are differences in the *qirāʾāt*. See Ibn al-Jazarī, *al-Nashr fī al-qirāʾāt al-ʿashr*, ed. ʿAlī Muḥammad al-Ḍabbāʿ (Beirut: DKI, n.d.), 1:270–71. Jalāl al-Dīn al-Suyūṭī explains this opinion to mean that the *basmalah* is a verse in one *qirāʾah* and not a verse in another. See al-Suyūṭī, *Nawāhid al-abkār wa shawārid al-afkār* (Mecca: Umm al-Qurā, 2005), 1:63.

22 *Jāmiʿ al-Tirmidhī*, no. 3789, *ḥasan*.

23 See Aḥmad al-ʿUmrānī, *Mawsūʿat madrasat Makkah fī al-tafsīr* (Cairo: Dār al-Salām, 2010), 1:13. See also al-Ṭabarī, *Comprehensive Exposition*, 112–13.

as one praises Allah not only for the blessings received and His benevolence but also because of His attributes of majesty (*jalāl*), beauty (*jamāl*), greatness (*ʿaẓamah*), and grandeur (*kibriyāʾ*).[24] This is the distinction between *ḥamd* (praise) and *shukr* (gratitude). Moreover, the use of the word *ḥamd* instead of *madḥ* (another word for praise) is important because the former denotes praise that can only be applied for one who is living and acts voluntarily, with knowledge and capability.[25] The Andalusian scholar Imam Ibn Juzayy al-Kalbī (d. 741 AH) mentioned that *alḥamdulillāh* is a phrase

24 See Ibn ʿAṭiyyah, *al-Muḥarrar al-wajīz*, 66.

25 Al-Bayḍāwī, *Anwār al-tanzīl wa asrār al-taʾwīl* (Beirut: Dār Iḥyāʾ al-Turāth al-ʿArabī, n.d.), 1:27. See also Ṣāliḥ Al-Zahrānī, *"Aḍwāʾ ʿalā al-iʿjāz al-balāghī fī Sūrat al-Fātiḥah," Majallat al-buḥūth wa al-dirāsāt al-qurʾāniyyah* 4, no. 2 (2007): 127.

that encompasses the meaning of Allah's ninety-nine Beautiful Names; it is a single phrase that encompasses what volumes cannot contain and extends beyond the intellects of all creation.[26]

Atheism
The ideology that rejects belief in the existence of God.

This single phrase liberates the human mind from a narcissistic culture obsessed with self-aggrandisement and self-glorification. We are increasingly witnessing the transformation of society into digital narcissists who crave self-praise:

> [S]cores on a clinical measure of narcissism increased by 30% in the U.S. between the late 1970s and the mid 2000s. One of the statements used as a measurement tool in [the researcher's] analysis was: "I am important and famous." In the 60s, around 12% of young people endorsed it. By the 90s, that number had increased to 80%... [T]echnology has normalized narcissism by legitimizing public displays of self-promotion, entitlement, and self-centeredness. In a real-world office, if you walk around telling everybody how great you are, ignoring what they say, and sharing everything you do with others (including what your cat had for breakfast), you'd be deemed quite obnoxious as a colleague. But in the digital world this will make you an influencer. In that sense, we are all nudged to behave like narcissists when we are on the internet. Though we may criticize those who show narcissistic tendencies on Snapchat, Instagram, TikTok, and the like, the algorithms on these platforms reward those behaviors with viral exposure in the form of likes and views.[27]

26 Ibn Juzayy, *al-Tashīl li-ʿulūm al-tanzīl* (Beirut: Dār al-Arqam, 1416 AH), 1:63.

27 Tomas Chamorro-Premuzic, "Are You a Digital Narcissist?," *Harvard Business Review*, April 10, 2023, https://hbr.org/2023/04/are-you-a-digital-narcissist. See Jean M. Twenge et al., "Egos Deflating with the Great Recession: A Cross-Temporal Meta-Analysis and Within-Campus Analysis of the Narcissistic Personality Inventory, 1982–2016," *Personality and Individual Differences* 179 (2021): 110947.

In a godless culture, people worship and praise themselves and think little of the One who bestowed upon them their blessings and obligated upon them a moral duty. Professor Ahmad Zaki Hammad notes that "by cultivating a grateful relationship with the Creator, the believer also becomes disposed to show due gratitude to creation,"[28] as the Prophet Muhammad ﷺ taught, "Whoever does not thank people has not truly thanked Allah."[29] The phrase "*alḥamdulillāh*" (all praise belongs to Allah) establishes the existence of a Divine Creator and rescues the human mind from both doctrinal and behavioral atheism.[30] In other words, it saves one from *believing* that God does not exist or from *acting* like God does not exist. The very next phrase *Rabb al-ʿālamīn* (Lord of the universe) directs one's attention to the abundant evidence of God in His creation.[31] Of course, one must possess the correct framework to recognise what constitutes evidence, and the atheist will need to abandon radical skepticism in order to benefit from such evidence (see author's previous article on atheism

In a godless culture, people worship and praise themselves and think little of the One who bestowed upon them their blessings and obligated upon them a moral duty.

28 Hammad, *Opening*, 14–15.

29 *Sunan Abī Dāwūd*, no. 4811; *Jāmiʿ al-Tirmidhī*, no. 1954.

30 See Badr al-Dīn ibn Jamāʿah, *al-Fawāʾid al-lāʾiḥah min maʿānī al-Fātiḥah* (Kuwait City: Dār al-Ẓahiriyyah, 2009), 30 and Ṭaha ʿĀbidīn Ṭaha, *al-Jāmiʿ fī hidāyāt al-Qurʾān: Sūrat al-Fātiḥah* (Mecca: Muʾassasat al-Nabaʾ al-ʿAẓīm, 2020), 5.

31 Al-Biqāʿī, *Naẓm al-durar fī tanāsub al-āyāt wa al-suwar* (Cairo: Dār al-Kitāb al-Islāmī, n.d.), 1:27.

and radical skepticism).[32] The phrase *alḥamdulillāh* itself guides one to restore the theocentric worldview necessary to understand the meaning of one's existence and pursue one's journey of moral purpose and rectification. The more one examines this phrase, the more one appreciates the wisdom and reasoning that underlie its negation of atheism.[33] Imam Fakhr al-Dīn al-Rāzī (d. 606 AH) explains that our very existence is a blessing from the Benefactor:

> Since existence is a favour, every existent being in the spiritual and corporeal worlds, or the lofty and lowly worlds, is indebted to God's favour, mercy and kindness: and these favours and mercies necessitate praise and thanks.[34]

The phrase *alḥamdulilāh* is expressed as a statement of fact (*jumlah khabariyyah*) and it also serves as an instruction (*jumlah inshāʾiyyah ṭalabiyyah*). The fact implies the instruction; since all praise ultimately belongs to Allah, one should seek nearness to Allah through loving praise and adoration.[35] In addition to being interpreted as an instruction or description, the statement can also be interpreted as a pronouncement initiated by God Himself. Imam Abū Ḥafṣ al-Nasafī (d. 537 AH) and others explain that

32 Nazir Khan, "Atheism and Radical Skepticism: Ibn Taymiyyah's Epistemic Critique," Yaqeen Institute for Islamic Research, July 7, 2020, https://yaqeeninstitute.ca/read/paper/atheism-and-radical-skepticism-ibn-taymiyyahs-epistemic-critique.

33 In his *tafsīr*, al-Rāzī interprets the phrase "All Praise is due to God" as comprising two claims: (1) God exists and (2) He deserves our praise. He locates the proof for the first in the phrase "Lord of the universe," while the proof of the second claim is in the verses "the Most Compassionate, the Most Merciful/Master of the Day of Judgement." See al-Rāzī, *Great Exegesis,* 1:281. Later in his commentary on the *sūrah,* he alludes to the fact that the phrase "*alḥamdulillāh*" itself establishes God's existence (see *Great Exegesis,* 1:418). This latter approach coincides with the outline I have developed, although both techniques serve to augment one another. On the first approach, see also al-Sanūsī, *Tafsīr Sūrat al-Fātiḥah* (Tunis: Dār al-Imām Ibn ʿArafah, 2023), 10 and ʿAbd al-Salām al-Majīdī, *al-Islām fī sabʿ āyāt* (Istanbul: Dār al-Uṣūl, 2021), 80–81.

34 Al-Rāzī, *Great Exegesis,* 1:352–353.

35 Al-Hararī, *Tafsīr ḥadāʾiq ar-rūḥ wa al-rayḥān fī rawābī ʿulūm al-Qurʾān* (Beirut: Dār Ṭawq an-Najāt, 1421/2001), 1:91; Wahbah al-Zuḥaylī, *al-Tafsīr al-munīr fī al-ʿaqīdah wa al-sharīʿah wa al-manhaj* (Beirut: Dār al-Fikr al-Muʿāṣir, 1411/1991), 1:55; Sulaymān al-Lāḥim, *al-Lubāb fī tafsīr al-istiʿādhah wa al-basmalah wa Fātiḥat al-kitāb* (Riyadh: Dār al-Muslim li an-Nashr wa al-Tawzīʿ, 1420/1999), 220.

God gives us the instruction to praise Him, but knowing our deficiencies in doing so, He mercifully expresses praise of Himself directly on our behalf.[36] It is also educational, as He is teaching us how to praise Him and call upon Him.

Praise occurs in the context of recognising something to be good. The evaluation of a particular state of affairs as praiseworthy or blameworthy cannot occur if the universe is just a vast collection of material elements that exist pointlessly without a Maker. For something to be praised as good invites the question: good with respect to what meaning, goal, or context? This presupposes that there is a purpose for which all things exist. Nihilism, the denial of any purpose or meaning to existence, is therefore also explicitly negated by this statement. Atheism and nihilism go hand-in-hand. Without a Creator, our existence is an unintended byproduct of aimless particle interactions. Any notion of purpose becomes a comforting illusion to shield ourselves from the brutal pointlessness of existence. American atheist philosopher Alex Rosenberg provides the following answers for atheists: "What is the purpose of the universe? There is none. What is the meaning of life? Ditto. Why am I here? Just dumb luck."[37]

By denying God's existence, the atheist lives in an existential bubble, disconnected from any transcendent reality or ultimate source of value. Any meaning derived from within the bubble is manufactured by the individual, and amounts to nothing more than an exercise in self-deception. Every endeavour becomes self-referential and bereft of any ultimate significance. Bound by one's own existential narcissism, one becomes trapped within the bubble, confined to an image of reality that is fundamentally meaningless.

36 See al-Nasafī, *al-Taysīr fī al-tafsīr* (Istanbul: Dār al-Lubāb, 2019), 1:94–95; cf. al-Qurṭubī, *al-Jāmiʿ li-aḥkām al-Qurʾān*, 1:135 and al-Sanūsī, *Tafsīr Sūrat al-Fātiḥah*, 8.

37 Alex Rosenberg, *The Atheist's Guide to Reality: Enjoying Life Without Illusions* (NY: WW Norton, 2011), 2–3.

Islam **Atheism**

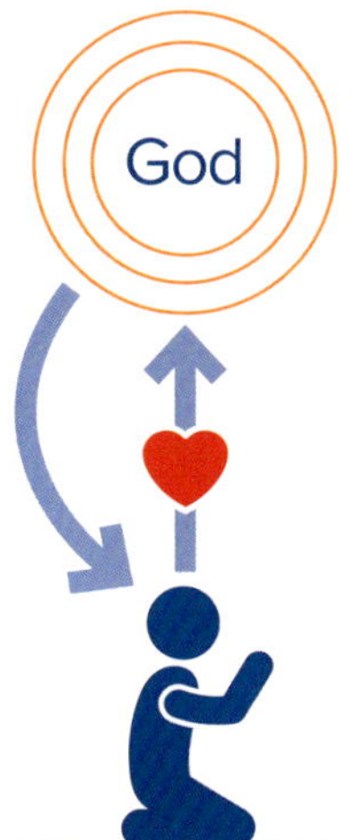

Recognising that all blessings are gifts that come from a Benefactor to whom love and praise is due. All of reality is meaningful through God.

Our universe is a meaningless bubble that exists without rhyme or reason. The existence of God is denied as well as anything beyond the bubble. There is nothing to praise but oneself or the bubble.

Within this bubble, one loses not only God but also oneself. What does it mean to be a human being? Is one nothing more than a collection of particles? Atheism dissolves the very notion of the human being. Allah says, "Do not be like those who forgot Allah, so He made them forget their own selves" (Qur'an 59:19).

Enabling us to recognise the meaning of our existence and fulfil the purpose of our lives is the central aim of the Qur'anic discourse. The Qur'an invites the human being to ponder: "Do you think that We created you without any purpose and that you will not return unto Us?" (Qur'an 23:115). To be human is to be entrusted with a sacred mission. As the Qur'anic scholar Imam al-Rāghib al-Iṣfahānī (d. 431 AH) notes, the Qur'an teaches that human beings have been created for lofty spiritual, moral and intellectual aims: devotion to God (*ʿibādah*, Qur'an 51:56), serving as custodians on earth to establish justice (*khilāfah*, Qur'an 27:62), and cultivating the earth and building civilisation (*ʿimārat al-arḍ,* Qur'an 11:61).[38] These divinely appointed goals render our human endeavours meaningful and praiseworthy.

Imam Ibn Taymiyyah (d. 728 AH) explains that all goal-directed human behavior must ultimately connect back to what is sought for its own sake (*maṭlūb li-dhātihi*) and not as a means to something else (*maṭlūb li-ghayrihi*). The former is what serves as the pinnacle of one's value hierarchy; for some people it may be money, fame, power, or pleasure. This becomes a person's "god," and he lives his life subservient to it, as the Qur'an indicates (25:43, 45:23). However, none besides the Creator of all existence is worthy of being the ultimate priority and loftiest goal in one's life.[39] Any other choice leads back to nihilism. This is also indicated by the fact that the phrase "*alḥamdulillāh*" has been expressed as a nominal sentence (*jumlah ismiyyah*), rather than a sentence with a verb (*jumlah fiʿliyyah*). A nominal sentence linguistically connotes permanence, constancy, and continuity.[40] This has an important implication: we cannot locate the source of life's meaning or ultimate value in something that is temporary and characterised by eventual obsolescence. In order for there to be anything meaningful in our statement of praise, it must be directed towards the One who is Eternal and Transcendent.

For anything to be praised as good inevitably invites the question of to whom the praise is ultimately due. True praise is due to the One who is the ultimate source of all blessings encountered in

38 Al-Rāghib al-Iṣfahānī, *al-Dharīʿah ilā makārim al-Sharīʿah* (Beirut: DKI, 1980), 31–32.

39 Ibn Taymiyya, *Darʾ taʿāruḍ al-ʿaql wa-al-naql,* ed. Muḥammad Rashād Sālim (Riyadh: Jāmiʿat al-Imām Muḥammad b. Saʿūd al-Islāmiyyah, 1411/1991), 8:465; *Qāʿida fī al-maḥabba* (Cairo: Maktabat al-Turāth al-Islāmī, 1987), 45; *al-Jawāb al-ṣaḥīḥ li-man baddala dīn al-Masīḥ* (Riyadh: Dār al-ʿĀṣima, 1999), 6:38; *al-Istiqāmah* (Riyadh: Jāmiʿat al-Īmām, 1403H), 2:149; *al-ʿUbūdiyyah* (Beirut: al-Maktaba al-Islāmiyya, 2005), 100–102; *Minhāj al-sunnah al-nabawiyyah* (Riyadh: Jāmiʿat al-Īmām, 1986), 3:165–66, 332–34; *Majmūʿ al-fatāwā,* 1:34, 2:37.

40 Al-Lāḥim, *al-Lubāb,* 1:301.

existence, He who possesses absolute perfection and is free of any deficiency or flaw.[41] Pakistani Islamic scholar, Mufti Muḥammad Shafīʿ (d. 1976) says the phrase "*alḥamdulillāh*" reminds us "that all praise in reality belongs to One whose power is absolute, and that it is only in our ignorance or indifference that we regard this praise to be due to anyone else."[42] Allah says, "Whatever blessing you have is from Allah, yet it is only when misfortune touches you that you cry to Him for help" (Qur'an 16:53).

Modern culture's narcissism transforms even something as deeply relational as gratitude into a self-centred act, stripping it of its original context within a loving relationship with the Divine. Such a hollow 'gratitude' is devoid of any logic. How can one recognise something as a blessing without recognising that there must also therefore be a Benefactor? To do so would be a clear contradiction.

Unfortunately, many people seem keen to ignore this glaring contradiction and instead thank the "universe" for "manifesting" the blessings in their life. Directing one's thanks and gratitude towards inanimate, insentient matter is nonsensical, akin to thanking the pots and pans after one has enjoyed a delicious meal. There is no sense in the sailor thanking winds or waves, nor in the farmer thanking crops or grain. Just as insentient matter cannot be the ultimate source of good, neither can human beings. Human efforts towards good are themselves dependent on a multitude of factors beyond their control, including possessing a motivation to do good that is instilled within them by God.[43] Islamic revivalist, Sayyid Abū al-Aʿlā

41 Abū Manṣūr al-Māturīdī, *Ta'wīlāt Ahl al-Sunnah* (Beirut: DKI, 2005), 1:358.

42 Muḥammad Shafīʿ, *Maʿārif al-Qur'ān*, trans. M. Hasan Askari and M. Shamim (Karachi: Maktaba-e Darul Uloom 1996), 1:64.

43 Al-Rāzī, *Great Exegesis*, 1:349.

Directing one's thanks and gratitude towards inanimate, insentient matter is nonsensical, akin to thanking the pots and pans after one has enjoyed a delicious meal.

al-Mawdūdī (d. 1979) devoted special attention to the profound implications of recognising God as *al-Rabb*:

> The fulfillment of the needs of human beings, the removal of their distress, the granting to them of refuge or protection, the extension of any needed help or assistance, their bringing up or preservation, and the acceptance of their prayers—none of these matters are so simple as people seem to assume them to be and hence mistakenly regard them as within the competence of human beings. All are dependent, inextricably and ultimately, upon the creative power and the controlling and managing authority being exercised over the entire universe by its one and only Lord and Master.
>
> Even the smallest need depends, for its fulfillment, on the combined results of a vast multitude of factors. Take, for example, the provision of just one glass of drinking water, or even just one grain of wheat used by men for food. Neither would come about but for incalculable and multifarious and, in many cases, hidden activity on the part of the sun and the earth and the oceans and the winds.
>
> Therefore, the authority or power which is actually required for listening to our prayers is no ordinary authority but, rather, super-extraordinary and unique authority or power, not less than that required for creating the heavens and earth and for ordering the movement of the heavenly bodies and of the winds and of causing rain, and so on—in short, that needed for governing the entire universe itself.[44]

---

44 Al-Mawdūdī, *Four Basic Qur'anic Terms,* trans. Abū Asad (Lahore: Islamic Publications, 1979), 25–26. On this treatise, see also Abū al-Ḥasan ʿAlī al-Nadwī, *Appreciation and Interpretation of Religion in the Modern Age* (Lucknow, 1982) and Usaama al-Azami, "Locating Ḥākimiyya in Global History: The Concept of Sovereignty in Premodern Islam and Its Reception after Mawdūdī and Quṭb," *Journal of the Royal Asiatic Society* 32, no. 2 (2022): 355–76.

Human beings are themselves dependent entirely on a vast existing order of blessings to survive. Moreover, while human beings are certainly capable of pursuing good, they are also capable of perpetrating tremendous evil. If humans are not mere biological automatons and possess true voluntary moral agency, then their choice to recognise and pursue good is itself a blessing with which they have been endowed by their Maker.

How the recognition of good leads to praise of God

Observe and recognise
that **good** *exists.*

Good fulfils a
beneficial purpose.

Good is meaningless without
an intended purpose.

***Intentional* good** *motivates*
love, gratitude, and praise.

***Intentional* good** ultimately
comes from the Creator—
not unconscious matter.

All praise
belongs to God.

Imam Ibn Juzayy explains that a higher station of gratitude is to thank Allah not only for one's blessings but also for one's tribulations, which exist for a wise purpose and offer unique opportunities for cultivating virtue and moral goodness. Moreover, he explains that thanking Allah does not only occur with one's tongue, but rather gratitude also manifests in one's actions and in one's heart.[45] Expressing gratitude to Allah through one's actions entails following His guidance, obeying His commandments, and striving to live virtuously in the world, sharing one's blessings with others. Thankfulness with the heart entails recognising that one's blessings come solely from Allah, thus abandoning any sense of entitlement, and filling one's heart with love and reverence for Allah and compassion for His creation.

Scholars of Islam are unanimously in agreement that the obligation of thanking the Benefactor (*wujūb shukr al-munʿim*) is one of the most fundamental concepts in the religion. Many scholars have argued further that this obligation is known to the intellect even prior to receiving revelation.[46] Ibn al-Qayyim writes, "There is no greater good known to the intellect (*ʿaql*) and sound human nature (*fiṭrah*) than thanking the Benefactor, nor anything more beneficial to the servant than it."[47] Recognising that there is good in the world directs one to praise Allah, the Creator and Benefactor. To recognise a blessing in one's life is to reject the nihilistic view that the universe is bereft of purpose

45 Ibn Juzayy, *al-Tashīl*, 1:64.

46 One group of scholars affirmed that the intellect can discern the obligation to thank the Benefactor, while the other held that no obligation can be known without recourse to revelation. For the various schools, see Abū Salama al-Samarqandī, *Jumal min uṣūl al-dīn* (Beirut: DKI, 2015), 14; al-Juwaynī, *al-Burhān fī uṣūl al-fiqh* (Beirut: DKI, 1997), 1:11; al-Ghazālī, *al-Mankhūl min taʿlīqāt al-uṣūl* (Beirut: Dār al-Fikr 1998), 71; al-Rāzī, *al-Maḥṣūl fī ʿilm uṣūl al-fiqh* (Beirut: Muʾassasat al-Risālah, 1997) 1:147; al-Āmidī, *al-Iḥkām fī uṣūl al-aḥkām* (Beirut: al-Maktab al-Islamī, 1986), 1:87; Ibn Ḥazm, *al-Iḥkām fī uṣūl al-aḥkām* (Beirut: Dār al-Āfāq al-Jadīdah), 4:75–76; Abū al-Khaṭṭāb al-Kalwadhānī, *al-Tamhīd fī uṣūl al-fiqh* (Mecca: Umm al-Qurā, 1985), 4:305.

47 Ibn al-Qayyim, *Miftāḥ Dār al-Saʿādah* (Beirut: Dār Ibn Ḥazm, 2019), 2:1089. See also Ibn ʿUthaymīn, *Tafsīr al-Fātiḥah wa al-Baqarah* (Riyadh: Dār Ibn al-Jawzī, 1423 AH), 1:197.

or meaning, the mere outcome of a cascade of aimless particle interactions. All gratitude is meaningless if we fail to recognise the true source of all blessings. Everything in life is a gift from Allah, our Creator. Imam Ibn Taymiyyah explained that this concept is in fact rooted in the nature of the human soul:

> Indeed, the servant is invited to the worship of Allah by the call of gratitude and the call of knowledge. Witnessing the blessings of Allah upon him is inherently a call to be grateful for them. Moreover, souls are naturally inclined to love those who are kind to them. Allah the Exalted is the Bestower of blessings and the Benefactor from whom all the blessings bestowed upon the servants come, and they are solely from Him.[48]

Fiṭrah

Fiṭrah is the Qur'anic term that refers to the natural, innate disposition or the original state of purity and goodness with which every human being is born. It represents the inherent inclination towards truth, morality, and belief in one God. It is the natural state of humans that aligns with the guidance of Islam before external inference by one's environment, culture, or socialisation.

Praising one's Benefactor and Creator is the natural tendency of human beings rooted in the *fiṭrah* (the primordial human nature). The *fiṭrah* not only leads one to believe in God but also affords the human being all the basic axioms of thought, including belief in morality, causation, the intelligibility of the world, and even the distinction between truth and falsehood. Do we need proof to convince a person that good and evil exist or that truth and falsehood exist? To deny such foundational matters is a form of radical skepticism. In the same way, belief in God is foundational to our understanding of

48 Ibn Taymiyyah, *Majmūʿ al-fatāwā* (al-Manṣūrah: Dār al-Wafāʾ li-l-Ṭibāʿa wa-l-Nashr, 1998), 8:32.

reality, a necessary axiom for making sense of all existence.[49] Ibn Taymiyyah says, "Even though the creation is a proof (*dalīl*) that establishes the existence of the Creator, knowledge of God is already present in human nature (*maʿrūf fi al-fiṭrah*) before this reasoning (*istidlāl*); and knowledge of the Creator is innate, embedded in sound nature, axiomatic, self-evident, and primary."[50] Similarly, al-Shahrastānī (d. 548 AH) writes:

> I do not count this issue (i.e., God's existence) among the inferential matters (*naẓariyyāt*) that are to be substantiated with proof (*burhān*). For verily, sound human nature (*al-fiṭrah*) testifies necessarily by virtue of its nature and its intuitive thought (*badīhat fikratihā*) that there is a Wise, All-Knowing, and All-Powerful Maker. "Is there any doubt concerning God, Creator of the heavens and the earth?" (Qur'an 14:10).[51]

Atheism is radical skepticism selectively applied to belief in the Creator. Like the basic axioms of human rationality and morality, recognising the Creator is a prerequisite to making sense of existence and our purpose in life. It is actually the starting point for any meaningful endeavour towards true understanding. Belief in the Divine serves as the fundamental conviction that grounds and renders meaningful all other beliefs and commitments.

---

49 Scholars of the *kalām* tradition hold that belief in God is *naẓarī* (inferential) knowledge, which means that it is proven with reference to other facts that are self-evident; this is sometimes referred to as theistic evidentialism. Meanwhile, other scholars hold that belief in God is a basic and necessary (*ḍarūrī*) axiom that one must possess in order for reality to make sense. Ibn al-Qayyim notes that both directions of proof are correct: creation proves the Creator and the Creator proves the creation. The natural sequence, however, is to proceed from that which is more obvious to that which is less obvious, and the existence of the Creator is more obvious than broad daylight. See Ibn al-Qayyim, *Ranks of the Divine Seekers,* 1:181.

50 Ibn Taymiyyah, *Majmūʿ al-fatāwā,* 16:324.

51 Muḥammad b. ʿAbd al-Karīm al-Shahrastānī, *Nihāyat al-iqdām fī ʿilm al-kalām* (Cairo: Maktabat al-Thaqāfah al-Dīniyyah, 2009), 119. See also Ibn Taymiyyah's elaboration on this comment in *Darʾ taʿāruḍ,* 3:129.

There can be no certainty in anything without this fundamental conviction.[52] This is precisely how *Sūrah al-Fātiḥah* is structured, beginning with the statement *alḥamdulillāh*. It is significant to note that the chapter does not express this in the imperative form, either 'praise God' (*iḥmadū Allah*)[53] or 'say: praise belongs to God' (*qul Alḥamdulilah*), but simply makes the declaration directly. It shows us that praising the Creator is the most natural human impulse.

Moreover, it is through our recognition of Allah and His divine nature that all else becomes intelligible and meaningful. The Alexandrian jurist and spiritual sage Ibn ʿAṭāʾ Allāh al-Iskandarī (d. 709 AH) writes about the distinction between the one who knows God through His creation versus one who knows the creation through God:

> What a difference between one whose inference proceeds from God (*yastadillu bihī*) and one whose inference proceeds towards Him (*yastadillu ʿalayhi*)! He who has Him as his starting point knows the Truth as it is and proves any matter with reference to the existence of its source. But inferential argumentation comes from being unable to reach Him. Otherwise, when was it that He was absent such that one has to proceed inferentially to Him? Or when was it that He was distant so that created things are required to lead us to Him?[54]

Rather than beginning by casting doubt on God and seeking to prove Him through obscure lines of reasoning, we would do better to look at how all existence makes sense only through a theocentric worldview. We are able to perceive meaning, purpose, and wisdom

52 Ibn Taymiyyah derives this point from the dialogue between Prophet Mūsā and Pharaoh. See Ibn Taymiyyah, *Majmūʿ al-fatāwā*, 16:332–35.

53 See al-Rāzī's comments in this regard, *Great Exegesis*, 1:351.

54 Ibn ʿAṭāʾ Allāh, *Kitāb al-ḥikam*, trans. Victor Danner (Leiden: Brill, 1973), 28, translation modified.

in the structure of reality and in every aspect of creation. This is precisely what our *fiṭrah* directs us to do, and it results in our ability to recognise the signs all around us. The Syrian scholar Shaykh ʿAbd al-Raḥmān Ḥasan Ḥabannakah al-Maydānī (d. 2004) writes:

> The first feeling that arises in the depths of a person when he reflects on himself and the universe around him is the sense of a powerful force controlling the cosmos that grants it order and organization, governs life and death, formation and disintegration, change and development, movement and stillness, and all the wise transformations that occur within it. A person senses this truth and believes in it deeply, whether he can provide deductive evidence for this feeling or not. The evidence of the innate disposition (*fiṭrah*) and intuitive insight is a truthful witness that precedes theoretical evidence and is often more precise.[55]

He also writes:

> This is the undeniable truth of the existence of Allah, whose signs are evident in everything. Allah has naturally constituted minds and thoughts to perceive this reality and has endowed them with the means to discover Him and the scales with which to weigh the evidence, affirming the truth and nullifying falsehood.[56]

The very structure of our thoughts is organised in a way that is naturally oriented towards seeking God. Recognising God is the default state for every soul and the logical beginning of rational inquiry and moral reflection. Conversely, every worldview that does not take into consideration our relationship with our Creator

55 ʿAbd al-Raḥmān Ḥasan Ḥabannakah al-Maydānī, *al-ʿAqīdah al-Islāmiyyah wa ususuhā* (Damascus: Dār al-Qalam, 2009), 85–86.

56 Al-Maydānī, *al-ʿAqīdah al-Islāmiyyah*, 93.

is a logical and moral dead end; it fails to guide humanity to true ethical cultivation and spiritual nourishment. Therefore, *Sūrah al-Fātiḥah* reinstates the *fiṭrah* and restores within one's mind the conceptual landscape necessary for spiritual development, moral decisions, and rational evaluation.

In fact, the Andalusian Berber exegete and grammarian, Imam Abū Ḥayyān (d. 745 AH) noted that atheism is refuted in *Sūrah al-Fātiḥah* by the simple word *iyyāka* (You alone), indicating that we are addressing Allah directly because His existence and presence are already known to us.[57] If we really want to know Allah, we just need to make an earnest effort to speak to Him. The statement *alḥamdulillāh* illustrates this as well. The very fact that we can begin our relationship with God through such a statement without the need for convoluted philosophical arguments is because we already have an internalised awareness of Him. The journey of our guidance to Him begins with the simple yet profound declaration of *alḥamdulillāh*, understanding that all our blessings and all goodness in existence are from Him.

All gratitude is meaningless if we fail to recognise the true source of all blessings. Everything in life is a gift from Allah, our Creator.

57 Abū Ḥayyān, *al-Baḥr al-muḥīṭ* (Beirut: Dār al-Fikr, 2010), 1:44. A similar point has been made by Ibn Taymiyyah concerning the opening to the ninety-sixth chapter of the Qur'an, *Sūrah al-ʿAlaq*. He observes that the passage states, "Read in the name of *your* Lord" (rather than simply "the Lord"), which implies that the human subject is already familiar with God. See Ibn Taymiyyah, *Majmūʿ al-fatāwā*, 16:324.

Rabb al-ʿālamīn

Lord of the Worlds

Materialism dismantled

The second phrase of this verse describes Allah as the Lord of the Worlds.[58] In particular, the Arabic word used here to describe Allah is the word *Rabb*. The meaning of *Rabb* encompasses God's complete sovereignty over all creation. It also carries the connotation of nurturing, guiding, and correcting.[59] The meaning of *Rabb* is therefore connected to the discussion in the previous section as the bestowal of blessings and guidance warrants praise and gratitude. Moreover, the term for providing one's children with an ethical upbringing is *tarbiyah* (nurturing) which is linguistically related. Al-Rāghib al-Iṣfahānī writes, "The term *al-Rabb* originally means 'to nurture,' which refers to bringing something into being stage by stage until it reaches completion."[60]

58 Abū Ḥafṣ al-Nasafī explains that grammatically the word *Rabb* has been connected via the genitive construct (*iḍāfah*) to "*al-ʿĀlamīn*" as if to say, "How magnificent am I that all creation belongs to Me, and how magnificent are My beloved servants that I am theirs!" See al-Nasafī, *al-Taysīr fī al-tafsīr*, 1:109–10.

59 Abū Ḥayyān, *al-Baḥr al-muḥīṭ*, 1:33.

60 See al-Rāghib al-Iṣfahānī, *al-Mufradāt fī gharīb al-Qurʾān*, ed. Ṣafwān ʿAdnān al-Dāwdī (Damascus: Dār al-Qalam, 1412/1991), 336 and *Tafsīr al-Rāghib al-Iṣfahānī* (Tanta: University of Ṭanṭā, 1999), 1:54; al-Bayḍāwī, *Anwār al-tanzīl*, 1:28. For a linguistic analysis of *tarbiyah*, see Khālid al-Ḥāzimī, *Uṣūl al-tarbiyah al-islamiyyah* (Riyadh: Dār ʿĀlam al-Kitāb, 2000), 17–20.

Therefore, we learn that we have a benevolent Lord who wishes for us to be guided towards righteousness, virtue, and ethical conduct.[61] It is no coincidence that the majority of supplications in Islam begin by invoking God as "our nurturing Lord" (*rabbanā*).[62]

One lesson that can be immediately drawn from the meaning of the word *Rabb* is that Allah has made the creation with purpose and meaning. Allah nurtures us and provides for us so that we can grow morally and spiritually. Life is all about this purpose and meaning which God has assigned His creation. The universe does not simply exist pointlessly.[63] The fact that there is a message behind our existence means that there is more to life than the physical stuff of matter. Atheism, discussed in the previous section, is most frequently motivated by an underlying presumption of

61 Divine providence encompasses nurturing the creation in its physical growth (*tarbiyah khalqiyyah*) as well as nurturing it towards knowledge and virtuous deeds (*tarbiyah sharʿiyyah*). See Muḥammad Rashīd Riḍā, *Tafsīr al-manār* (Cairo: al-Hayʾa al-Miṣriyyah al-ʿĀmmah li-l-Kitāb, 1990), 1:43.

62 Al-Qurṭubī, *al-Jāmiʿ li-aḥkām al-Qurʾān*, 1:137.

63 Muḥammad Shafīʿ, *Maʿārif al-Qurʾān*, 1:65.

materialism, which says that there is nothing beyond physical matter. Just like atheism can be doctrinal or behavioural, materialism can as well. There is philosophical (metaphysical) materialism that denies the existence of anything beyond the material realm, and then there is psychological (consumer) materialism that diminishes the importance of anything beyond the material realm. Although the rise of philosophical materialism created the conditions for a culture of consumer materialism, it is important to remember that on an individual level the latter does not require the former. Thus, there are people who are very *materialistic* in their mindset and attitude regardless of their self-professed religious beliefs: they care only about worldly possessions, expensive clothes, lavish homes, fancy cars, or jewelry. The Qur'an teaches us:

Philosophical materialism
"Nothing exists besides matter."

Psychological materialism
"Nothing matters besides matter (i.e., materialistic possessions and wealth)."

> In the eyes of men, the love of things they covet has been made alluring: desire for women and children, vast hoards of gold and silver, branded horses, cattle, and fertile land. These are the pleasures of this worldly life, but with Allah is the best return. (Qur'an 3:14)

Taking this section in consideration alongside the previous one, we see that the full verse "*Alḥamdulillāhi Rabb al-ʿālamīn*" establishes first the negation of atheism and then the negation of the underlying materialistic mindset that most often motivates atheism. Moreover, recognising that there is a moral purpose behind all of existence established by the One Creator negates both polytheism and nihilism, which are also negated elsewhere in this *sūrah*.[64]

64 The negation of nihilism has already been discussed under *alḥamdulillāh*, and the negation of polytheism will be discussed below under *iyyāka naʿbudu*.

"The real religion of the West today, the religion that rules over its mind and spirit, is not Christianity but materialism."

Sayyid Abū al-Ḥasan ʿAlī al-Nadwī (d. 1999)

In his celebrated 1950 Arabic work entitled *Mādhā khasira al-ʿālam bi-inḥiṭāṭ al-Muslimīn* (What did the world lose with the decline of Muslims?), the Indian Muslim scholar Sayyid Abū al-Ḥasan ʿAlī al-Nadwī (d. 1999) diagnosed materialism as the principal malady of modern Western civilsation. He wrote, "The real religion of the West today, the religion that rules over its mind and spirit, is not Christianity but materialism."[65] Materialism is evident within the value hierarchy of people's choices. It is the metaphysical lens by which people view the world and organise their priorities. However, this state of affairs is one that came about gradually in the Western world. Al-Nadwī explains:

> Provoked by the intellectual stagnation of the clergy and the heinous atrocities perpetrated by the Inquisition, the enlightened sections among the Europeans developed a strong aversion to all knowledge, morality and truth associated with the Church and religion in general. They could not help connecting religion with all the misdeeds of the Papacy and the brutal sufferings of the secular scholars. A dismal disbelief crept over the Continent.

---

65 Sayyid Abū al-Ḥasan ʿAlī Nadwī, *Islam and the World: The Rise and Decline of Muslims and Its Effect on Mankind*, trans. Muhammad Asif Kidwai (Leicester: UK Islamic Academy, 2005), 121.

> ...In this spiritual vacuum, Europe took a tragic turn. It descended by degrees into the depths of materialism. Its social thinkers and scientists investigated the nature of the world and of life as if there were no absolute power which created them and ruled over them according to some plan and purpose without itself being subject to any laws. They interpreted the material universe and its manifestations along mechanical lines and called it objective and scientific, rejecting as slavery to tradition whatever was based on belief in the existence of God. One by one, they disowned everything that existed apart from matter and energy, everything that was not realizable in experience, or could not be weighed or measured.
>
> For a long time the Europeans did not openly reject the notion of God—all Europeans are not atheists, even today—but the intellectual and moral position they had adopted definitely precluded all claim of religion upon life. Attempts were made after the Renaissance to produce a reconciliation between Religion and Science, as some sort of religious arrangement was thought necessary to preserve the tranquility of society by influencing the social relations of men. But the pace set by materialistic civilization was so hot that religion could not stand it. It also entailed a good deal of inconvenience to keep materialism in harmony with transcendental truths. As decades and centuries advanced, the ceremony was waived, and much of Europe took unconditionally to the worship of matter.[66]

The worship of matter indeed became the reigning dogma amongst the European intelligentsia that displaced recognition of divine lordship. The loss of a theocentric worldview had

66 Nadwī, *Islam and the World*, 118–20.

costly ethical consequences. Viewing everything through a materialistic lens entails organising societies around power and wealth without any regard for moral and spiritual development. Communism and capitalism are merely two sects of the false religion of materialism. The Syrian Islamic thinker and revivalist Shaykh Muṣṭafā al-Sibāʿī (d. 1964) concludes: "Thus both branches of western civilization, capitalism and communism, have taken away man's peace of mind, security and moral standards and replaced that ideal with materialism."[67] Concerning communism, Abū al-Ḥasan ʿAlī al-Nadwī also writes:

> Karl Marx is one example of the total immersion of the Western mind in materialism. He developed the doctrine of class struggle to maintain that all history was merely the result of economic conditions, under whose influence all other life-phenomena had received form and imprint. He recognized only the economic aspect of human existence, denying the validity of other factors such as religion, ethics, soul and intellect.[68]

Viewing everything through a materialistic lens entails organising societies around power and wealth without any regard for moral and spiritual development.

67 Muṣṭafā al-Sibāʿī, *Civilization of Faith: A Journey through Islamic History*, trans. Nasiruddin al-Khattab (Riyadh: IIPH, 2005), 21.

68 Nadwī, *Islam and the World*, 129.

The erasure of religion at any cost became a paramount focus within the communist movement. In 1929, at the second congress of the League of Militant Atheists, Yemelyn Yaroslavsky, a Bolshevik revolutionary said:

> It is our duty to destroy every religious world-concept... If the destruction of ten million human beings, as happened in the last war, should be necessary for the triumph of one definite class, then that must be done and it will be done.[69]

Indeed, the Soviet communist regime murdered thousands of clergymen and destroyed churches, monasteries, mosques, and religious schools in an effort to eradicate religion and construct its envisioned utopia.[70] The total bloodshed carried out under the Soviet communist reign was astonishing: an estimated 62 million were killed, a large portion including those who died from coerced labor in the lethal conditions of the Gulag (forced labor camps).[71] Muhammad Asad, a translator of the Qur'an and an Austro-Hungarian Jewish convert to Islam, wrote in 1933:

> No doubt, there are still many individuals in the West who feel and think in a truly religious way and make the most desperate efforts to reconcile their beliefs with the spirit of their civilization; but they are exceptions only. The average Occidental—be he a Democrat or a Fascist, a Capitalist or a Communist, a manual worker or an intellectual—knows only one positive "religion," and that is the worship of material progress, the belief that there is no other goal in life than

---

69 Alfred McClung Lee and Elizabeth Briant Lee, *The Fine Art of Propaganda* (New York: Octagon Books, 1972), 90.

70 Peter Watson, "The Bolshevik Crusade for Scientific Atheism," in *The Age of Atheists: How We Have Sought to Live Since the Death of God* (New York: Simon and Schuster, 2014), 200–219. He cites as a source Paul Froese, *The Plot to Kill God: Findings from the Soviet Experiment in Secularization* (Berkley: University of California Press, 2008).

71 R. J. Rummel, *Death by Government* (Rutgers, NJ: Transaction Publishers, 1994), 24.

> to make that very life continually easier or, as the current expression goes, "independent of Nature." The temples of this "religion" are the gigantic factories, cinemas, chemical laboratories, dance-halls, hydro-electric works, and its priests are bankers, engineers, film stars, captains of industry, record sportsmen. The unavoidable result of this craving for power and pleasure is the creation of hostile groups armed to the teeth and determined to destroy each other whenever and wherever their respective interests clash. And on the cultural side, the result is the creation of a human type whose morality is confined to the question of practical utility alone, and whose highest criterion of good and evil is material success.[72]

Capitalist nation-states are ambivalent towards moral aims and ethical goals. Abū al-Ḥasan ʿAlī al-Nadwī writes:

> Godless states are, in fact, trade societies or cartels whose real job is to extort, not to confer, benefits. They have no spiritual roots, no ethical ideals, and they are supremely unconcerned with the inner selves of their peoples and the welfare of humanity at large. Their attention is focused only on material gain. Whenever there is a clash between morality and economic gain, these states will always give preference to the latter... Prostitution is, for example, a legal trade; usury is practiced by governments; gambling flourishes under respectable names; alcohol is freely available and the industry is extolled as a source of national wealth. Radio, cinema and television function solely as an instrument of entertainment. Instead of educating the masses and refining them morally, it perverts their tastes and makes them frivolous.[73]

---

72 Muhammad Asad, *Islam at the Crossroads* (Gibraltar: Dar al-Andalus, 1982), 44.

73 Nadwī, *Islam and the World*, 136–37.

In the phrase "Lord of the Worlds" we have the Arabic word *ʿālamīn*. The word *ʿālamīn* is a plural of another plural (or collective noun), *ʿālam* (world), which has no singular.[74] It encompasses everything in existence besides Allah, including all the species of creation existing in every time period, encompassing both the seen and unseen realms.[75] It is linguistically derived from *ʿalāmah* (sign) because everything in creation serves as a sign of God.[76] Many scholars have explained that it refers especially to the sentient creations endowed with moral choice, namely, the *jinn* and humankind.[77] Allah created us with the opportunity to strive for moral virtue and use the blessings He has given us to fulfil the rights of others. He is our *Rabb* and He wishes for us to develop ethically. Given that creation is composed of sentient beings with moral faculties capable of virtue and vice, it becomes clear that the materialist paradigm is gravely in error.

On the mechanistic worldview of materialism, reality is nothing but the interactions of physical matter, and human beings are nothing more than glorified meat machines (or "lumbering robots" as Richard Dawkins put it).[78] For the materialist, there is nothing sacred that defines the human being as distinct from the physical

---

74 Al-Ṭabarī, *The Comprehensive Exposition*, 117–19. Some scholars observe that *ʿālamīn* is a minor plural (*jamʿ al-qillah*) rather than a major plural (*jamʿ al-kathrah*) because when attributed to God, all the worlds are miniscule in comparison with His vast omnipotence and omniscience. See al-Ṭībī, *Futūḥ al-ghayb* (Dubai: DIHQA, 2013), 1:733 and al-Sanūsī, *Tafsīr Sūrat al-Fātiḥah*, 11.

75 Ibn ʿAṭiyyah, *al-Muḥarrar al-wajīz*, 67. Muḥammad al-Ghazālī includes "everything that has ever existed or shall ever exist" (*Thematic Commentary*, 2).

76 Al-Naḥḥās, *Maʿānī al-Qurʾān* (Mecca: Umm al-Qurāʾ University, 1988), 1:61; al-Bayḍāwī, *Anwār al-tanzīl*, 1:28. Al-Bayḍāwī notes that this verse proves that contingent entities require a cause for the perpetuation of their existence and not only for their origination.

77 This has been reported by Ibn ʿAbbās among others. See al-Ṭayyār, *Mawsūʿat al-tafsīr al-maʾthūr*, 2:26 and al-ʿUmrānī, *Mawsūʿat madrasat Makkah fī al-tafsīr*, 1:14. See also al-Samarqandī, *Baḥr al-ʿulūm* (Beirut: DKI, 1993), 1:80; al-Thaʿlabī, *Kashf al-bayān ʿan tafsīr al-Qurʾān* (Jeddah: Dār al-Tafsīr, 2015), 2:391–93.

78 Richard Dawkins, *The Selfish Gene* (Oxford: Oxford University Press, 2006), 19. See also Conor Cunningham, *Genealogy of Nihilism* (London and New York: Routledge, 2005), 246.

The emergence of materialism provided the thought structure through which the project of colonialism became fathomable.

objects of the world that surround him.[79] The human body is but another object of the world to be acted upon, subjugated, and dominated. The human being sees himself as a lord over the natural world and rejects his moral responsibility towards the one True Lord, the *Rabb*. The emergence of such notions provided the thought structure through which the project of colonialism became fathomable. The colonisers, being convinced of their own enlightenment, proceeded to engage in the subjugation of other nations, exploiting their resources and enslaving or massacring their populations as they saw fit. British colonialism killed 100 million Indians in 40 years between 1880 to 1920.[80] The ruthless violence of colonialism merged with the insatiable greed of capitalism: "Drawing on nearly two centuries of detailed data on tax and trade, Patnaik calculated that Britain drained a total of nearly $45 trillion from India during the period 1765 to 1938."[81] Together, these forces enabled the decimation of indigenous

79 Caner Dagli writes, "We are told to believe that all human beings are 'equal in dignity,' but we are given absolutely no explanation of why these beings have this attribute of dignity... We want to say that people are equal but do not want to acknowledge that what makes human beings equal is that very spiritual nature that we now deny them." Caner K. Dagli, "Dignity Is for the Heart, Not the Ego," *Renovatio* 7, no. 1 (2023), https://renovatio.zaytuna.edu/article/dignity-is-for-the-heart-not-the-ego.

80 Dylan Sullivan and Jason Hickel, "How British Colonialism Killed 100 Million Indians in 40 Years," Al Jazeera, December 22, 2022, https://www.aljazeera.com/opinions/2022/12/2/how-british-colonial-policy-killed-100-million-indians. Cf. Dylan Sullivan and Jason Hickel, "Capitalism and Extreme Poverty: A Global Analysis of Real Wages, Human Height, and Mortality Since the Long 16th Century," *World Development* 161 (2023): 106026.

81 Jason Hickel, "How Britain Stole $45 Trillion from India," Al Jazeera, December 8, 2018, https://www.aljazeera.com/opinions/2018/12/19/how-britain-stole-45-trillion-from-india.

populations and the exploitation of vast amounts of natural resources. In North, South, and Central America, European settlers killed 56 million indigenous people over the course of one century—enough to produce a shift in global temperature.[82]

The current genocide unfolding in Gaza provides another stark reminder of the brutal violence of colonialism. As Israeli historian Ilan Pappé explains,

> Zionism is the last remaining active settler-colonialist movement or project. Settler colonialism is, in a nutshell, a project of replacement and displacement, settlement and expulsion. Since this is the project, that you take over someone's homeland and you're not satisfied until you feel you've taken enough of the land and you've gotten rid of enough of the native people, as long as you feel that this is an incomplete project, you will continue with the project.[83]

This was a reality openly acknowledged before colonialism became a negative word in the West. "Zionism is a colonizing adventure," wrote Vladimir Jabotinsky (d. 1940), one of its founding fathers.[84] A *New York Times* article in 1899 featured a headline expressing that Zionists "will colonize Palestine."[85]

---

82 Lauren Kent, "European Colonizers Killed So Many Native Americans That It Changed the Global Climate, Researchers Say," CNN, February 2, 2019, https://www.cnn.com/2019/02/01/world/european-colonization-climate-change-trnd/index.html. B. B. Chaudhuri, Shubhra Chakrabarti, and Utsa Patnaik, *Agrarian and Other Histories: Essays for Binay Bhushan Chaudhuri* (New Delhi: Tulika Books, 2017).

83 Eli Masse, "Ilan Pappe: Israel Is the Last Remaining, Active Settler-Colonialist Project," In These Times, May 5, 2016, https://inthesetimes.com/article/ilan-pappe-bernie-sanders-noam-chomsky-bds-israel-palestine. See also Ilan Pappé, "Zionism as Colonialism: A Comparative View of Diluted Colonialism in Asia and Africa," *South Atlantic Quarterly* 107, no. 4 (October 1, 2008): 611–33.

84 From a 1925 essay Jabotinsky wrote entitled "The Iron Law," as cited in Nur Masalha, *Expulsion of the Palestinians* (Washington, DC: Institute for Palestine Studies, 1992), 45.

85 "Conference of Zionists; Elect Delegates at Their Meeting in Baltimore. Will Colonize Palestine Rabbis Gottheil and Wise Were Chosen Members of the International Executive Committee," *New York Times*, June 20, 1899, https://www.nytimes.com/1899/06/20/archives/conference-of-zionists-elect-delegates-at-their-meeting-in.html.

Islam

God

God is the Lord of the Universe and He created all things with purpose. Everything has been provided by Him. He wants us to live ethically and use the gifts He has given us to help others. Everything ultimately belongs to God.

Materialism

No acknowledgment of the Creator.

Nothing exists except the material world. So, in a lifestyle without accountability, acquiring material things is the ultimate success.

Professor Adam Stern describes Zionism as "a tradition within which an essential connection between messianism and colonialism has developed and continues to exist."[86] During the Nakba, a total of 531 Palestinian villages were destroyed and over 70 massacres were committed against innocent civilians, resulting in the deaths of more than 15,000 Palestinians between 1947 and 1949 and the expulsion of 750,000 Palestinians from their ancestral lands.[87] The Gaza genocide is a continuation of the Nakba and the underlying hubris and self-aggrandisation that animate all forms of ethnic cleansing, land theft, colonialisms,

86 Adam Y. Stern,"On Zionism and the Concept of Deferral," *Critical Times* 5, no. 1 (April 1, 2022): 20–49.

87 "Israeli Apartheid: The Legacy of the Ongoing Nakba at 75," ReliefWeb, May 15, 2023, https://reliefweb.int/report/occupied-palestinian-territory/israeli-apartheid-legacy-ongoing-nakba-75-enar.

and genocides. Journalist Chris Hedges describes the mentality of the perpetrators of the Gaza genocide in the following terms:

> We revel in our *libido dominandi*—our lust for domination.
>
> ...We may feel insignificant in Israel, but here, in Gaza, we are King Kong, a little tyrant on a little throne. We stride through the rubble of Gaza, surrounded by the might of industrial weapons, able to pulverize in an instant whole apartment blocks and neighborhoods, and say, like Vishnu, "Now I have become death, the destroyer of worlds."
>
> But we are not content simply with killing. We want the walking dead to pay homage to our divinity.
>
> ... Rafah is the prize at the end of the road. Rafah is the great killing field where we will slaughter Palestinians on a scale unseen in this genocide. Watch us. It will be an orgy of blood and death. It will be of Biblical proportions. No one will stop us. We kill in paroxysms of excitement. We are gods.[88]

When US senators threatened to invade the Hague if it held Israel responsible for war crimes, Francesca Albanese, the UN Special Rapporteur on the occupied Palestinian territories, asked in astonishment at their audacity, "Who do they think they are, the lords of the world?"[89]

88 Chris Hedges, "Israel's Willing Executioners," Consortium News, May 14, 2024, https://consortiumnews.com/2024/05/14/chris-hedges-israels-willing-executioners/.

89 Middle East Eye (@MiddleEastEye), "'Who do they think they are, the lords of the world?' Francesca Albanese, the UN special rapporteur on occupied Palestinian territories, talked to Abby Martin on @EmpireFiles about the threats by some US senators against the ICC after its chief prosecutor, Karim Khan, requested arrest warrants for Israeli officials.," X, May 25, 2024, 4:07 p.m., https://x.com/MiddleEastEye/status/1794475415769166141.

Man is not his own lord, nor can any man be lord of the world by any stretch of the imagination. God alone is our Lord, and He is the Lord of all the worlds. Everything belongs ultimately to Allah and therefore our purpose in life is not to chase materialistic pleasures but to pursue the pleasure of our Creator. In this simple opening declaration of *al-Fātiḥah*, the Qur'an eloquently eviscerates the ideological organs behind every tyrannical and totalitarian regime throughout history. It was Pharaoh who declared to his people, "I am your *Rabb* (Lord) Most High" (Qur'an 79:24), of whose genocidal actions the Qur'an frequently reminds us (Qur'an 2:49, 7:141, 14:6, 28:4). Every tyrant is threatened by the liberating message of Allah's lordship (*rubūbiyyah*). "Do you kill a man simply because he says my *Rabb* is Allah?," a believing man from Pharaoh's family asks (Qur'an 40:28). The early Muslims saw such liberation at the heart of Islam's message. This is eloquently expressed in the words of the Muslim emissary sent to the Persian army, Rib'ī ibn 'Āmir:

> Allah has sent us in order to liberate His servants from servitude to other servants to the servitude of God alone, from the narrowness of this worldly life to the vastness of this life and the next, and from the injustice of false ideologies to the justice of Islam."[90]

Only God holds sovereignty over His servants. In insisting that all human beings bow only to their Maker, that they all have One Lord, and that they all stand equally before Him as morally accountable sentient beings, Islam eliminated the very roots of human subjugation and dehumanisation, including one of its most pernicious forms, namely, racism. Syed Naquib al-Attas

90 Rib'ī ibn 'Āmir was sent by the commander of the Muslim army Sa'd ibn Abī Waqqāṣ to Rustum, general of the Persian army, prior to the Battle of Qadisiyya in the year 15/636. See Ibn Jarīr al-Ṭabarī, *Tārīkh al-rusul wa-l-mulūk* (Cairo: Dār al-Ma'ārif, 1967), 3:520. Ibn Kathīr, *al-Bidāya wa al-nihāya* (Cairo: Dār Hajr, 1998), 9:622.

explains that one of the implications of recognising God's divine lordship is that "all souls have the same status in relation to their Lord."[91] And as the American Muslim author Shaykh Jamaal Zarabozo likewise comments, "Since Allah is the *Rabb* of all people, there is no tribe or race that has a special status just because they are from that tribe or race."[92] In fact, this is an ethical principle that can only be coherently grounded with theology. The Bosnian Muslim philosopher and politician Alija Izetbegović (d. 2003) explained, "The equality and brotherhood of people is possible only if man is created by God. The equality of men is a spiritual and not a natural, physical, or intellectual fact."[93] He further observes that in contrast to many ancient philosophers, "only the ethics of the revealed religions postulated clearly and without ambiguity the equality of all men as God's creatures."[94]

The prohibition of racism is made very explicit in Islam and is established in both the Qur'an and the Prophetic teachings. Allah says in the Qur'an:

> O mankind, indeed We have created you from a male and a female and made you peoples and tribes that you may know one another. Indeed, the noblest of you in the sight of Allah is the most righteous of you. Indeed, Allah is Knowing and Acquainted. (Qur'an 49:13)

---

91 Syed Naquib al-Attas, *Islam and Secularism* (Kuala Lumpur: ISTAC, 1993), 73.

92 Jamaal Zarabozo, *Al-Fatihah: An In-Depth Study of Surah al Fatiha,* 28 Audio CD set (Boulder, CO: SoundKnowledge Audio Publishers, 2006), disc 5.

93 Alija Izetbegović, *Islam between East and West* (Indianapolis: American Trust Publications, 1989), 36.

94 Izetbegović, *Islam between East and West,* 37.

Allah has sent us in order to liberate His servants from servitude to other servants to the servitude of God alone, from the narrowness of this worldly life to the vastness of this life and the next, and from the injustice of false ideologies to the justice of Islam.

Ribʿī ibn ʿĀmir, the Muslim emissary sent to the Persian army

The Prophet Muhammad ﷺ said:

> O people, indeed your Lord is one. Verily, there is no superiority of an Arab over a non-Arab, nor of a non-Arab over an Arab, nor of a white person over a black person, nor of a black person over a white person, except by piety. Indeed, the most honourable of you in the sight of God is the most righteous among you.[95]

The very term *ʿālamīn* eliminates any notions of racial superiority, recognising that our moral essence as created beings is to serve our Creator alone. The American Muslim civil rights activist Malcolm X wrote in his letters, "America needs to understand Islam because this is the one religion that erases from its society the race problem... I have never before seen sincere and true brotherhood practiced by all colors together, irrespective of their color."[96] When one witnesses how deeply embedded the dehumanisation of people of colour is within the Western psyche and the thought structures that animate it, the importance and relevance of this teaching becomes apparent. In Gaza, when Israel targeted and killed seven aid workers associated with the US-based World Central Kitchen charity, many noted with disappointment that it was only when Israel's victims were white that those in positions of power in the West seemed to show any concern.

95 Al-Bayhaqī, *Shuʿab al-īmān* (Riyadh: Maktabat al-Rushd, 2003), 7:132.

96 Malcolm X and Alex Haley, *The Autobiography of Malcolm X: As Told to Alex Haley* (New York: Grove Press, 1964), 345.

British journalist Peter Oborne wrote:

> It is fair to say that, among the western media and political classes, there has been more noise made in the past 24 hours about the Israeli killing of seven aid workers than about all the 32,000 dead Palestinians put together... The real crime in the eyes of the West was Israel's slaughter of white people. What happened yesterday is a terrible human tragedy for the aid workers and their families. But it is also a story of western racism.[97]

These horrors further highlight to us the imperative of restoring a true moral order to the world, rooted not in materialistic myths, colonial legacies, or racist sentiments but in the divine guidance of the One who is *Rabb al-ʿālamīn*.

Allah is our *Rabb* indicating that He nurtures us and provides for us so that we can grow morally and spiritually and fulfil our purpose in life.

97 Peter Oborne, "Israel's Slaughter of Aid Workers Is a Tragedy. But It Is Also a Story of Western Racism," Middle East Eye, April 3, 2024, https://www.middleeasteye.net/opinion/israel-slaughter-aid-workers-tragedy-western-racism.

al-Raḥmān al-Raḥīm

The All-Merciful, the Ever-Merciful

Deism dismantled

As we noted in the preceding verse of *Sūrah al-Fātiḥah*, Allah is described as the *Rabb*, the Lord who is nurturing and wishes for our guidance. His benevolence towards creation is expressed further in this verse by two divine names: *al-Raḥmān* and *al-Raḥīm*. Both these names describe God with the attribute of *raḥmah* (mercy), meaning that He is compassionate, benevolent, caring, loving, merciful, and kind.[98] The word is linguistically linked to the word *raḥim* (womb), which emphasises the profound nature of the compassion of Allah towards His creation, greater than a mother's love and care for her child.[99] In terms of the distinction between these two names, some scholars have explained that the name *al-Raḥmān* describes the scope of His mercy for

Deism
Belief in a God who created the world but is not involved in it and does not send guidance or answer prayers.

98 See also Jinan Yousef, "Understanding the Qur'an Through the Names and Attributes of Allah," Yaqeen Institute for Islamic Research, March 30, 2023. https://yaqeeninstitute.org/read/paper/approaching-the-quran-through-the-names-of-allah.

99 See *Ṣaḥīḥ al-Bukhārī*, no. 5988; *Sunan Ibn Mājah*, no. 4297.

الرحمن
الرحيم

all creation, while *al-Raḥīm* describes the immensity of His mercy for the faithful.[100] Imam Abū Ḥāmid al-Ghazālī (d. 505 AH) observes that the mercy mentioned in this verse relates to both the preceding and the succeeding verses. His divine mercy connects to the fact that Allah is "Lord of the Worlds," for every facet of His creation exemplifies the divine providence and care which He has afforded even the smallest of creatures like the honeybee. His divine mercy also connects to the fact that Allah is "Master of the Day of Judgement," as He will judge His creation in accordance with His immense mercy towards them.[101]

Understanding the mercy of the Creator dismisses the idea of deism, that there is a "higher power" who fashioned this world but who does not care to involve himself in human affairs. There is a connection between the repudiation of deism and the repudiation of secularism, discussed under the next verse. In his commentary on al-Fātiḥah, the Syrian Islamic scholar and revivalist Saʿīd Ḥawwā (d. 1989) writes, "One of the presumptions of Greek philosophy was that God does not enter into the affairs of creation. Currently, we find that most people also assume that God has nothing to do with the affairs of people, and the ideology of separating religion and state is nothing but a manifestation of this thought process."[102]

How does understanding divine mercy show us the error in deism? God's mercy entails that He would never deprive His creation of the knowledge needed for their prosperity.[103] Once, the Companions of the Prophet witnessed a mother searching

---

100 This is the opinion of al-Ṭabarī, *Comprehensive Exposition,* 1:103–4. For a summary of the various opinions, refer to Abu Rumaysah, *The Spiritual Cure: An Explanation to Surah al-Fātiḥah* (Birmingham: Daar us-Sunnah Publishers, 2006), 86–91.

101 Al-Ghazālī, *Jawāhir al-Qurʾān* (Beirut: Dār Iḥyāʾ al-ʿUlūm, 1986), 65–68.

102 Saʿīd Ḥawwā, *al-Asās fī al-tafsīr* (Cairo: Dār al-Salām, 1985), 1:47.

103 Al-Zahrānī, *"Aḍwāʾ ʿalā al-iʿjāz al-balāghī fī Sūrat al-Fātiḥah,"* 131.

God's mercy entails that He would never deprive His creation of the knowledge needed for their prosperity.

desperately for her lost infant; upon finding her infant she immediately began to nurse him. The Prophet ﷺ asked his Companions, "Do you think this woman would ever throw her child into the fire?" When the Companions replied no, the Prophet said, "Allah is more merciful to His servants than this mother is to her infant."[104] The loving care and concern a mother has for her infant is an infinitesimal fraction of Allah's mercy for His creation. A parent who negligently abandons his children would be considered morally irresponsible. No one can impose any obligation upon Allah, yet Allah has ordained upon Himself a moral responsibility towards His creation just as the creation has a reciprocal moral responsibility towards Him:

> Muʿādh said, "I was riding behind the Prophet, peace and blessings be upon him, on a donkey named ʿUfayr. He said, 'O Muʿādh, do you know the right of Allah upon His servants and the right of the servants upon Allah?'
>
> I said, 'Allah and His Messenger know best.'
>
> He said, 'Indeed, the right of Allah upon the servants is that they worship Him and not associate anything with Him. And the right of the servants upon Allah is that He not punish those who do not associate anything with Him.'

104 *Ṣaḥīḥ Bukhārī*, no. 5999; *Ṣaḥīḥ Muslim*, no. 2754.

> Then I said, 'O Messenger of Allah, shall I not then inform the people?' He said, 'Do not inform them lest they rely on this alone.'"[105]

Likewise, God does not do injustice:

> The Messenger of Allah reported that his Lord has said, "O My servants, verily I have forbidden oppression upon Myself and have made it forbidden amongst you, so do not wrong one another."[106]

Deism presents either a deity who has a purpose but is unjust and unmerciful or a deity who has no purpose at all. In the case of the former, why would a benevolent God bring into existence a creation capable of discerning guidance but abandon them without it? In the case of the latter, Allah says:

> And We did not create the heaven and earth and that which is between them in play. If it had been Our wish to take a pastime, We should surely have found it in Our presence, if We were to act in such a manner. (Qur'an 21:16–17)

> And We did not create the heavens and earth and what is between them in play. We did not create them except with true purpose, but most of them do not know. (Qur'an 44:38–39)

---

105 *Ṣaḥīḥ Bukhārī*, no. 2856; *Ṣaḥīḥ Muslim*, no. 30b.

106 *Ṣaḥīḥ Muslim*, no. 2577; al-Bukhārī, *al-Adab al-mufrad*, no. 490.

If our existence has no purpose, then we fall back to nihilism. And if it does have a purpose, then by what rationale would it not be communicated to us? Imam Ibn al-Qayyim writes:

> First, being "Lord of the worlds," it does not behoove Him to leave His servants without guidance, failing to inform them of what is beneficial and what is harmful in their earthly life as well as afterlife. This would be a deficiency in lordship, and it would not be appropriate to attribute it to God; whosoever does so has failed rightfully to honor God.[107]

Similarly, Sayyid Quṭb writes concerning the meaning of *Rabb al-ʿālamīn*:

> This living and dynamic relationship between the Creator and the created is the perpetual fountain of life for all creation. God has not created the world and abandoned it to its own devices. He continues to be an active living authority over His creation, giving it what it needs for its continued and meaningful life.[108]

It is precisely because of the incapacity of deism to offer any "why" to existence that it fails to offer any persuasive rationale in its favour and garners its adherents largely through dissidence within the ranks of other religions. Indeed, deism arose out of dissatisfaction with religion as it was experienced in European history as *unmerciful* and oppressive. People wanted to distance themselves from "organised religion" altogether. Interestingly, the Qur'an hints at this underlying diagnosis:

---

107 Ibn al-Qayyim, *Ranks of the Divine Seekers*, 1:84.

108 Sayyid Quṭb, *In the Shade of the Qur'an* trans. Adil Salahi (Leicester: The Islamic Foundation, 2007), 1:3.

> It is by the mercy (*raḥmah*) of Allah that you [Prophet Muhammad] were gentle with them. Had you instead been cruel or hard-hearted, they would have certainly abandoned you. So pardon them and ask forgiveness for them and consult them in the matter. And when you have decided, then rely upon Allah. Indeed, Allah loves those who rely upon Him." (Qur'an 3:159)

This verse indicates that when religious authority is experienced as cruel and unmerciful, people will inevitably turn away from it. The verse also illustrates that the Islamic model of leadership must be a manifestation of mercy and compassion, as we see in the example of the Prophet Muhammad ﷺ. Leadership that is cruel, harsh, and unforgiving is not in keeping with the Islamic model of governance nor is it an effective path to winning the hearts and minds of people when calling them to Allah. Islam therefore rejects the idea of ruling others through fear, subjugation, and repression, all of which characterise totalitarianism. Moreover, the Prophet was asked to consult with others (*shūrā*) despite having no need to do so, which indicates that Islam does not espouse an autocratic style of leadership that does not care about the opinions of others, in contrast to authoritarianism. The Moroccan Islamic jurist Shaykh Ahmed Raïssouni explains that a clear principle established in the Qur'an, Sunnah, and practice of the companions is that the ruler (*al-ḥākim*) should serve as a *wakīl* (entrusted agent) of the Muslim community, i.e., a representative delegated to act in the community's best interests in accordance with the divinely revealed law.[109] Hence, there is no basis in Islam for dictatorial overlords who disregard the sacred law and the rights of the community.

---

109 Ahmed Raïssouni, *Fiqh al-thawrah: Murājaʿāt fī al-fiqh al-siyāsī al-Islāmī* (Cairo: Dār al-Kalimah 2013), 21.

Islam

God

Constant praise, devotion, love, gratitude, and worship of the Single Almighty Creator.

Deism

Acknowledgment of the existence of God but no involvement from Him in governing the creation or answering our prayers.

God's mercy is not only mentioned in this verse, but the names *al-Raḥmān* and *al-Raḥīm* are repeated in the *basmalah*, the formula that begins nearly every chapter in the Qur'an.[110] The Qur'an therefore insists that human beings formulate their understanding of the world in a manner that sees the mercy of God everywhere. This is the basis of all compassion among creation. The Prophet Muhammad ﷺ said:

> Allah divided mercy into one hundred parts. He kept ninety-nine parts with Himself and sent down one part to the earth, and because of that [one single part], His creations are merciful to one another, so that even the mare lifts up its hoofs away from its baby animal lest it should trample on it.[111]

---

110 The only chapter that does not begin with the *basmalah* is the ninth chapter, *Sūrah al-Tawbah*. According to ʿAlī ibn Abī Ṭālib, this is because the *basmalah* is a declaration of mercy while the ninth chapter opens with a declaration of war. See *Mustadrak al-Ḥākim*, no. 3673. See also al-Ṭayyār, *al-Muḥarrar fī ʿulūm al-Qurʾān* (Jeddah: Maʿhad al-Imām al-Shāṭibī, 2008), 201–2.

111 *Ṣaḥīḥ al-Bukhārī*, no. 6000.

> "If one is certain that God is beneficent and merciful, as indicated in *Sūrah al-Fātiḥah*, then one will also be benevolent to others (whether believers or disbelievers) and treat them with compassion." Dr. Tallal Zeni

It is through that single share of divine mercy that "mothers show compassion to their children and wild animals and the birds show compassion to one another."[112] In fact, contrary to what the ancient Greek philosophers thought, the basis of ethical action and true altruism is not philosophical arguments or definitions but rather compassion, which motivates empathy. The Libyan Muslim theologian Aref Ali Nayed explains:

> If one is challenged to define compassion, therefore, one better not try to provide a rational definition.The best strategy is to say, "Compassion is what you felt in your mother's arms!" We literally drink compassion in our mothers' milk. It grows in our hearts as we grow in our mothers' nourishing love. That is the creaturely source of our compassion and the source of our deep pre-understanding of it.[113]

---

112 *Sunan Ibn Mājah*, no. 4294.

113 Aref Ali Nayed, "Does Moral Action Depend on Reasoning? No, It Does Not!," in *Does Moral Action Depend on Reasoning? Thirteen Views on the Question* (Templeton Foundation, 2010).

In the image that deism presents, the world is generated by a prime mover unconcerned with our prosperity and morally indifferent to our struggles. The mechanical clockwork of the universe is simply set in motion and then abandoned. The psychological configuration that arises from such a worldview is one that gives us every reason to be apathetic and indifferent ourselves. There is no substantive basis for true ethical growth. Deism eliminates divine mercy from the universe, and what is left is only cold and uncaring materialism and determinism. The fact that the mechanistic worldview of modernity fails to provide any basis for compassion and mercy has prompted many in the Western world to look elsewhere for an alternative paradigm. The American historian of science Anne Harrington writes:

> I am moved to say that the world that comes into view through the focusing lens of science is, at its deepest explanatory level, one in which compassion is irrelevant. We understand ourselves to be emergent products of indifferent physicochemical processes; and—though we have always admitted our capacity to experience and practice compassion— there is little in the stories we tell of our origins and emergence that is likely to incline us to see compassion as fundamental to our nature.[114]

Indeed, the New Atheist Richard Dawkins writes, "In a universe of electrons and selfish genes, blind physical forces and genetic replication, some people are going to get hurt, other people are going to get lucky, and you won't find any rhyme or reason in it, nor any justice."[115] In his words, the universe possesses "nothing but pitiless indifference." There could not be a greater contrast

114 Anne Harrington, "A Science of Compassion or a Compassionate Science? What Do We Expect from a Cross-Cultural Dialogue with Buddhism?," in *Visions of Compassion: Western Scientists and Tibetan Buddhists Examine Human Nature*, ed. Richard J. Davidson and Anne Harrington (New York: Oxford Academic, 2002), online ed.

115 Richard Dawkins, *River Out of Eden: A Darwinian View of Life* (London: Weidenfeld and Nicolson, 1995), 133.

between this desolate view of reality and the view of the Qur'an which describes reality as a manifestation of divine compassion and an opportunity to receive and embody mercy.

The Qur'anic worldview's emphasis on divine mercy also addresses the age-old philosophical question known as the problem of evil: if God is good, then why do evil and suffering exist in the world?[116] Seeing reality through the lens of God's mercy allows us instead to conceive every instance and occurrence of suffering as an opportunity for us to be a vehicle of divine mercy and compassion. It is an opportunity to emulate the divine attributes—just as God is the Most Merciful, He loves those who show mercy.[117] In a famous hadith, the Prophet Muhammad ﷺ said, "The Most Merciful shows mercy to those who show mercy. Show mercy to all those on earth and the One in heaven will show mercy to you."[118] Tallal Zeni writes, "If one is certain that God is beneficent and merciful, as indicated in *Sūrah al-Fātiḥah,* then one will also be benevolent to others (whether believers or disbelievers) and treat them with compassion. This mercy leads to a decrease in harm, injustice, and evil on a societal level."[119]

---

116 On responses to the problem of evil, see for instance Suleiman Hani, "The Problem of Evil: A Multifaceted Islamic Solution," Yaqeen Institute for Islamic Research, April 20, 2020, https://yaqeeninstitute.ca/read/paper/the-problem-of-evil-a-multifaceted-islamic-solution; Mohammed Elshinawy, "Why Do People Suffer? God's Existence & the Problem of Evil," Yaqeen Institute for Islamic Research, July 2, 2018, https://yaqeeninstitute.ca/read/paper/why-do-people-suffer-gods-existence-the-problem-of-evil; Tallal Zeni, "The Divine Wisdom in Allowing Evil to Exist: Perspectives from Ibn al-Qayyim," Yaqeen Institute for Islamic Research, December 6, 2018, https://yaqeeninstitute.ca/read/paper/the-divine-wisdom-in-allowing-evil-to-exist-perspectives-from-ibn-al-qayyim.

117 See al-Ghazālī, *al-Maqṣad al-asnā* (Beirut: Dār Ibn Ḥazm, 2003), 63. See also Ibn al-Qayyim, *ʿUddat al-ṣābirīn* (Beirut: Dār Ibn Ḥazm, 2019), 1:544; *al-Wābil al-ṣayyib* (Beirut: Dār Ibn Ḥazm, 2019), 1:78; *Ṭarīq al-hijratayn* (Beirut: Dār Ibn Ḥazm, 2019), 1:273.

118 *Jāmiʿ al-Tirmidhī*, no. 1924; *Sunan Abī Dāwūd*, no. 4941.

119 Tallal Zeni, *Revival of Piety through an Islamic Theodicy* (Seattle: KDP, 2020), 4.

Our goal is to become a source of mercy in alleviating the suffering of others. Moreover, in our own suffering we also have the opportunity to experience divine mercy and deepen our connection with Allah. When we turn to Him and pray to Him in times of distress and calamity, demonstrating our hope in His mercy, we feel even more intensely the meaning and significance of His mercy. The Turkish Muslim revivalist Bediuzzaman Said Nursi (d. 1960) comments:

> Whenever I encounter some afflicted youth, I find that he is more concerned with his religious duties and the hereafter than are his peers. From this I deduce that illness does not constitute a misfortune for such people, but rather a bounty from God. It is true that illness causes him distress in his brief, transient and worldly life, but it is beneficial for his eternal life. It is to be regarded as a kind of worship.[120]

Adversity reminds us that we were not created for this transient physical abode, but rather that we will ultimately return to Allah. It recalls within us the vision of God's mercy and the everlasting life with Him, strengthening us to rise above our pain and turmoil. "One should not resent misfortune but love it," Nursi says.[121] He explains that physical misfortune is ultimately a favor from God and a means of spiritual purification.[122] When we turn to Allah in times of distress, He causes our suffering to erase and expiate our sins and moral shortcomings. As the Prophet Muhammad ﷺ taught, "No fatigue, nor disease, nor sorrow, nor sadness, nor hurt, nor distress befalls a Muslim, even if it were the prick he receives from a thorn, but that Allah expiates some

120 Bediuzzaman Said Nursi, *The Flashes*, trans. Sukran Vahide (Istanbul: Sozler Publications, 2009), 28.

121 Nursi, *Flashes*, 25.

122 Nursi, *Flashes*, 26.

of his sins."[123] Moreover, all suffering will appear as illusory upon receiving the infinite mercy of God's reward in the next life. The Prophet Muhammad described this when he said, "The most destitute person in this world will be brought and dipped once into Paradise, and it will be said to him: 'O son of Adam, did you ever see anything bad? Did you ever experience any hardship?' He will say: 'No, by God, O Lord. I never saw any hardship nor experienced any distress.'"[124]

It is the Greek philosopher Epicurus (d. 270 BCE) who is most famously associated with formulating the problem of evil, and it is no coincidence that he also espoused hedonism (the idea that pleasure is the aim of human life). If there is no point to our existence other than maximizing bodily pleasure, then suffering will undoubtedly seem pointless. Consequently, Epicurus was incapable of fathoming that God could decree the existence of suffering to allow for opportunities for human spiritual and moral growth, in line with the very aims of creation. Imam Ibn al-Qayyim explains that were there no challenges or adversaries, the true nature of worship and devotion would never come to light. True devotion and worship (*ʿubūdiyyah*) entails placing one's spiritual and moral duty above the most intense personal needs, sacrificing one's time, wealth, and life for virtue and going against the crowd for a higher truth. Without these struggles, the depth of one's moral and spiritual commitment would never truly show.[125]

Just as one begins reciting each chapter of the Qur'an with the declaration of divine mercy, the believer pursues every moment in life with the aim of becoming a source of mercy.

---

123 *Ṣaḥīḥ al-Bukhārī*, no. 5641.

124 *Ṣaḥīḥ Muslim*, no. 2807.

125 Ibn al-Qayyim, *Ṭarīq al-hijratayn* (Beirut: Dār Ibn Ḥazm, 2019), 255.

The Anatolian Islamic scholar al-Kāfījī (d. 879 AH) writes:

> The servant's share of mercy is to awaken the heedless among God's servants without violence, to look upon sinners with the eye of mercy, to gently lead them away from their sins, to aid the needy by fulfilling their needs to the best of his ability, to support the poor with the wing of his assistance to relieve their distress, or to intercede on their behalf if he lacks the means, or to help them through his supplications when he lacks influence and wealth.[126]

This mercy and compassion brings human beings into harmony with the creation around them. Shaykh Muṣṭafā al-Sibāʿī writes:

> The Islamic legislative system achieved the utmost humane outlook by establishing the unity of all worlds—human, animal, plant, inanimate, earth, and celestial bodies—in their common servitude to Allah and submission to the natural laws of the universe. And how magnificent is what the Qur'an asks the Muslim to recite in every unit of his prayer, "All praise is due to Allah, the Lord of the Worlds, the Most Merciful, the Most Compassionate." Indeed, it is incumbent upon the Muslim to remember that he is a part of the universe, created by One God characterized by profound and all-encompassing mercy. Thus, in the world in which he lives and upon which he depends, let the Muslim be a model of the mercy that characterizes Allah, who is independent of all worlds.[127]

126 Marzūq ʿAlī Ibrāhīm, *"al-Ghurrah al-wāḍiḥah fī tafsīr Sūrat al-Fātiḥah li-Shaykh al-Islām Muḥammad ibn Sulaymān ibn Saʿd al-Kāfījī (788–879 AH): Taḥqīq wa dirāsah," Majallah al-Buḥūth al-Dirāsāt al-Qurʾāniyyah* 10, no. 16 (2015): 230 (cited henceforth as "al-Kāfījī, *al-Ghurrah*").

127 Al-Sibāʿī, *Civilization of Faith*, 90, translation modified based on the original; see al-Sibāʿī, *Min rawāʾiʿ ḥaḍāratinā* (Riyadh: Dār al-Warrāq 1999), 99–100.

Mercy and compassion are etched into every facet of the Islamic worldview and way of life. Imam Ibn al-Qayyim writes:

> The Sharīʿah is founded upon wisdom and the well-being of humanity in this life and the next. It is in its entirety justice, compassion (*raḥmah*), prosperity, and wisdom, and therefore anything that deviates from justice to injustice, from compassion to its opposite, from welfare to harm, or from wisdom to nonsense is not part of the Sharīʿah, even if it is included therein by dint of misinterpretation.[128]

This is one of the clearest antidotes to the misuse and misinterpretation of religious teachings, which scholars have addressed at many levels (see the author's previous article *Is Islam a Violent Religion? Debunking the Myth*).[129] This is, in fact, something intuitive for anyone who understands the basic message of Islam. The average Muslim requires no jurisprudential erudition to recognise that cruelty can never belong to the religion of compassion (*dīn al-raḥmah*), nor can it ever represent the way of the Prophet of mercy (*nabī al-raḥmah*) ﷺ, nor can it ever be considered a commandment of our Lord, the Most Compassionate and Most Merciful (*al-Raḥmān al-Raḥīm*).

Every civilisation that loses *raḥmah* eventually crumbles, every society deprived of *raḥmah* degenerates, every family that forgets *raḥmah* falters, and every person who neglects *raḥmah* ultimately suffers a life of misery and discontent. The Prophet Muhammad stated, "Mercy is not removed except from the most miserable."[130] He also said, "Kindness is not to be found in anything except that

128 Ibn al-Qayyim, *Iʿlām al-muwaqqiʿīn* (Dammam: Dār Ibn al-Jawzī, 2002), 4:337.

129 Nazir Khan, *"Is Islam a Violent Religion? Debunking the Myth,"* Yaqeen Institute for Islamic Research, November 16, 2016. https://yaqeeninstitute.org/read/paper/is-islam-a-violent-religion-debunking-the-myth.

130 *Jāmiʿ al-Tirmidhī*, no. 1923; *Sunan Abī Dāwūd*, no. 4942.

it beautifies it and it is not withdrawn from anything except that it debases it."[131] Any serious spiritual revival must begin with reiterating the message of mercy that inaugurates the divine revelation and is ubiquitous in the Islamic faith. Any moral or humanitarian ambition must focus on cultivating compassion in the hearts of people. Any intellectual endeavour must ultimately be linked with bettering the human condition in a complete sense.

Islam will never capitulate to the modern ideologies which have only spawned cruelty and indifference to the suffering of others. If the aim of our existence is to worship the Most Merciful and spread mercy among His creation, then this is not achieved, for instance, by constructing society on the principle of profit maximization. The capitalist world in which we live today is one governed entirely by industries that have no care or concern for the suffering of the poor or needy but exist only to increase the wealth of a select privileged class. Divine mercy rescues humanity from the merciless cruelty of the greedy and affords us true opportunities for spreading mercy and compassion in the world.

Every civilisation that loses *raḥmah* eventually crumbles, every society deprived of *raḥmah* degenerates, every family that forgets *raḥmah* falters, and every person who neglects *raḥmah* ultimately suffers a life of misery and discontent.

131 *Ṣaḥīḥ Muslim*, no. 2594a.

مَلِكِ يَوْمِ الدِّينِ

Māliki yawm al-dīn

Sovereign of the Day of Judgement

Secularism dismantled

In the next verse of the *sūrah*, we are informed that God is the Sovereign of the Day of Judgement. Al-Māwardī (d. 450 AH) explains that just as the preceding verses informed us of His sovereignty in this life as *al-Rabb*, He is likewise the complete sovereign in the next life.[132] There are two readings (*qirāʾāt*) of this verse, as follows: ***maliki** yawm al-dīn* (**King** of the Day of Judgement) and ***māliki** yawm al-dīn* (**Master** of the Day of Judgement).[133] This verse establishes belief in the Day of Judgement and reminds us that in the next life, all human pretences of authority and power will vanish in the presence of the One True King, the Sole Master and Owner of everything

Secularism

The ideology that seeks to remove religion from the public domain and confine it to the private affairs of the individual.

132 Al-Māwardī, *al-Nukat wa-l-ʿuyūn* (Beirut: Dār al-Kutub al-ʿIlmiyah, 2012), 1:57.

133 It is recited as *māliki* by ʿĀṣim and al-Kisāʾī (among the seven reciters) as well as Yaʿqūb al-Ḥaḍramī and Khalaf al-Bazzār (among the ten reciters). The remaining canonical reciters read *maliki*.

in existence.[134] The prolific Egyptian Islamic scholar Shaykh Muḥammad al-Ghazālī (d. 1996) writes:

> The concept of a Day of Judgment has been all but obliterated and forgotten in today's materialistic society. It has become a subject for satire and ridicule. In areas of education, law, and national and international politics, it has been deliberately omitted or swept aside. Nevertheless, it represents a most basic and fundamental fact of human existence and should be cherished and reckoned with.[135]

Likewise, Mufti Muḥammad Shafīʿ (d. 1976) writes:

> [I]n possessing lands or money or power, which has been given to him by way of trial, man has always been prone to get drunk with pride and vanity (specially the modern man living in the so-called 'humanistic civilization' where the sole drive and motivating force is the complacent belief in man's mastery).[136] The phrase "Master of the Day of Judgment" is a warning to man reeling in his forgetfulness and self-conceit, and an intimation that all his possessions, all his relationships with things and men are only short-lived, and that there shall come a Day when masters will no more be masters and slaves no more slaves, when no one will own anything even in appearance, and the ownership and mastery, apparent as well as real, of the whole universe will be seen to belong to none but Allah, the Exalted.[137]

---

134 Al-Rāghib al-Iṣfahānī, *Tafsīr,* 1:56; al-Thaʿlabī, *al-Kashf wa al-bayān,* 2:425. See also Zohair Abdul-Rahman and Jinan Yousef, "Mercy and Might on Judgment Day: Allah's Name Maliki Yawm al-Din," Yaqeen Institute for Islamic Research, March 29, 2022. https://yaqeeninstitute.org/read/paper/mercy-and-might-on-judgment-day-allahs-name-maliki-yawn-al-din.

135 Muḥammad al-Ghazālī, *Thematic Commentary,* 2.

136 The text in parentheses is found in a footnote.

137 Muḥammad Shafīʿ, *Maʿārif al-Qurʾān,* 1:69.

Ibn ʿAbbās, the Prophet's cousin and early Qur'anic exegete, said, "On that Day, no one will possess any ownership alongside God as they used to possess in the *dunyā* (worldly life)."[138] The Qur'an also teaches:

> The Day when they shall rise up from their graves, nothing will be hidden from God. To whom does the kingdom belong today? To God, the One, the Supreme. (Qur'an 40:16)

In both the cosmic order and the civic order, true sovereignty belongs only to God, whose laws and ordinances are supreme, while political reign is entrusted to man only as a matter of moral custodianship and service.[139] The Egyptian Muslim thinker Sayyid Quṭb writes:

> Belief in the hereafter is essential because it engages the human soul and mind and concentrates man's attention on a future existence. This in turn helps to rein in man's obsession with the present life, and to transcend his immediate earthly desires. He is no longer anxious to reap all his rewards here and now; he can conquer his selfishness and develop altruistic feelings and interests. Man is able to go through life as a motivated, tolerant, confident and optimistic being.[140]

Accepting the absolute sovereignty of God on the Day of Judgement entails that our moral duties, our sense of right and wrong, and our accountability are determined by God and not the political interests of the state. Secularism, by contrast, dismisses religion and belief in God as irrelevant to the moral order of society.

---

138 See al-Ṭayyār, *Mawsūʿat al-tafsīr al-ma'thūr,* 2:33; al-ʿUmrānī, *Mawsūʿat madrasat Makkah fī al-tafsīr,* 1:14.

139 Al-Attas, *Islam and Secularism,* 66.

140 Quṭb, *In the Shade of the Qur'an,* 1:5.

Modern secularism is, in actuality, a form of atheism.[141] The term "secularism" was actually coined by George Jacob Holyoake in 1851 as a more palatable substitute for "atheism" due to the connotations of immorality associated with the latter term in society.[142] Secularism seeks a rupture between man and the moral order established by God but ultimately opens the door to man's subordination to the state. Secularism substituted one oppression for another: the oppression suffered in Christian Europe under religious tyranny for the oppression of the state.[143] The sovereign powers of the secular world are not themselves beholden to a higher authority. There is no "rules-based international order" in the secular world when the powerful nation-states can decide upon a whim that the rules are non-binding, for instance, using veto powers to allow a genocide to continue unimpeded.

The Egyptian Qur'anic scholar Muḥammad ʿAbdullāh Dirāz (d. 1958) eloquently pointed out, "How can one possibly conceive of a moral rule without an obligation? Is this not a contradiction in terms?"[144] In his work on ethics, he explained that an ethical system is not possible without the five Qur'anic prerequisites of obligation (*ilzām*), accountability (*masʾūliyyah*), sanction (*jazāʾ*), proper intention (*niyyah*), and effort (*juhd*). Without the

141 Joseph Kaminski, *Islam, Liberalism, and Ontology* (London and New York: Routledge, 2021), 131.

142 See Michael Rectenwald, "Mid-Nineteenth-Century Secularism as Modern Secularity," in *Organized Secularism in the United States: New Directions in Research*, ed. Ryan T. Cragun, Christel Manning, and Lori L. Fazzino (Berlin: De Gruyter, 2017), 31–56.

143 The attempt to relegate religion to its own private sphere cleared a space for the state in modern ethics. See Talal Asad, *Formations of the Secular*, 255. As secularism was transplanted from the West to the East, intervention of the state was also required. Joseph Kaminski writes, "While in Europe the development toward secularism was more of a bottom-up process, driven by civil society over a steady period of time, in the Muslim world, it was the opposite. The imposition of secularism in Muslim lands was a rushed, top-down process driven by elites who inherited both their power and penchant toward cruelty from their former colonizers. As a matter of fact, civil society was almost completely excluded from the forced secularization process that transpired in the Middle East. Instead, secularism was thrust upon the masses by 'enlightened' despots who were assisted by the military elite in crushing dissent and cementing their own power." Kaminski, *Islam, Liberalism, and Ontology*, 185.

144 M. A. Draz (Muḥammad ʿAbdullāh Dirāz), *The Moral World of the Qur'an* (London: I.B. Tauris, 2008), 13.

Accepting the absolute sovereignty of God on the Day of Judgement entails that our moral duties, our sense of right and wrong, and our accountability are determined by God and not the political interests of the state.

ontological prerequisites of a moral discourse, there is no basis for true ethical conduct and moral sacrifice, but only conformity to existing power structures and social conventions.

These five Qur'anic concepts form the basis of morality

1 Obligation

ilzām

There are rules one must follow.

2 Accountability

masʾūliyyah

We will be judged by God.

3 Sanction

jazāʾ

There are consequences to acting rightly or wrongly.

4 Intention

niyyah

Actions must be performed with the right intention.

5 Effort

juhd

Morality requires sacrifice and struggle against one's own desires.

Secularism is closely related to a variety of other ideologies, including those that pertain to ownership and distribution of wealth, namely capitalism and communism, discussed earlier. In this verse of *al-Fātiḥah*, we note that true ownership of everything one possesses belongs only to God since He is *al-Mālik*. He is the real Owner of all property and wealth, and they must be utilised according to His guidance for the benefit of His creation. In contrast, capitalism regards the individual as the complete owner over his wealth to be expended according to the dictates of his whims, lusts, and desires.[145] Communism assigns complete

145 Zarabozo, *Al-Fatihah*, disc 7.

ownership to the state, affording people effectively no rights over their wealth. Both arise from a common failure to accord true ownership to God.

Secularism also fails to provide adequate conceptions of sovereignty. Democracy promises to free mankind from tyranny by granting citizens political representation and enabling the electorate to choose the ruling party. In actual fact, however, the ruling elite is molded to the interests of wealthy corporations and lobby groups, which in turn mold the public to their interests.[146] Through the relentless manipulation of information in corporate-owned mass media and the distractions of the entertainment industry, the ordinary citizen becomes exploited and indeed enslaved. A democracy turns into a cleverly disguised dictatorship. Four decades ago, Neil Postman offered the following powerful comparison of Orwell's *1984* and Huxley's *Brave New World*:

> Contrary to common belief even among the educated, Huxley and Orwell did not prophesy the same thing. Orwell warns that we will be overcome by an externally imposed oppression. But in Huxley's vision, no Big Brother is required to deprive people of their autonomy, maturity and history. As he saw it, people will come to love their oppression, to adore the technologies that undo their capacities to think.
>
> What Orwell feared were those who would ban books. What Huxley feared was that there would be no reason to ban a book, for there would be no one who wanted to read one. Orwell feared those who would deprive us of information. Huxley feared those who would give us so much that we would be reduced to passivity and egoism. Orwell feared that the truth would be concealed from us. Huxley feared

146 Asad, *Formations of the Secular*, 4–5.

> the truth would be drowned in a sea of irrelevance. Orwell feared we would become a captive culture. Huxley feared we would become a trivial culture, preoccupied with some equivalent of the feelies, the orgy porgy, and the centrifugal bumblepuppy. As Huxley remarked in *Brave New World Revisited,* the civil libertarians and rationalists who are ever on the alert to oppose tyranny "failed to take into account man's almost infinite appetite for distractions." In *1984,* Huxley added, people are controlled by inflicting pain. In *Brave New World,* they are controlled by inflicting pleasure.[147]

These words were written before the advent of smartphones, social media algorithms,[148] zombie scrolling, online bots, and the various highly sophisticated digital forms of "manufacturing consent." With such an arsenal, the subjugation of human beings seems almost guaranteed. The greatest threat to such a system, however, is a community that refuses to be subordinated to man's authority, one that recognises no authority higher than that of its Maker and the morality of His dictates.

The loss of an ethical foundation is not an accidental consequence of secularism but is, in fact, deeply embedded within its internal logic. Perhaps none understood this better than Niccolo Machiavelli, the "inventor of secular politics" and the originator of the modern concept of the state as an instrument of power and domination.[149] His thought exemplifies the maxim "the ends justify the means." Machiavelli wrote that cruelty can be used effectively "out of the necessity to secure one's power,"[150] that "a wise ruler cannot and

147 Neil Postman, *Amusing Ourselves to Death* (London: Penguin Books, 1985), xix–xx.

148 Studies have demonstrated that fake news travels faster than real news on social media platforms such as X. Soroush Vosoughi et al., "The Spread of True and False News Online," *Science* 359, no. 6380 (2018): 1146–51, https://doi.org/10.1126/science.aap9559.

149 Emmet Kennedy, *Secularism and Its Opponents from Augustine to Solzhenitsyn* (New York: Palgrave Macmillan, 2006), 57, 63–64.

150 Niccolo Machiavelli, *The Prince,* trans. Peter Constantine (New York: Random House, 2007), 43.

should not keep his word when it would be to his disadvantage to do so,"[151] and "that when a populace no longer believes, a prince can compel them to believe by force."[152] It is not merely the case that secularism fails to sustain an ethical order but rather that it deliberately undermines it. Compare Machiavelli's statements with Ibn al-Qayyim's observations concerning someone whose value structure is ultimately tied to worldly ambitions rather than to the worship of God:

> This is the condition of anyone whose ultimate pursuit is anything other than Allah and His servitude—whether they are idolaters or those who follow their desires without any goal beyond them, or those in positions of power who are determined to maintain their authority by any means, whether right or wrong. When the truth comes in the way of their power, they obliterate it and trample it underfoot. If they are unable to do so, they repel it with tyranny. If they still cannot overcome the truth, they block its path and divert others from it to another route. They are always ready to resist the truth by any means possible.[153]

The loss of an ethical foundation is not an accidental consequence of secularism but is, in fact, deeply embedded within its internal logic.

151 Machiavelli, *Prince*, 82.

152 Machiavelli, *Prince*, 28.

153 Ibn al-Qayyim, *Ranks of the Divine Seekers*, 1:168, translation modified based on original. See Ibn al-Qayyim, *Madārij al-sālikīn* (Beirut: Dār Ibn Ḥazm, 2019), 1:85.

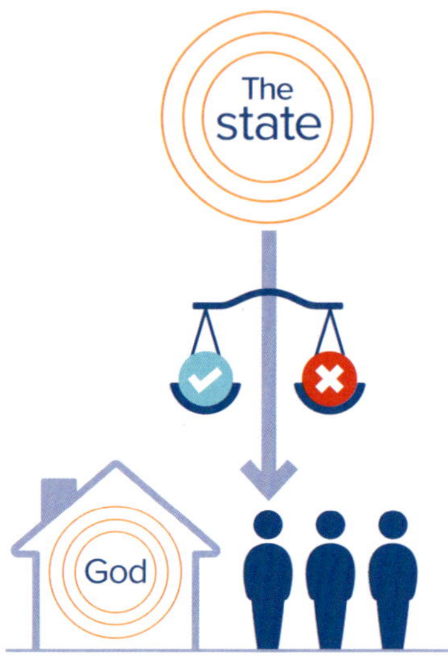

Humanity is under God's authority and sovereignty. We are morally accountable to God both in this life and in the afterlife.

Legislation and right versus wrong is determined by those in power. No accountability to God. Belief in God is a private matter which is irrelevant to public life.

In contrast, the ethical order established by God is one that recognises the absolute imperative of justice and accountability and cultivates these values in the hearts and minds of its subjects. One of the meanings of *māliki yawm al-dīn* is "Master of the Day of Pure Justice," because that is the day on which God's perfect justice will be fully manifest.[154] Further, we learn from the Qur'an that the very purpose for which God sent messengers is so that people may establish justice: "Verily, We sent Our messengers with clear signs and sent down with them the Scripture and the balance that people may uphold justice in their affairs" (Qur'an 57:25). Commenting on this verse, Ibn al-Qayyim writes, "Whenever a path to justice becomes clear, it is part of the religion and law of God and can never be opposed to it."[155]

154 Ibn ʿĀshūr, *al-Taḥrīr wa al-tanwīr* (Tunis: Dār al-Tunīsiyya, 1984), 1:177.

155 Ibn al-Qayyim, *al-Ṭuruq al-ḥukmiyyah* (Beirut: Dār Ibn Ḥazm, 2019), 1:31.

Establishing justice is an obligation that follows naturally from understanding the attributes of God. God is the Most Just and He loves those who exercise justice. The Prophet ﷺ related that God says, "O My servants, I have made injustice forbidden upon Myself and have made it forbidden amongst you, so do not commit injustice."[156] The Prophet Muhammad explained that those who establish justice will be in the company of God on the Day of Judgement on pulpits of light, "those who practise justice in their judgements, with their families, and in all that they have authority over."[157]

Islam's vision of justice is all-encompassing and multi-faceted and provides a robust form of guidance for social justice (see author's previous article on Islam and Social Justice).[158] It is important to recognise that Islam does not merely posit justice as an abstract lofty ethical ideal but actively legislates the means towards achieving justice as well, providing a comprehensive accounting of the rights of both Creator and creation. Islam actively constructs a programme to develop human minds spiritually and morally to live according to the ethical requirements of justice, individually and societally. In a secular society there is no shared ethical curriculum to partake in: everyone is simply left to his own devices.

The opening verses of *al-Fātiḥah* indicate that in the past, the present, and the future, the human being owes everything to Allah alone.[159] We were created by the Lord of the Worlds in the past, we are nurtured by His mercy in the present, and we will stand accountable before Him on Judgement Day in the future.

---

156 *Ṣaḥīḥ Muslim*, no. 2577.

157 *Ṣaḥīḥ Muslim*, no. 1827.

158 Nazir Khan, "A Sacred Duty: Islam and Social Justice," Yaqeen Institute for Islamic Research, February 4, 2020. https://yaqeeninstitute.org/read/paper/a-sacred-duty-islam-and-social-justice.

159 Muḥammad Shafīʿ, *Maʿārif al-Qurʾān*, 1:70. See also al-Rāzī, *Great Exegesis*, 1:353.

Islam actively constructs a programme to develop human minds spiritually and morally to live according to the ethical requirements of justice, individually and societally.

In this verse, the Day of Judgement is called *yawm al-dīn*, which means the day of recompense, requital, and reckoning, when everyone will receive their due reward or punishment.[160] A linguistically related name of God is *al-Dayyān* (the One True Judge). There is a *ḥadīth qudsī* in which Allah uses both the names *al-Malik* and *al-Dayyān*, also in the context of the Day of Judgement. On that Day, God will say:

al-Dayyān
One of the names of Allah. This name emphasises Allah's role in administering absolute justice on the Day of Judgement, where every action is weighed and rewarded or punished accordingly.

> I am the true King (*al-Malik*), I am the true Judge (*al-Dayyān*); it is not fitting for anyone from the people of Paradise to enter Paradise, nor for anyone from the people of Hell to enter Hell, until I judge any grievance of his, even if it be as little as a slap.[161]

This is the perfect justice and absolute accountability that Islam teaches, such that in the court of Divine Justice there will be retribution for even the slightest infraction against the rights of another. In combination with the emphasis on compassion in the previous verse and the present verse's emphasis on justice, we find that the value structure of Islam is direly needed in an era where the reigning ideologies and forces have run amok with cruelty and injustice.

---

160 Al-Ṭabarī, *Comprehensive Exposition*, 127–28. Abū al-Ḥasan al-Ḥarālī (d. 638 AH) makes the observation that in reality, one's day of recompense is a process that begins inconspicuously with the effects of the sin in this life until its outward manifestation on the Day of Judgement. See al-Ḥarālī, *Turāth Abū al-Ḥasan al-Ḥarālī al-Marākushī fī al-tafsīr* (Rabat: al-Markaz al-Jāmiʿī lil-Baḥth al-ʿIlmī, 1997), 146.

161 *Musnad Aḥmad*, no. 16042; *Mustadrak al-Ḥākim*, no. 3690. The companion who reported this hadith, Jabir ibn ʿAbdullāh, purchased a camel and traveled for one month to Egypt hearing that someone knew a hadith which he did not know, whereupon he learned this narration. This shows the importance with which the Companions regarded learning hadith and seeking guidance from the Prophet's ﷺ words.

Iyyāka naʿbudu
You alone do we worship

Polytheism dismantled

From the Islamic perspective, acquiring sound knowledge of God and His divine attributes is the basis for knowing how to live in this world and pursue ethical conduct. We see this mirrored in *al-Fātiḥah*. After establishing the foundations of knowledge about God, the chapter turns to the required duty of the servants of God.[162] This begins with the statement "You alone do we worship" (*iyyāka naʿbudu*). This also demonstrates a grammatical shift (*iltifāt*) from third-person tense to second-person, signaling a concomitant shift in the human psyche prepared to address God directly after acquiring a sound understanding of His attributes of perfection.[163] The one who has properly internalised the meanings of Islam's theocentric vision has prepared himself for the intimacy and immediacy of a direct relationship with the Divine.[164]

162 Al-Rāzī divides *Sūrat al-Fātiḥah* into knowledge of the Lord and knowledge of servitude, and further divides the latter into acts of the servant and the effects of those acts. Al-Rāzī, *Great Exegesis,* 1:418–19.

163 Al-Rāzī, *Great Exegesis,* 1:449.

164 Al-Qūnawī and Ibn al-Tamjīd, *Ḥāshiyat al-Qūnawī ʿalā tafsīr al-Bayḍāwī wa-maʿahu ḥāshiyat Ibn al-Tamjīd,* (Beirut: DKI, 2001), 1:223–29.

The chapter also teaches the etiquettes of supplicating to Allah, in that one begins first with due praise and worshiping Allah alone before proceeding with one's request.[165] Shaykh Mohammed Elshinawy writes:

> In the opening chapter of the Qur'an (*al-Fātiḥa*), it is meaningful that God placed the phrase 'Only You do we worship' after the verses praising and extolling Him. This sequence captures how servitude is an offshoot of recognition, and hence a Muslim is moved to worship God both internally and externally. The external motivation is the revealed command of God which obligates people to perform ritual worship, while the internal motivation results from an appreciation of God's Perfection and one's own imperfection and appreciation of His benevolence.[166]

---

165 Al-Thaʿlabī, *Kashf al-bayān ʿan tafsīr al-Qurʾān*, 2:508; al-Nasafī, *al-Taysīr fī al-tafsīr*, 1:149; Saʿīd Ḥawwā, *Asās fī al-tafsīr*, 1:48–49.

166 Mohammad Elshinawy, "Why Does God Ask People to Worship Him?," Yaqeen Institute for Islamic Research, December 26, 2017, https://yaqeeninstitute.ca/read/paper/why-does-god-ask-people-to-worship-him.

Polytheism
The belief in or worship of more than one god.

In addition to teaching the etiquettes of worship and supplication, the categories of *tawḥīd* (monotheism) are also found in the opening verses of *al-Fātiḥah*. One finds *tawḥīd al-rubūbiyyah* (oneness of Allah's Lordship) in the description of God as the *Rabb*, the sole Lord and Creator of the universe, *tawḥīd al-asmāʾ wa-l-ṣifāt* (oneness of Allah's divine names and attributes) in the verses describing His uniquely great mercy as well as His sovereignty on Judgement Day, and *tawḥīd al-ulūhiyyah* (oneness of Allah's exclusive right to be worshiped) in describing our worship of Him alone.[167]

The statement "You alone do we worship" (*iyyāka naʿbudu*) comprises the essence of the Islamic faith, namely, that there is none worthy of worship except God alone. It summarises the entirety of divine revelation. There is a statement from Imam al-Ḥasan al-Baṣrī (d. 110 AH) that Allah gathered the knowledge of 104 divine scriptures in the *Tawrāh, Injīl, Zabūr,* and the Qur'an, and gathered the knowledge of the former three in the Qur'an itself, and gathered the knowledge of the Qur'an in the short (*mufaṣṣal*) chapters, and gathered the knowledge of these chapters in *al-Fātiḥah*.[168] An additional portion of the statement mentioned by Ibn Taymiyyah and Ibn al-Qayyim says that God gathered the knowledge of *al-Fātiḥah* in the phrase "You alone do we worship, and You alone do we ask for help."[169]

---

167 See, for instance, Sulaymān ibn al-Lāḥim, *al-Lubāb fī tafsīr al-istiʿādhah wa-l-basmalah wa-Fātiḥat al-Kitāb* (Riyadh: Dār al-Muslim, 1999), 302–5; Khalid Sabt, *Dalāʾil al-Fātiḥah ʿalā uṣūl al-dīn*, 1436 AH, https://khaledalsabt.com/interpretations/3624/12-%D8%AF%D9%84%D8%A7%D9%84%D8%A9-%D8%A7%D9%84%D9%81%D8%A7%D8%AA%D8%AD%D8%A9-%D8%B9%D9%84%D9%89-%D8%A7%D8%B5%D9%88%D9%84-%D8-%A7%D9%84%D8%AF%D9%8A%D9%86.

168 See al-Bayhaqī, *al-Sunan al-kubrā* (Cairo: Markaz Hajr, 2011), 19:23; al-Thaʿlabī, *al-Kashf wa-l-bayān*, 2:269.

169 Ibn al-Qayyim, *Madārij al-sālikīn*, 1:115.

The call to worship God alone is the central message of all the Prophets and Messengers: “And We certainly sent unto every nation a messenger proclaiming: Worship Allah and avoid false deities (*ṭāghūt*)” (Qur’an 16:36). Imam Ibn Jarīr al-Ṭabarī explains that the word *ṭāghūt* refers to “anything revered in worship or obeyed or submitted to besides Allah, regardless of whether that revered thing is a stone, a human, or a devil.”[170] It includes every falsehood that leads people away from Allah’s guidance.[171] The principal moral failing and spiritual malady of humanity has been its devotion to other than God. When God is no longer the focal point of people’s lives, they begin to worship themselves as well as all manner of idols in their obedience, love, veneration, and devotion. As we read in the Qur’an, “Have you not seen the one who takes his own desires as his god?” (Qur’an 25:43, 45:23). The declaration “You alone do we worship” is a complete negation of all forms of polytheism (*shirk*).[172] One who completely commits himself to the worship of Allah alone has achieved total liberation from the tyranny of all ideological and political forces in this world.[173]

The principal moral failing and spiritual malady of humanity has been its devotion to other than God, which invites all forms of tyranny and oppression.

170 Ibn Jarīr al-Ṭabarī, *Jāmiʿ al-bayān* (Cairo: Dār Hajr, 2001), 7:140.

171 Ibn Taymiyyah, *Majmūʿ al-fatāwā*, 28:201 and al-Rāghib al-Iṣfahānī, *Tafsīr*, 3:272.

172 Polytheism is also negated in the phrase “All Praise belongs to Allah, Lord of the Universe.” See Muḥammad Shafīʿ, *Maʿārif al-Qurʾān*, 1:64–65.

173 Quṭb, *In the Shade of the Qur’an*, 1:6; al-Sibāʿī, *Civilization of Faith*, 62–63.

Devotion to the One Creator. Every action done seeking the pleasure of God is considered an act of worship.

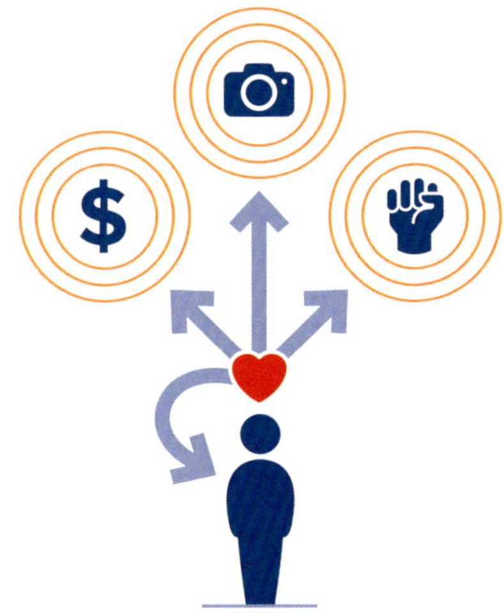

Devotion to multiple deities which may include worship of money, fame, power, and the self.

While many think of worship only in terms of the ritual acts in Islam like prayer (*ṣalāh*), fasting (*ṣiyām*), or major pilgrimage (*ḥajj*), the Islamic understanding of worship is actually far broader than this. When asked about *ʿibādah* (worship), Imam Ibn Taymiyyah replied:

> *ʿIbādah* is a comprehensive term for everything that Allah loves and is pleased with, including both inward and outward speech and actions. It encompasses prayer, charity, fasting, pilgrimage, truthful speech, fulfilling trusts, being kind to parents, maintaining family ties, honoring agreements, enjoining what is right, and forbidding what is wrong. It also includes striving against disbelievers and hypocrites, being kind to neighbors, orphans, the needy, travelers, slaves, and animals, as well as supplication, remembrance, recitation of the Qur'an, and similar acts of worship.

> Additionally, love of Allah and His Messenger, fear of Allah, turning to Him in repentance, sincerity in religion, patience with His decree, gratitude for His blessings, contentment with His judgement, reliance on Him, hope in His mercy, and fear of His punishment—all of these are acts of worshiping Allah.
>
> This is because worship of Allah is the beloved aim for which all of creation was created, as Allah said: "And I did not create the jinn and mankind except to worship Me." And it is for this purpose that all the prophets were sent.[174]

Viewed through this lens, worship is as broad as life itself. Any seemingly small action in our lives becomes an act of worship when connected to our broader mission and vision in life of serving God and striving for moral virtue. By performing one's daily activities with the intention of pleasing Allah and striving to follow His guidance, a person becomes a perpetual worshipper of God. Every goal in life is meaningful insofar as it leads towards the fulfilment of the purpose for which we were created by God. Therefore, as Zarabozo observes, worship is not only the most important goal in life but "in reality, no other goal has any value or meaning to it whatsoever."[175]

Worship combines ultimate love with complete submission. Love is the foundation of a believer's relationship with God. Ibn al-Qayyim explains, "If you love someone but are not submissive and humble toward him, you are not his worshiper, and if you are submissive toward someone without love, you are not his worshiper. You worship someone if you are loving as well as submissive."[176] Every occurrence and experience in life

174 Ibn Taymiyyah, *Majmūʿ al-fatāwā*, 10:149–50.

175 Jamaal Zarabozo, *Al-Fatihah*, disc 10.

176 Ibn al-Qayyim, *Ranks of the Divine Seekers*, 1:206.

reminds the believer of his Lord and intensifies his love for Him. Many scholars note that by saying, **"You alone** do we worship" instead of "We worship none **but you,"** the words have been deliberately structured in a manner that directs one's attention first to God rather than one's own actions.[177] Rather than focusing on one's own virtuous deeds, one focuses instead on the fact that God has honoured one with the opportunity to be connected to Him through such a precious relationship of love. In order to earn God's love, one must first fulfil the basic requirements of one's spiritual and moral obligations. Beyond the obligatory actions, one's love for Allah can also manifest through a diverse array of voluntary deeds. The Prophet Muhammad said:

The emotional ingredients of worship

Ibn al-Qayyim says, "The heart in its journey towards Allah is like a bird: love is its head, and fear and hope are its wings." (*Madārij al-sālikīn* 2:188)

> Indeed, Allah has said, "Whoever shows enmity to a friend of Mine, I have indeed declared war against him. My servant does not draw near to Me with anything more beloved to Me than the duties I have made obligatory upon him, and My servant continues to draw closer to Me with voluntary deeds (*nawāfil*) until I love him. Then, when I love him, I become his hearing with which he hears, his sight with which he sees, his hand with which he strikes, and his foot with which he walks. If he asks of Me, I will surely give to him; and if he seeks My protection, I will surely protect him. I do not hesitate in doing anything as I hesitate in [taking the life of] a believer, for he hates death, and I hate to disappoint him."[178]

177 Al-Thaʿlabī, *al-Kashf wa-l-bayān,* 2:428; al-Nasafī, *al-Taysīr fī al-tafsīr,* 1:127; al-Bayḍāwī, *Anwār al-tanzīl,* 1:29.

178 *Ṣaḥīḥ al-Bukhārī,* no. 6502

The voluntary deeds (*nawāfil*) one can choose to perform are of numerous types and categories, catering to the diversity of human personalities. The Prophet's Companions were not all clones; they each excelled in different areas. Some of the Companions distinguished themselves by their unique scholarship and teaching (e.g., Ibn ʿAbbās, ʿĀʾishah, Zayd ibn Thābit), others through their intense devotion in voluntary prayers and fasting (e.g., ʿAbdullāh ibn ʿAmr ibn al-ʿĀṣ, al-Juwayriyyah, Abū al-Dardāʾ). Some stood out for their charity and philanthropy (e.g., ʿAbd al-Raḥmān ibn ʿAwf, Zaynab bint Khuzaymah), while others excelled in their courage in standing up for justice (e.g., Ṣafiyyah bint ʿAbd al-Muṭṭalib, ʿUmar ibn al-Khaṭṭāb), among many other diverse qualities of virtue. In a previous study on this topic, we described this concept as "spiritual personality types" (see author's previous co-authored article *Souls Assorted: An Islamic Theory of Spiritual Personality*).[179] Imam Mālik (d. 179 AH) was once asked why he was busy in circles of knowledge rather than simply isolating himself in voluntary prayer. He replied by explaining the diversity of spiritual personalities:

> Certainly, Allah has divided good actions like he has divided His providence (*rizq*). It may be that voluntary prayer has been facilitated for a person, but voluntary fasting has not. Another person may have a tendency for voluntary charity (*ṣadaqah*) but not voluntary fasting, and some are granted ease in *jihād* (a just struggle in the cause of God) and not in voluntary prayers. And I am pleased with what Allah has facilitated for me (the pursuit of knowledge). I do not think what I am focused on is of less value than what you are focused on. Rather, I hope that we are both upon goodness and righteousness.[180]

179 Zohair Abdul-Rahman and Nazir Khan, *"Souls Assorted: An Islamic Theory of Spiritual Personality,"* Yaqeen Institute for Islamic Research, October 18, 2018. https://yaqeeninstitute.org/read/paper/souls-assorted-an-islamic-theory-of-spiritual-personality.

180 See Ibn ʿAbd al-Barr, *al-Tamhīd limā fī al-Muwaṭṭā min al-maʿānī wa-l-asānīd* (London: Furqan Institute, 2017), 5:202; Ibn ʿAbd al-Barr, *al-Istidhkār* (Beirut: DKI, 2000), 5:146.

The great Andalusian hadith scholar Imam Ibn ʿAbd al-Barr (d. 463 AH) links the above statement of Imam Mālik with the fact that *jannah* has multiple gates for different acts of worship, as we are informed in the following hadith:

> Narrated by Abu Hurayra, the Messenger of Allah, peace be upon him, said, "Whoever spends a pair (of anything) in the way of Allah will be called from the gates of Paradise, 'O servant of Allah, this is good.' Whoever is among the people of prayer will be called from the gate of prayer, whoever is among the people of *jihād* will be called from the gate of *jihād*, whoever is among the people of charity will be called from the gate of charity, and whoever is among the people of fasting will be called from the gate of *Rayyān*."
>
> Abū Bakr al-Ṣiddīq asked, "O Messenger of Allah, is it necessary that one be called only from one of these gates? Is it possible that one may be called from all of them?" The Prophet replied, "Yes, and I hope that you will be among them."[181]

Therefore, diversity in spiritual personality is accommodated in the very architecture of *jannah* itself—it is cosmologically grounded. There are multiple entrances into *jannah*. Imam Ibn ʿAṭiyyah explains this regarding why the plural "ways" is used in the verse "And as for those who strive for Our sake, We will surely guide them to Our ways, for indeed, Allah is with those who do good" (Qur'an 29:69). He writes:

> And "the ways" (*subul*) here could mean the paths of Paradise and its routes, or it could mean the multiplicity of deeds and the illuminated beliefs leading to Paradise. Abū Sulaymān al-Dārānī said: *Jihād* in this verse does not mean only fighting

181 *Muwaṭṭā* Mālik, no. 1009; *Ṣaḥīḥ al-Bukhārī*, no. 3666. See Ibn ʿAbd al-Barr, *al-Tamhīd*, 5:201–2.

> the enemy, but it also includes supporting the religion, refuting the falsifiers, countering the oppressors, and greatly emphasizing enjoining what is good and forbidding what is evil. It includes struggling against oneself in obedience to Allah, exalted and glorious, which is the greater *jihād*.[182]

This multiplicity of voluntary actions must be built upon the foundations of the obligatory actions and in keeping with the correct creed of Islam, which is the straight path (*al-ṣirāṭ al-mustaqīm*). The word *ṣirāṭ* is never used in the Qur'an in the plural.[183] *Sabīl* (way) on the other hand can sometimes be used to refer to subroutes along the straight path.[184] It is pluralised as *subul* (ways), which can be thought of as many lanes on the same highway; i.e., *ṣirāṭ* (path).[185] As we will discuss in a subsequent chapter, it is necessary to acknowledge the singularity of the straight path to avoid falling into relativism. The fundamental message of the straight path is the emphasis on *tawḥīd* (monotheism) and rejecting *shirk* (polytheism).

Whenever humans deify or worship other than God, it is considered a form of *shirk*, the ultimate moral transgression.[186] In one hadith, the Prophet mentioned the three greatest sins as follows: (1) that you assign a partner to God when He alone created you, (2) that you kill your own child fearing he will share your food, and (3) that you commit adultery with your neighbor.[187] All of these transgressions

182 Ibn ʿAṭiyyah, *al-Muḥarrar al-wajīz*, 4:326.

183 See Qur'an 1:6–7; 2:142, 213; 3:51, 101; 4:68, 175; 5:16; 6:39, 87, 126, 153, 161; 7:16, 86; 10:25; 11:56; 14:1; 15:41; 16:76, 121; 19:36, 43; 20:135; 22:24, 54; 23:73–74; 24:46; 34:6; 36:4, 61, 66; 37:23, 118; 38:22; 42:52–53; 43:43, 61, 64; 48:2, 20; 67:22.

184 When *sabīl* is used synonymously with *ṣirāṭ* to refer to the religion, then it is only used in the singular for Islam and in the plural for the various paths of misguidance. See, e.g., Qur'an 6:153.

185 Zarabozo, *Al-Fātiḥah*, disc 18.

186 Zohair Abdul-Rahman, "Why is Shirk the Greatest Sin?," Yaqeen Institute for Islamic Research, July 25, 2022, https://yaqeeninstitute.org/read/paper/why-is-shirk-the-greatest-sin-of-all.

187 *Ṣaḥīḥ al-Bukhārī*, no. 4477.

share a similar theme of betrayal of one's duty and moral responsibility towards one to whom one owes a dutiful bond of devotion.[188] In another sense, the injustice of betraying one's moral contract with God opens up the door to all other forms of injustice and moral depravity, as the human being becomes subjugated to false gods and ideologies and detached from his or her true purpose in life as a moral custodian (*khalīfah*).

In the time of the Prophet, the idolatry of the pagan Arabs took the form of worshipping idols carved out of stone or wood. The prevailing idols today take the form of material riches, the entertainment industry, celebrity worship, social media influencers, false ideologies, and misguided ideologues. A compelling portrait of contemporary idol worship in American culture, for instance, is provided by Chris Hedges in *Empire of Illusion*:

> We all have gods, Martin Luther said, it is just a question of which ones. And in American society our gods are celebrities. Religious belief and practice are commonly transferred to the adoration of celebrities. Our culture builds temples to celebrities the way the Romans did for divine emperors, ancestors, and household gods. We are a de facto polytheistic society. We engage in the same kind of primitive beliefs as older polytheistic cultures. In celebrity culture, the object is to get as close as possible to the celebrity. Relics of celebrities are coveted as magical talismans. Those who can touch the celebrity or own a relic of the celebrity hope for a transference of celebrity power. They hope for magic.[189]

---

188 Zohair Abdul-Rahman, "Why is Shirk the Greatest Sin?".

189 Chris Hedges, *Empire of Illusion: The End of Literacy and the Triumph of Spectacle* (Toronto: Vintage Canada, 2010), 17.

The prevailing idols today take the form of material riches, the entertainment industry, celebrity worship, social media influencers, false ideologies, and misguided ideologues.

The Russian novelist Fyodor Dostoyevsky (d. 1881) also wrote:

> There exists no greater or more painful anxiety for a man who has freed himself from all religious bias than how he shall soonest find a new object or idea to worship... And so will they do till the end of this world; they will do so even then, when all the gods themselves have disappeared, for then men will prostrate themselves before and worship some idea.[190]

People continue to flock to theaters and stadiums of mass distraction even as the mass slaughter of thousands of children in Gaza continues unabated. The world's descent into flagrant moral derangement is all but guaranteed by such a state of affairs. Obsessed with fictional worlds and attached to frivolous pursuits, people's capacity for discerning reality itself deteriorates. One's essential purpose in life as custodians serving God alone is entirely forgotten, one's moral duties rendered derelict. Imam Ibn al-Qayyim poignantly notes, "Such is the ego that if you do not occupy it with what is true, it will occupy you with what is false.

190 Fyodor Dostoyevsky, *The Grand Inquisitor,* trans. H. P. Blavatsky, Project Gutenberg, 2010, https://www.gutenberg.org/files/8578/8578-h/8578-h.htm.

And such is the heart that if the love of God does not reside in it, the love of creatures will, without fail."[191]

When humanity forgets God and turns to the worship of false deities, or to the self and the idols of its own making, it becomes ethically unmoored and epistemically detached. Attributing divine qualities to other than Allah leads to a distorted view of reality and a misinterpretation of the natural order and the moral responsibilities that accompany it. Dependence on false deities or conflicting sources of guidance results in irrational and incoherent beliefs and practices. The cognitive disarray that arises from an incoherent mix of beliefs hinders one's ability to think clearly and act ethically. A person becomes ideologically subordinated to manufactured sources of authority, which leads to ethical and moral confusion. Islam presents every single human being with the possibility of equal access to God, free of any intermediaries. It provides a clear worldview that identifies the reason for which we were created and establishes our moral responsibility in the world and our accountability before God in the afterlife. This, in turn, provides the basis for the rational, spiritual, and ethical cultivation of humanity.

When society becomes disconnected from its singular moral commitment to God, deleterious consequences ensue. Those who spend their lives studying the bloodied chapters in human history often have the most revealing insights into this process. The Russian author and Soviet dissident Aleksandr Solzhenitsyn (d. 2008) writes:

> Over a half century ago, while I was still a child, I recall hearing a number of old people offer the following explanation for the great disasters that had befallen Russia:

191 Ibn al-Qayyim, *Ibn Qayyim Al-Jawzīya on the Invocation of God : Al-Wabil al-Sayyib*, trans. M. Youssef Slitine and M. Abdurrahman Fitzgerald (Cambridge: Islamic Texts Society, 2000), 107.

> "Men have forgotten God; that's why all this has happened." Since then I have spent well-nigh 50 years working on the history of our revolution; in the process I have read hundreds of books, collected hundreds of personal testimonies, and have already contributed eight volumes of my own toward the effort of clearing away the rubble left by that upheaval. But if I were asked today to formulate as concisely as possible the main cause of the ruinous revolution that swallowed up some 60 million of our people, I could not put it more accurately than to repeat: "Men have forgotten God; that's why all this has happened."[192]

Society's ethical erosion is precipitated by the collective and consistent cognitive refusal to accept that there is none worthy of worship but our Creator. There is nothing greater than God and therefore no duty supersedes the moral obligation to Him. It is through this commitment that we recover the value of what is sacred and the urgency of introspection. There is a way one's life *should* be lived, and there is a need for guidance from one's Maker. As Syed Naquib al-Attas explains, one's "whole ethical life is one continuous *ʿibādah* (worship), for Islam itself is a complete way of life."[193] We are servants with value and with a singular purpose, and we will stand before our Creator to account for our deeds. The journey of worship in Islam is intricately tied to the concept of self-discipline and spiritual purification, and this is the source of true liberation.[194] As Professor ʿAbd al-Salām al-Majīdī explains:

> Worship in the simplest terms entails paving the way for humanity to achieve true freedom, which has otherwise

192 Edward E. Ericson, Jr., "Solzhenitsyn: Voice from the Gulag," *Eternity* (October 1985): 23–24.

193 Al-Attas, *Prolegomena*, 59.

194 Al-Attas, *Prolegomena*, 59–60.

The true vision of freedom that the Qur'an provides is one that allows human beings to return to their moral and ethical purpose in life and uplift themselves from the tyranny of all forms of enslavement and subjugation to other creatures.

> been exhausted by the deprivation of its rights through various schemes. Is there any real freedom except when a person liberates himself from the servitude of creatures to be only a servant of God who created and perfected him? Reflect on God's words to see that the Qur'an did not use the word "freedom" except in the context of freeing slaves from their bondage. After that, their complete freedom is to be servants of God. Does a person think he will find comfort while straying from the system his Creator prepared for him to attain happiness and sovereignty?
>
> ...Here, one must express amazement at some people who may bow to humans, worship sheep and cattle, submit to the sun and moon, or worship stones. You might even see them glorifying tyrannical rulers, granting titles and grand descriptions to the magicians of the media and the criminals of tyranny, all while failing to exalt God, the Sovereign, the Holy, the Peaceful. Then they claim to be advocates of peace and protectors of the world's general security! "It is naught but lies" (Qur'an 18:5).[195]

The true vision of freedom that the Qur'an provides is one that allows human beings to return to their moral and ethical purpose in life and uplift themselves from the tyranny of all forms of enslavement and subjugation to other creatures. One should also not lose sight of the fact that the verse expresses our commitment in the plural: "You alone do *we* worship." Shaykh Saʿīd Ḥawwā writes:

> The *sūrah* indicates to us in its usage of the collective voice (i.e., You alone do *we* worship, Guide *us*) that the default for the Muslim is to be a part of a whole, which is the collective

195 Al-Majīdī, *al-Islām*, 190–91.

> Muslim community, and that Islam's moral cultivation (*al-tarbiya al-Islāmiyya*) is predicated upon the cultivation of the collective community (*al-tarbiya al-jamāʿiyya*).[196]

Likewise, Muhammad Asad comments on Islam's vision for the human collective:

> The continuity of an individual's rise in spiritual stature (the fundamental objective of every religion) depends on whether he is helped, encouraged and protected by the people around him—who, of course, expect the same cooperation from him. This human interdependence was the reason why in Islam religion could not be separated from economics and politics. To arrange practical human relations in such a way that every individual might find as few obstacles and as much encouragement as possible in the development of his personality: this, and nothing else, appeared to be the Islamic concept of the true function of society. And so it was only natural that the system which the Prophet Muhammad enunciated in the twenty-three years of his ministry related not only to matters spiritual but provided a framework for all individual and social activity as well. It held out the concept not only of individual righteousness but also of the equitable society which such righteousness should bring about.[197]

Jamaal Zarabozo observes that the collective voice in this verse should remind Muslims that they should support one another in their journey towards God, offering corrections aimed at helping one another improve rather than refutations aimed at undermining one another's efforts.[198] The collective voice in these verses

---

196 Saʿīd Ḥawwā, *Asās fī al-tafsīr,* 1:39.

197 Muhammad Asad, *The Road to Mecca* (Louisville: Fons Vitae 2005), 302.

198 Zarabozo, *Al-Fatihah,* disc 11.

reminds us of the fallacy underlying the individualism of modern society: the quest for moral virtue and justice requires a collective movement. Joseph Kaminski notes, "A society that prioritizes positive communal bonds is bound to produce a different moral agent and a different public conceptualization of moral agency than one that does not."[199] The collective voice is also a reflection of humility, as the individual recognises that he or she is merely one soul among the multitudes of worshippers of Allah.

This *sūrah* provides the theological and ethical principles that underscore a vision for humanity that can achieve true ethical prosperity by reaffirming the covenant with God and liberating us from the tyranny of man-made ideologies. Without the aforementioned commitments as prerequisites, the horizons for our collective moral cultivation diminish considerably. The declaration of one's worship of God alone constitutes "a moral contract touching every sphere, comprehending each act, and outlasting death."[200]

Any seemingly small action in our lives becomes an act of worship when connected to our broader mission and vision in life of serving God and striving for moral virtue.

199 Kaminski, *Islam, Liberalism, and Ontology*, 175.

200 Hammad, *Opening*, 20.

Wa iyyāka nastaʿīn

And You alone do we ask for help

Naturalism dismantled

In the verse "You alone do we worship, and You alone do we ask for help," two concepts are mentioned: *ʿibādah* (worship) and *istiʿānah* (seeking help). These correspond respectively to the divine names Allah (the One who alone is worthy of worship) and *al-Rabb* (the nurturing Lord).[201] The Mauritanian scholar Shaykh Muḥammad al-Amīn al-Shinqīṭī (d. 1973) observes that these two concepts are frequently linked in the Qur'an (cf. Qur'an 12:123, 9:129, 73:9, 67:29), emphasizing that we only place our trust in the One who is deserving of our worship.[202] Lest we think that we have been able to worship Allah of our own accord, we are reminded that it is Allah who enabled us to worship Him and therefore we seek His help, as the West African scholar Shaykh ʿAbdullāh ibn Fūdī (d. 1829) observes.[203] Moreover, *ʿibādah* and *istiʿānah* provide

201 Riḍā, *Tafsīr al-manār,* 1:50. As we note in the conclusion, al-Rāzī shows how all the actions of the servant mentioned in *al-Fātiḥah* align with the divine attributes mentioned.

202 Al-Shanqīṭī, *Aḍwāʾ al-bayān fī īḍāḥ al-Qurʾān bi-l-Qurʾān* (Cairo: Dār al-Ḥadīth, 2006), 1:59.

203 Ibn Fūdī, *Ḍiyāʾ al-taʾwīl fī maʿānī al-tanzīl* (Sokoto: Al-Hajj Muhammad Ali Agha, n.d.), 1:9. For more on this work, see Dawud Walid, "How to Deal With Racism: Lessons From West African Scholars' Tafsīr of Sūrah al-Ḥujurāt," Yaqeen Institute for Islamic Research, June 23, 2023, https://yaqeeninstitute.ca/read/paper/how-to-overcome-racism-lessons-from-west-african-scholars-tafsir-of-surat-al-hujurat.

sincerity and humility, respectively, as the antidotes to ostentation (*riyāʾ*) and arrogance (*kibr*), two of the most prevalent diseases of the heart.[204] It has also been noted that the meaning of *lā ilāha illā Allāh* (there is none worthy of worship except Allah) has been affirmed when we say *iyyāka naʿbudu* and that the meaning of *lā ḥawla wa-lā quwwata illā bi-llāh* (there is no power or might except in Allah) has been affirmed when we say *iyyāka nastaʿīn*.[205] Furthermore, *iyyāka naʿbudu* entails developing gratitude and *iyyāka nastaʿīn* encompasses developing patience, two essential ingredients of Islamic spirituality.[206] The word *iyyāka* ("You alone") has been repeated in the verse to emphasise

Naturalism
The philosophical belief that everything can be explained through the properties and forces of nature without the need to invoke Divine intervention or supernatural explanations.

204 Al-Zahrānī, "*Aḍwāʾ ʿalā al-iʿjāz al-balāghī fī Sūrat al-Fātiḥah*," 133.

205 Al-Rāzī, *Great Exegesis,* 1:385. See also ʿAbd al-Razzāq al-Badr, *Sharḥ al-durūs al-muhimmah li-ʿāmmat al-ummah* (Kuwait City: Maktab al-Shuʾūn al-Fanniyyah, 2016), 15.

206 Al-Nasafī, *al-Taysīr fī al-tafsīr,* 1:137.

that what is most significant in this commitment to Allah is the exclusivity of these actions with respect to Him.[207]

After mentioning "You alone do we worship," we recognise that we need Allah's help in order to be able to worship Him, hence we say "You alone do we ask for help."[208] Asking for help is, however, not limited to help in religious matters. Rather, it includes seeking help in all aspects of our lives. Ibn ʿAbbās explained *iyyāka nastaʿīn* saying, "You alone do we ask for help in obeying You and in all our affairs."[209] Both our spiritual and physical affairs are ultimately dependent upon Allah. Of course, based upon the comprehensive understanding of worship discussed in the preceding section, all our physical affairs become spiritual acts of worship when connected to our journey to serve Allah. As the Ottoman-era Iraqi Qur'anic exegete Abū al-Thanāʾ Maḥmūd al-Ālūsī (d. 1270 AH) explains, seeking God's assistance encompasses every facet of life connected with our worship and our mission to walk the straight path.[210] Thus, in a certain sense, for the believer operating at the level of complete faith (*al-īmān al-kāmil*), there is nothing regarding which to ask for help other than worship. In our spiritual affairs, we focus on striving to come closer to Allah through our acts of prayer, supplication, recitation of the Qur'an, fasting, and so forth. In our physical affairs, we live every moment of our lives

---

207 Al-Thaʿlabī, *al-Kashf wa al-bayān*, 2:430.

208 Shams al-Dīn Aḥmad ibn al-Khalīl al-Khuwayyī (d. 637 AH), a student of al-Rāzī, writes, "You alone do we ask for help so that our worship will be according to what You are pleased with, as it is not possible for us to extract categories of worship befitting Your majesty based solely on our limited rational faculties and limited actions." See ʿAbd al-Hādī ʿAlī Muḥammad al-Qarnī, "*Yanābīʿ al-ʿulūm (aqālīm al-taʿālīm) li-Shams al-Dīn qāḍī al-quḍāh bi-l-Shām Aḥmad ibn al-Khalīl ibn Saʿādah ibn Jaʿfar ibn ʿĪsā al-Muhallabī 583–637 A.H. dirāsah wa-taḥqīq*," *al-Majallah al-ʿIlmiyyah li-Kullīyat Uṣūl al-Dīn wa-l-Daʿwah bi-l-Zaqāzīq* 33, no. 2 (2021): 285–356 (henceforth "al-Khuwayyī, *Yanābīʿ al-ʿulūm*").

209 Al-Ṭayyār, *Mawsūʿat al-tafsīr al-maʾthūr*, 1:35, no. 144; al-ʿUmrānī, *Mawsūʿat madrasat Makkah fī al-tafsīr*, 1:15.

210 Al-Ālūsī, *Rūḥ al-maʿānī fī tafsīr al-Qurʾān al-ʿaẓīm wa-l-sabʿ al-mathānī* (Beirut: Dār al-Kutub al-ʿIlmiyyah, 1995), 1:93.

Levels of faith

Deficient faith	Required faith	Complete faith
al-īmān al-nāqis	*al-īmān al-wājib*	*al-īmān al-kāmil*
Falling short of one's obligatory duties or engaging in major sins.	Performing the obligatory duties.	Performing both the obligatory duties and recommended actions.

striving to do virtuous deeds for His sake, whether working to support our families, build communities, help people, study the world, and even partake in permissible forms of enjoyment to rejuvenate ourselves for the spiritual task ahead.

In all our worldly interactions and the occurrences of life, we are conscious of the fact that it is God who is in control and that the appropriate response, therefore, is to seek His aid (*istiʿānah*) and place our absolute trust in Him (*tawakkul*), while utilizing the worldly means that He has established (*ittikhādh al-asbāb*). Understanding this verse properly allows us to recognise the error of naturalism, which is the presumption that the forces of nature alone account for the occurrences in life.[211] Note that naturalism is closely related to materialism, discussed earlier, but they are not synonymous. Materialism is the narrow position that reality is made of nothing more than matter. Naturalism is the view that all phenomena in the universe are determined by processes that can be studied by scientific investigation; in other words, that everything can be explained through nature. Some have suggested that "you can have naturalism without materialism, but not materialism without naturalism."[212]

211 See Zarabozo, *al-Fātiḥah*, disc 14.

212 Peter Atkins, "Naturalism and Materialism," *Think* 19, no. 56 (2020): 121–32. Some also distinguish between metaphysical naturalism and methodological naturalism. For a discussion on the relation of the concept of *tawakkul* to an understanding of methodological naturalism, see Edward Omar Moad, "Tying Your Camel: An Islamic Perspective on Methodological Naturalism," Yaqeen Institute for Islamic Research, March 28, 2018, https://yaqeeninstitute.org/read/paper/tying-your-camel-an-islamic-perspective-on-methodological-naturalism. One should note that even methodological naturalism cannot be entirely divested of metaphysical commitments.

This verse is of critical importance to understand where our priorities and hopes lie as a global Muslim community (*ummah*). Who will save us from oppression? When and from where will the help come? In the case of stopping the genocide in Gaza, all hopes in man-made institutions have continued to fail. The Arab League, the Organisation of Islamic Cooperation, the International Court of Justice, the International Criminal Court, the UN Security Council, the UN General Assembly—all these institutions have proven themselves either appallingly unwilling or woefully incapable of ending the mass slaughter of thousands of children. Any efforts that have ensued have been too little or too late. So whom do we ask for help? The answer is to trust in the Creator and not the creation. When Banī Isrāʾīl were subjected to mass slaughter of their children and persecution ordered by Firʿawn, Prophet Musa advised his people, "Seek Allah's help and be patient! Verily, the earth belongs to Allah alone, He grants it to whomever He chooses from His servants, and the final victory belongs to the righteous" (Qur'an 7:128). In the other two instances in the Qur'an where the command to seek help from God is mentioned, it is also mentioned alongside patience (cf. Qur'an, 2:45, 2:153). We continue to petition God for His help and raise our hands in prayer because we understand that this world is governed by a reality that extends beyond material elements and the physical forces of nature. As Allah reminds us, "Whoever is mindful of Allah, He will surely make a way out for him and provide for him from sources he could never imagine. Whoever puts his trust in Allah, Allah suffices him. Allah will surely accomplish His purpose, and Allah has decreed for everything its fate" (Qur'an 65:2–3).

One may ask, why appeal to God instead of just attending to the physical causes in nature alone? Part of the answer is epistemological: there are always factors and causes beyond our knowledge.[213] Studying the physical causes can certainly afford knowledge of a range of potential outcomes and associated probabilities based on past experiences. However, our past data will always be limited in predicting future outcomes. Many processes are not deterministic but stochastic, which means the cause increases the likelihood of the effect but each occurrence is subject to random variation (e.g., smoking causes lung cancer, but not every smoker gets lung cancer). Even processes that are deterministic may be described mathematically by chaos theory, which means that slight variations in the initial conditions can produce massive variations in the final state. All in all, even the best real-world predictions about future outcomes will always be fallible. In medicine, in spite of our best therapies, there is always the potential for adverse outcomes and treatment failure. One trusts in God over and above the physical means because the complete panoply of possibilities and the eventual actuality are determined solely by His divine will.

We continue to petition God for His help and raise our hands in prayer because we understand that this world is governed by a reality that extends beyond material elements and the physical forces of nature.

213 Riḍā, *Tafsīr al-Manār*, 1:49. He explains, "Allah has granted human beings the knowledge and capacity to overcome some obstacles and secure some causes while veiling others from them."

The other part of the answer as to why we look beyond the physical causes is metaphysical. In the modern era, many people are drawn to the notion of *scientism*, the idea that science alone provides us with knowledge of the truth. It is often presumed that science provides a complete account of reality such that there is no need for any appeal to factors beyond the natural realm. However, one cannot make sense of the natural realm without an appeal to some set of metaphysical commitments that lie beyond the scope of empirical inquiry. Cosmologist Paul Davies writes about the problematic gap in scientific thinking as follows:

> The most refined expression of the rational intelligibility of the cosmos is found in the laws of physics, the fundamental rules on which nature runs. The laws of gravitation and electromagnetism, the laws that regulate the world within the atom, the laws of motion—all are expressed as tidy mathematical relationships. But where do these laws come from? And why do they have the form that they do?
>
> ...Over the years I have often asked my physicist colleagues why the laws of physics are what they are. The answers vary from "that's not a scientific question" to "nobody knows." The favorite reply is, "there is no reason they are what they are—they just are." The idea that the laws exist reasonlessly is deeply anti-rational. After all, the very essence of a scientific explanation of some phenomenon is that the world is ordered logically and that there are reasons things are as they are. If one traces these reasons all the way down to the bedrock of reality—the laws of physics—only to find that reason then deserts us, it makes a mockery of science.[214]

214 Paul Davies, "Taking Science on Faith," *New York Times*, November 24, 2007, https://www.nytimes.com/2007/11/24/opinion/24davies.html.

As Davies also notes, the very notion of laws of nature arises from theology, from the notion that God created the world and ordered it in a rational way. That is a non-empirical metaphysical commitment that is needed in order for empirical science to work. Science must presuppose a fixed regularity and intelligible order to nature. As the American philosopher Thomas Nagel writes, "Science is driven by the assumption that the world is intelligible."[215] A portion of intelligible reality lies within the domain of our empirical investigation, while a portion lies beyond it. Even with complete empirical data on every entity and force in nature, one would not be able to predict the future. Part of seeking help from God is understanding that He controls all outcomes and that reality proceeds only by His permission—something that naturalism fails to account for. It is also important for the progress of scientific theorization that we have the capacity to relegate to God (*tafwīḍ*) aspects of reality beyond our empirical lens.[216] Theories function as maps that provide representations of certain features of external reality that are useful for certain insights. Just as there can be a variety of "true" maps emphasizing various features of reality (topographical, weather, traffic, etc.), so too can there be multiple levels of causal explanation even within the purview of natural science.[217]

As I have noted elsewhere, theology provides the metaphysical foundations for the philosophy of science.[218] The view that science provides a literal, true description of reality is called scientific realism and has been largely abandoned in the philosophy of science due to a variety of intractable failures.

---

215 Thomas Nagel, *Mind and Cosmos: Why the Materialist Neo-Darwinian Conception of Nature Is Almost Certainly False* (New York: Oxford University Press, 2012), 16.

216 Noam Chomsky has written about how the very notion of physical forces like gravitation, i.e., objects acting at a distance without contact, was regarded by Isaac Newton and John Locke as an absurdity necessary for scientific explanation. Noam Chomsky, What kind of creatures are we? (NY: CUP, 2016), 81–97.

217 For an example in mental causation, see Jaegwon Kim, *Mind in a Physical World* (Cambridge, MA: MIT Press, 1998), 38.

218 Nazir Khan, "Shades of Structural Realism in Post-Classical Islamic Thought," *Theology and Science* 21, no. 3 (2023): 376–89. I refer to this relationship between theology and science as "consolidation."

Part of seeking help from God is understanding that He controls all outcomes and that reality proceeds only by His permission—something that naturalism fails to account for.

Instead, many philosophers of science now accept a compromise between scientific realism and scientific anti-realism. In a previous co-authored article on the Islamic perspective on biological evolution, we elaborated on this subject:

> One of the most influential opponents of scientific realism has been philosopher Bas van Fraassen who has championed an anti-realist view called *constructive empiricism*. Essentially, instead of science telling us what is true or false about the real world, it makes no such metaphysical pretension but rather has a more modest objective: to arrive at theories that are 'empirically adequate,' i.e., theories that fit with our observations. Thus, we construct models and representations of the phenomena around us. When it comes to things that are directly observable, then empirical adequacy becomes the same as truth.[219] As for matters that are unobservable, then we rely on interpretations, inferences, models, extrapolations, and postulations that aim only to be empirically adequate. Attempting to retreat from many of the unwarranted

219 Constructive empiricism therefore affirms objective truth (as does structural realism) and should not be confused with postmodernism (discussed in a subsequent chapter) which negates objective truth and holds that reality itself is socially constructed.

> metaphysical excesses of scientific realism, there emerged a diverse set of offshoots of scientific realism including empiric structural realism (both direct and indirect), ontic structural realism, semi-realism, etc. However a key theme acknowledged by almost all groups is that what we can affirm as truth when it comes to the unobservable is considerably limited.[220]

Structural realism is a compromise between scientific realism and anti-realism. It says that our best scientific theories serve to represent some aspects of fundamental reality, like its causal relations or mathematical structure, for instance, while there are other questions concerning the essential nature of unobservable entities which will forever elude our grasp. Structural realism in fact recalls several theologically-informed approaches developed by Muslim theologians and scientists which allowed for the successful liberation of astronomy and other natural sciences from a variety of philosophical assumptions that impeded its progress.[221] A similar benefit may be achieved today. Reviving a theologically informed philosophy of science can guide scientific theorisation towards a more conceptually rigorous account of the empirically observable aspects of reality.

Another example of the metaphysical excesses of philosophical naturalism occurs in the study of history using the historical-critical method. The historian who adopts this method will exclude *a priori* any divine intervention, supernatural occurrence, or miraculous turn of events from his or her account.[222]

---

220 Nazir Khan and Yasir Qadhi, "Human Origins—Part 1: Theological Conclusions and Empirical Limitations," Yaqeen Institute for Islamic Research, August 31, 2018, https://yaqeeninstitute.ca/read/paper/human-origins-part-1-theological-conclusions-and-empirical-limitations.

221 See the examples cited in Khan, "Shades of Structural Realism."

222 Jonathan Brown writes, "The scientific revolution sealed the assumption that miracles or God's direct involvement could not be called on to explain history and scripture." Jonathan Brown, "Blind Spots: The Origins of the Western Method of Critiquing Hadith," Yaqeen Institute for Islamic Research, January 31, 2019, https://yaqeeninstitute.ca/read/paper/blind-spots-the-origins-of-the-western-method-of-critiquing-hadith.

The historical-critical method "cannot take such accounts of supernatural intervention at face value, because to do so would be a violation of the laws of historical study, namely acceptance of the laws of nature as understood by modern science and the operation of the law of cause and effect *within* history."[223] Certainly, divine intervention and supernatural matters lie beyond the scope of empirical enquiry and are therefore not objects within the realm of modern scientific theorisation. However, rather than simply acknowledging this as a limitation of one's method, the incautious historian commits an unjustified metaphysical leap by constructing an account predicated on the negation or absence of any factors beyond the forces of nature. By contrast, the balanced approach adopted by Ibn Khaldūn (d. 808 AH), the founder of sociology and a noted historian, is to consider both divine action and natural forces.[224] He explains that the general rule is that the historical plausibility of an event depends on what is within the realm of natural possibility:

> Thus, the principle in distinguishing truth from falsehood in reports by considering possibility and impossibility is to look at human social organization, which is civilization, and discern which conditions naturally pertain to it, which are incidental and not significant, and what cannot occur. If we do this, it will serve as a law for us in distinguishing truth from falsehood in reports and truth from lies with a definitive argument that leaves no room for doubt.[225]

223 David Law, *The Historical-Critical Method: A Guide for the Perplexed* (New York: Continuum, 2012), 22.

224 See Peter Adamson, "Ibn Khaldūn's Method of History and Aristotelian Natural Philosophy," *Journal of the History of Philosophy* 62, no. 2 (2024): 195–210.

225 Ibn Khaldūn, in the introduction ("*Muqaddimah*") to his work of history *al-ʿIbar wa-dīwān al-mubtadaʾ wa-l-khabar fī tārīkh al-ʿArab wa-l-Barbar wa-man ʿāṣarahum min dhawī al-shaʾn al-akbar*, ed. A. Khalīl Shihāda, rev. Dr. Suhayl Zakkār (Beirut: Dār al-Fikr, 1401/1981), 1:49.

Reliance on the Creator for all provision and sustenance. We make use of natural means and resources but we acknowledge the Creator and rely upon Him—not nature itself.

The natural realm is all there is. The universe is running on autopilot and there is no need to pray to anyone or give thanks.

However, when conclusive evidence points to the occurrence of miracles, rationality leads one to their affirmation.[226] Moreover, one should recognise that even naturalistic causation includes processes that are beyond direct empirical inquiry. Ibn Khaldūn explains:

> As these natural causes are traced back, they expand and multiply in both length and breadth, leaving the mind bewildered in comprehending and enumerating them... Moreover, the manner in which these causes effect many of their consequences is unknown because they are only perceived through customary association, relying on apparent linkage. The reality and manner of their influence are unknown, "and of knowledge you [mankind] have been given but little" (Qur'an 17:85).[227]

226 On miracles, see Ibn Khaldūn, *"Muqaddimah,"* 1:117.

227 Ibn Khaldūn, *"Muqaddimah,"* 1:580–81.

The restrictive approach of naturalism leads to significant interpretative shortcomings. For instance, any naturalistic explanation that denies the prophethood of Muhammad ﷺ by accusing him of deceit or mental illness fails on a cursory examination of his life or a study of the coherence of the Qur'an. Historical records consistently portray the Prophet as an individual of exceptional honesty and integrity, earning the title *al-Amīn* (the trustworthy) prior to his prophetic mission, and the intense persecution he and his followers endured belies any potential motive for deceit. Moreover, his life also demonstrates his leadership in navigating complex socio-political landscapes, mediating disputes, and establishing a cohesive community that formed the bedrock of a global civilization and a comprehensive legal tradition. Any suggestion of psychosis is therefore irrational and historically untenable. Ibn Ḥazm (d. 456 AH) writes:

> Anyone who contemplates the biography of Muhammad, peace be upon him, will inevitably conclude that he is truly the Messenger of Allah. Even if his life were his only miracle, it would suffice as proof. He grew up in a land of ignorance, unable to read or write, and never left his homeland except for two brief trips to the Levantine frontier, once as a child with his uncle and a second trip later which was short, after which he never left his people. Then, Allah caused all the Arabs to submit to his authority. In spite of this, he remained the same person and his character remained unchanged until his death. He died humbly, with his shield mortgaged for barley to feed his family, and he did not leave behind a single dinar or dirham. He would eat while sitting on the ground, mend his own shoes, patch his own clothes, and always preferred others over himself.
>
> When a distinguished Companion was killed, a loss that could demoralize any army, he did not retaliate against his enemies, as Allah had not commanded it. He did not seek their blood or

wealth, nor did he even blame them. Instead, he personally paid the blood money to the family on behalf of his enemies with a hundred camels of his own, despite needing just one for his strength.[228] Such actions are unimaginable for any earthly king or wealthy person. Such an action is also not in line with typical leadership or politics. It becomes clear, without a doubt, that he was following what his Lord, exalted is He, commanded him, whether it brought him great harm in this world or not. This is astonishing for anyone who contemplates it.[229]

Any objective assessment of the historical evidence and biographical accounts therefore reveals that the *a priori* exclusion of a divine explanation is a significant methodological failing in the historical critical method and will not yield a reliable narrative of the Prophet Muhammad's life. One cannot provide a historically accurate account of his life while failing to consider the veracity of the most important fact of it, namely, his prophethood. Similarly, pivotal moments in history—including the victory of the Muslims at Badr against a much larger and better equipped force—are inadequately understood through material explanations that do not take into consideration the universal patterns of divine action in the world (*al-sunan al-rabbāniyyah*) including cases of miraculous divine intervention (*muʿjizāt*). Allah says in the Qur'an:

> The patterns of divine action (*sunan*) have taken place before your time, so travel through the earth and observe the fate of those who denied the truth. (Qur'an 3:137)

228 This refers to the killing of ʿAbdullāh ibn Sahl ibn Zayd when he went to Khaybar while suffering extreme poverty. He was murdered and his body was found in a ditch. His family members did not witness the crime and therefore could not bear oath that the murder had been committed by the Jewish tribe of Khaybar, and since the latter party denied any involvement, the Prophet ﷺ elected to pay the compensation on their behalf. See *Ṣaḥīḥ al-Bukhārī*, no. 7192; *Ṣaḥīḥ Muslim*, no. 1669; *Muwaṭṭā Mālik*, "*kitāb al-qasāmah*," 1.

229 Ibn Ḥazm, *al-Fiṣal fī al-milal wa-l-ahwāʾ wa-l-niḥal* (Cairo: Maktabat al-Khānjī, 1903), 2:73–74.

Imam al-Baghawī (d. 510 AH) explains the meaning of this verse as follows:

> Indeed, there have transpired by My will certain patterns (*sunan*) among those before you from the past disbelieving nations, where I granted them respite and gradually led them to their doom until the decreed time for their destruction came, and I gave victory to My prophets over them. So travel through the earth and observe how the end of the deniers was.[230]

A purely naturalistic account of the rise and fall of civilisations inevitably fails to provide a comprehensive understanding of the forces driving the transformations in this world. It presents only a reductionistic account on the basis of economic and political factors but neglects that there are moral principles with divine consequences. Muslim scholars read history in a manner that integrated the empirical realities with an awareness of divine agency and the moral and theological principles governing change. Ibn Khaldūn has a chapter entitled "A new state typically overthrows an established state through prolonged effort, not sudden conquest," in which he comments on both the universal pattern of divine action and the exceptional, miraculous case of early Islam as follows:

> Such is the state of newly emerged dynasties in contention and prolonged struggle with established ones; this is the way (*sunnah*) of Allah with His servants, and you will find no change in the way of Allah.
>
> This is not contradicted by the Islamic conquests and how they took over Persia and Rome within three or four years after the Prophet's ﷺ death. Know that this was one of the

230 Al-Baghawī, *Maʿālim al-tanzīl* (Beirut: Dār Iḥyāʾ Turāth al-ʿArabī, 1420 AH), 1:513.

> miracles of our Prophet, the secret of which was the Muslims' determination in their struggle against their enemies, bolstered by their faith, and the fear and discord Allah cast into the hearts of their enemies.
>
> All of this was supernatural, breaking the usual pattern of prolonged conflict between newly emerged and established states. Since this was supernatural, it is among the miracles of our Prophet, peace be upon him, whose manifestation in the Islamic community is well known. One cannot compare miracles to ordinary matters nor use the exceptional occurrence of miracles as an objection to the existence of a natural order. Allah the Almighty knows best, and He is the granter of success.[231]

Sometimes secular historians seem oblivious to the ways in which their conclusions are entirely dependent on unsubstantiated presuppositions of the falsity of a religious doctrine or upon background philosophical assumptions like metaphysical naturalism. In a particularly egregious example, the New Testament historian Bart Ehrman writes about the Qur'an:

> The fact that later scribes accurately copied the Qur'an has no bearing on the question of whether the author(s) of the Qur'an had accurate information when they composed the book. With respect to Jesus they would have had no independent information—only what they had learned from earlier Christians and Christian sources.[232]

This exemplifies the logical fallacy known as begging the question by presupposing that the Qur'an is a human composition. The question of the accuracy of its content concerning Jesus is not

231 Ibn Khaldūn, "*Muqaddimah*," 1:375.

232 Bart Ehrman (@BartEhrman), X, April 24, 2024, https://x.com/BartEhrman/status/1783104679322255591.

Aside from helping scientists do better science and historians do better history, reconnecting empirical science with its theological foundations is also necessary to safeguard humanity from the unethical and harmful outcomes of scientific innovation.

tied to whether or not direct information was humanly available, but to whether or not its claim to be divine revelation is true. Moreover, the Qur'anic denial of Jesus's crucifixion, an element central to Christian doctrine, as well as its other subtle yet substantive differences from Judaeo-Christian sources refutes simplistic assumptions of "borrowing."[233] In a detailed study of several examples, Sharif Randhawa and Taha Soomro conclude:

> ...this mode of study also reveals that the Qur'an demonstrates an extremely profound, detailed, wide-ranging, and accurate knowledge of the Jewish and Christian scriptures and traditions across different languages, including Hebrew, Aramaic, Syriac, and even Greek. Yet, the Qur'an itself highlights the Prophet's ﷺ own lack of scriptural learning (29:48). Had he been known to have undertaken an education in the Jewish and Christian scriptural traditions—and the level of knowledge of these traditions evinced by the Qur'an would have required an extensive education under masters of these traditions, to say the least—it would not have been possible for the Qur'an to make this claim without being easily discredited. Yet, the Prophet's ﷺ opponents were hard pressed to explain how he acquired such knowledge, pointing, for example, to a foreigner who was scarcely able to communicate in Arabic (16:103; cf. 25:4–5). For Muslims, however, the Qur'an's deep familiarity with previous traditions should be far from surprising; after all, one would expect no less from a divine scripture revealed by God.[234]

233 See, for instance, Samuel Zinner, "The Qur'ān's Detailed Knowledge of the Bible: The Explanatory Inadequacy of the 'Conversational' or 'Christian Missionaries' Models," *Interdisciplinary Studies of Quran and Hadith* 1, no. 2 (2023): 109–26.

234 Taha Soomro and Sharif Randhawa, "The Qur'an's Engagement with Christian and Jewish Literature," Yaqeen Institute for Islamic Research, February 28, 2023, https://yaqeeninstitute.ca/read/paper/the-qurans-engagement-with-christian-and-jewish-literature.

By stepping beyond narrowly confined assumptions about the naturalistic origins of a text, scholarship can actually discover a great deal more about the sophisticated character of the Qur'an's correction and adjudication of minute details mentioned in Christian and Jewish sources.

Aside from helping scientists do better science and historians do better history, reconnecting empirical science with its theological foundations is also necessary to safeguard humanity from the unethical and harmful outcomes of scientific innovation. The production of hydrogen bombs was the first clue that science unhinged from ethical constraints can easily annihilate us. The continued devastation of the environment through relentless deforestation, fossil fuel consumption, and industrial pollution offers another stark example.[235] Technological innovation and scientific experimentation become harmful when directed towards the aims of colonial interests seeking to conquer natural resources and subjugate peoples. Sayyid Quṭb writes concerning the Islamic perspective on the natural sciences and how it differs from the colonial perspective:

> Man is specifically taught and directed to study the world around him, discover its potential and utilize all his environment for his own good and the good of his fellow humans. Any harm that man suffers at the hands of nature is a result only of his ignorance or lack of understanding of it and of the laws governing it. The more man learns about nature, the more peaceful and harmonious his relationship with nature and the environment is.

235 Ovamir Anjum, "Being a 'Good Person' is Not Enough: Why Ethics Need Islam," Yaqeen Institute for Islamic Research, January 27, 2022. https://yaqeeninstitute.ca/read/paper/being-a-good-person-is-not-enough-why-ethics-need-islam.

> Hence the notion of "conquering nature" can readily be seen as cynical and negative. It is alien to Islamic perceptions and betrays a shameless ignorance of the spirit in which the world has been created and the divine wisdom that underlies it.[236]

Today, cutting-edge technologies of surveillance and robotic warfare are placed in the hands of governments that utilise them for their political ends without the slightest moral compunction. Meanwhile, developments in artificial intelligence, including deep fakes, have opened a Pandora's box of illusions that threaten to obliterate the very distinction between reality and fiction altogether. As AI increasingly occupies a wider range of roles in labour and art, it will without a doubt accelerate the concentration of wealth and power in the hands of a select few. A recent MIT series discussing AI colonialism notes:

> The AI industry does not seek to capture land as the conquistadors of the Caribbean and Latin America did, but the same desire for profit drives it to expand its reach... [I]t has developed new ways of exploiting cheap and precarious labor, often in the Global South, shaped by implicit ideas that such populations don't need—or are less deserving of—livable wages and economic stability... AI is impoverishing the communities and countries that don't have a say in its development—the same communities and countries already impoverished by former colonial empires. They also suggest how AI could be so much more—a way for the historically dispossessed to reassert their culture, their voice, and their right to determine their own future.[237]

236 Quṭb, *In the Shade of the Qur'an*, 1:6.

237 Karen Hao, "Artificial Intelligence Is Creating a New Colonial World Order," MIT Technology Review, April 19, 2022, https://www.technologyreview.com/2022/04/19/1049592/artificial-intelligence-colonialism/.

Worse than AI colonialism is AI genocide, which has been taking place in Gaza. A recent investigation found that the Israeli army used an AI program called Lavender to mark thousands of Palestinians as targets without adequate verification, then enabled the military to bomb them when they entered their family homes.[238] They have also made use of so-called robot dogs, or Vision 60 units produced by the American company Ghost Robotics, in their campaign of destruction. As experts have noted, Israel's use of AI-enhanced weaponry raises ethical questions about how the technology can help facilitate violence and further Palestinian dispossession by reducing Israel's human cost of conducting warfare."[239]

The future of scientific innovation can be either one that serves humanity or one that threatens to exterminate it. Electing the former course requires restoring the theocentric value structure that enabled scientific innovation in the first place. Turning back to seek help and guidance from God in all our affairs allows for the prioritisation of ethical virtues necessary to ensure that the physical means are to our benefit and not to our detriment.

238 Yuval Ibrahim, "'Lavender': The AI machine directing Israel's bombing spree in Gaza," +972 Magazine, April 3, 2024, https://www.972mag.com/lavender-ai-israeli-army-gaza/.

239 "'Robodogs' Part of Israel's 'Army of Robots' in Gaza War," The New Arab, March 6, 2024, https://www.newarab.com/news/robodogs-part-israels-army-robots-gaza-war.

It is Allah who is always in control of our affairs. Therefore, the most appropriate course of action is to seek His aid and place our absolute trust in Him, while utilising the worldly means that He has established for us.

Ihdinā al-ṣirāṭ al-mustaqīm

Guide us on the straight path

Relativism dismantled

After the praise of God and expression of our commitment to Him, *Sūrah al-Fātiḥah* contains a supplication for guidance: "Guide us on the straight path." In describing Islam as a path, the image we receive about the nature of religiosity is radically different from the conventional discourse on religion in modernity. Religion is often represented today as an identity label, something that remains static and does not change throughout one's life. However, the language of direction exemplified in this verse differs significantly from the language of stasis. Islam is a commitment to a continuous process of self-improvement; it is about a journey towards God along the straight path. That is why believers must continue to ask for guidance, every time they recite this verse. God's guidance is necessary not only to embrace Islam but also to live according to its teachings in every part of our lives and to continue striving until we reach our destination.

Relativism

The doctrine that moral values and truth claims differ between cultures and peoples, and there is no absolute correct answer.

اهدنا
الصراط
المستقيم

Imam Ibn Juzayy says, "If it is asked, 'How should believers request guidance when they already possess it?' the answer is that it is a request for steadfastness in that guidance until death or for an increase in it, as the ascent through spiritual stations is endless."[240] Through divine guidance, all the experiences of life become part of a process of coming closer to God. Islam teaches that every day in life is a unique opportunity to take a step further along that path, aiming to come closer to the destination. "If two consecutive days in a person's life are the same, that person has cheated himself," a wise saying in the tradition counsels.[241] All the difficulties, hardships, and tragedies of life are also part of that arduous journey. As God says in the Qur'an, "O human being, indeed you are striving towards your Lord, with tremendous effort, and you will surely meet Him" (Qur'an 84:6).

The description of the path as straight (*mustaqīm*) indicates that it is free of error or distortion[242] and correlates with our aspiration for continued uprightness and steadfastness (*istiqāmah*) on it.[243] The Tunisian jurist and exegete Imam Ibn ʿĀshūr (d. 1973) also explained that the use of the descriptor *mustaqīm* indicates that "Islam is decisively clear in its proof (*wāḍiḥ al-ḥujjah*) and upright in its methodology (*qawīm al-maḥajjah*), such that its adherents do not descend into the abyss of error."[244] The straight path is the guidance provided by the Qur'an, the teachings of the

240 Ibn Juzayy, *al-Tashīl*, 1:65.

241 Al-Daylamī, *Kitāb al-firdaws* (Beirut: DKI, 1986), 3:611. Note that this is not a saying of the Prophet ﷺ.

242 Makkī ibn Abī Ṭālib, *al-Hidāyah ilā bulūgh al-nihāyah* (Sharjah: University of Sharjah, 2008), 1:111.

243 Al-Māturīdī, *Ta'wīlāt*, 1:367.

244 Ibn ʿĀshūr, *al-Taḥrīr wa-l-tanwīr*, 1:200. Al-Māturīdī explains that it is the path established with clear proofs and evidence (*bil-barāhīn wa al-adillah*) that cannot be undermined by any schemer or skeptic. See al-Māturīdī, *Ta'wīlāt*, 1:367.

Without a clear set of guiding principles concerning truth and justice, human beings inevitably succumb to relativism in the face of intractable moral disagreements.

Prophet Muhammad ﷺ, in other words, the way of Islam.[245] In this verse, guidance includes being shown the truth (*hidāyat al-irshād*) and being granted the ability and will to accept and follow the truth (*hidāyat al-tawfīq*).[246] In fact, were the verse to be worded with a preposition, such as *ihdinā ilā al-ṣirāṭ al-mustaqīm* (guide us *towards* the straight path) or *ihdinā li-l-ṣirāṭ al-mustaqīm* (guide us *to* the straight path), it would not have emphasised the importance of divine providence in following the path (*hidāyat al-tawfīq*).[247] Because it is a supplication to God for His divine guidance, it contains a humble acknowledgement that we are always in need of His aid in enabling us to accept the truth when it is shown to us. Moreover, we recognise that knowledge of the truth (*hidāyat al-irshād*) must ultimately be rooted in divine guidance as well. Without a clear set of guiding principles concerning truth and justice and a concrete programme of application, human beings inevitably succumb to relativism in the face of intractable moral disagreements.

245 There are several statements from the Companions and the early Muslims with mutually complementary meanings in this regard. See Ibn al-Jawzī, *Zād al-masīr fī ʿilm al-tafsīr* (Beirut: Dār Ibn Ḥazm, 2002), 34–35 and al-Ṭayyār, *Mawsūʿat al-tafsīr al-maʾthūr*, 2:37–41. This is a paradigmatic example of what is described as *ikhtilāf al-tanawwuʿ* (complementary differences) in *uṣūl al-tafsīr* (principles of Qur'anic exegesis).

246 Ibn al-Qayyim, *Badāʾiʿ al-fawāʾid* (Beirut: Dār Ibn Ḥazm, 2019), 447–48 and Ibn al-Qayyim, *Shifāʾ al-ʿalīl fī al-ḥikmah wa-l-taʿlīl* (Beirut: Dār Ibn Ḥazm, 2019), 1:265–68. See also Ibn ʿUthaymīn, *Tafsīr al-Fātiḥah wa-l-Baqarah*, 1:16.

247 Ibn al-Qayyim, *Badāʾiʿ al-fawāʾid*, 423–25.

There are, in fact, several levels at which human beings require divine guidance in order for moral values to be properly grounded.[248] The first level is **moral truths (ontology)**: do good and evil actually exist? Belief that good and evil have an objective, real existence is something affirmed by revelation and the human *fiṭrah*, but cannot be established by those who deny religion. Alija Izetbegović explains, "Moral conduct is either meaningless, or else, it has its meaning and sense in the existence of God. A third option is not possible."[249] Richard Garner, a contemporary atheist philosopher, argues that his fellow atheists have no grounds to believe in morality and should dispense with it altogether (a position he terms moral abolitionism). He writes, "Just as atheists claim that the beliefs of theists about the objective existence of a god are in error, moral error theorists claim that the beliefs of moral realists about the objective existence of moral rules, prohibitions, virtues, vices, values, rights, and duties are also in error, and for the same reason—what they are talking about doesn't exist."[250]

The second level is **moral knowledge (epistemology)**: how do I know which actions are good and which actions are evil? Culturally ingrained and emotionally conditioned moral responses are often defended with arbitrary reasons offered as post hoc justifications. American philosopher Jesse Prinz writes:

> People's reflective moral judgments seem to have an emotional foundation. If we ask people why they hold a particular moral view, they may offer some reasons, but those reasons are often superficial and post hoc. If the reasons are successfully challenged, the moral judgment often remains.

248 Zohair Abdul-Rahman and Nazir Khan, "Proving God's Existence | In Pursuit of Conviction II," Yaqeen Institute for Islamic Research, October 11, 2019. https://yaqeeninstitute.ca/read/paper/in-pursuit-of-conviction-ii-proving-gods-existence.

249 Alija Izetbegović, *Islam between East and West*, 110.

250 Richard Garner, "Morality: The Final Delusion?," *Philosophy Now*, 82 (2011): 18–20.

> When pressed, people's deepest moral values are based not on decisive arguments that they discovered while pondering moral questions, but on deeply inculcated sentiments.[251]

Ultimately, our values have to be grounded in something beyond the subjective and relativistic human whims. As Alija Izetbegović observes, "Reason can only examine and determine the relations between things; it cannot give a judgment of value when the question is of moral approval or moral renouncement."[252] If wealth and power are situated at the top of one's value hierarchy, then domination and exploitation of others will seem to be a rational conclusion. Even when altruistic virtues are incorporated into a secular value hierarchy, they are typically defined loosely in ways that leave them vulnerable to manipulation. When moral disagreements arise, having a common reference point anchored in divine revelation with a clearly defined value hierarchy prevents the inexorable slide towards self-interest or political manipulation. Professor Ovamir Anjum writes:

> ...[T]he secular overlords of the world have altered, and continue to alter, what counts as being good, and the perceptions of the masses are often shaped by propaganda. Just a century ago, for instance, serving one's parents would have been universally deemed among the most important ethical virtues throughout the world, from Europe and the Islamic world to China and India. Today, secular, liberal societies have dropped this virtue, if not turned it into a vice. Greed, similarly, had always been recognised as the greatest of evils and its particular form, usury or interest, the most hated crime in all cultures and all history until modern capitalism began to consider it both a virtue and a necessity.

---

251 Prinz, *The Emotional Construction of Morals* (Oxford: OUP, 2008), 29.

252 Alija Izetbegović, *Islam between East and West*, 116.

> This points to a deeper problem than economic exploitation and increasing inequality: it is our very sense of right and wrong that is mass manipulated by the elite. This I call epistemic imperialism—the colonization of knowledge-production, meaning, and values by certain key global institutions. Since the rise of globalism in the 1980s, these institutions are no longer merely "Western," but have extended to include the ultra-rich "global" elite in the global South, joining hands against the majority of people everywhere.[253]

The third level is **moral development (psychology)**: how do we develop within people the motivation to make tremendous sacrifices in order to strive for moral outcomes? There is nothing in the atheistic worldview or the materialistic picture of reality to motivate a person to endure discomfort or hardship for ethical aims. Alija Izetbegović writes:

> Atheism is quite helpless against the rush of purely utilitarian, selfish, and immoral or amoral claims. What can be done against this crippling logic? If I live only today and have to die tomorrow and be forgotten, why should I not live as I like and without obligations, if I can?[254]

Left to their own devices, human beings invariably act to maximise their own pleasure, demonstrating selfishness and greed. A person may be fully aware that a particular goal is noble and virtuous but may entirely lack the willpower to pursue it. He may affirm that a particular behavior is immoral but may still choose to indulge in it. By contrast, the entire theological system of Islam constantly motivates a human being to pursue spiritual

253 Ovamir Anjum, "Being a 'Good Person' is Not Enough: Why Ethics Need Islam," Yaqeen Institute for Islamic Research, January 27, 2022, https://yaqeeninstitute.ca/read/paper/being-a-good-person-is-not-enough-why-ethics-need-islam.

254 Alija Izetbegović, *Islam between East and West*, 139.

God's truth is singular. There is a defined 'straight path' to success, and we pray to God to guide us collectively upon it.

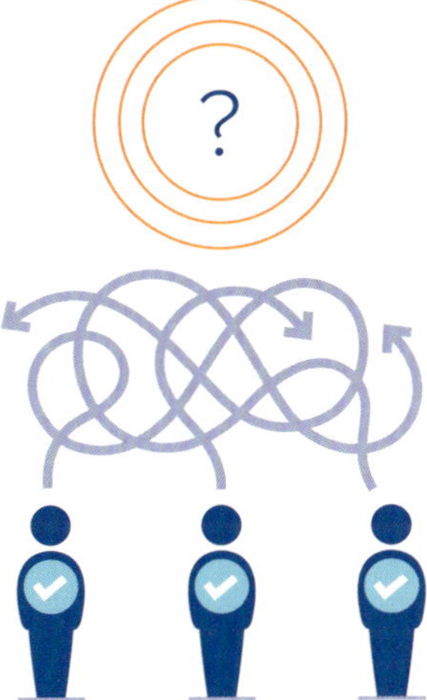

Each person is right in their own way. There is no fixed path set by God.

purification and moral development. The Qur'an indicates the relationship between beliefs and ethical restraint in many instances, for example: "As for one who fears standing before his Lord and restrains himself from evil desires, surely Paradise will be his refuge" (Qur'an 79:40–41).

In addition to problems with adhering to morals, in the absence of divine guidance there is also no psychological motivation to engage in moral introspection. The ability to assess one's own moral deficiencies is vital to moral growth. An aphorism in the Islamic tradition counsels, "Blessed is he who is preoccupied with his own defects rather than those of others."[255] If a person does not possess any guiding framework by which to revise his own behaviour, complacency kicks in and there is no psychological drive to improve and better oneself by eliminating bad character

255 *Musnad al-Bazzār,* no. 6237.

traits and replacing them with positive ones. While everyone agrees that there are good people and bad people in the world, the irony is that no one considers himself bad: even bad people think they are good. And why wouldn't they? Without guidance, the criteria for goodness can be as malleable as one wishes. Islam, on the contrary, provides the optimal rubric for self-evaluation in the form of the moral example of the Prophet Muhammad ﷺ: "Indeed in the Messenger of Allah you have an excellent role model to follow for one who hopes in Allah and the Last Day and remembers Allah much" (Qur'an 33:21).

The fourth level is that of **moral society (sociology)**: how do we create a society that cares about promoting virtue rather than just acting on the basis of pure selfishness? The early Muslim jurist Imam al-Shaʿbī (d. 104 AH) said:

> Social dealings were rooted in religion (*dīn*) for a long time until religion was gone. Then people lived according to honor until honor was gone. Then they lived according to a sense of shame, and then they lived according to reward and punishment, and I suspect that what is worse is yet to come.[256]

In his journey to find Islam, Muhammad Asad also expressed this sentiment poignantly:

> The world in which I was living—the whole of it—was wobbling because of the absence of any arrangement as to what is good and evil spiritually and, therefore, socially and economically as well. I did not believe that individual man was in need of 'salvation': but I did believe that modern society was in need of salvation. More than any previous time, I felt with mounting certainty, this time of ours was in need of an ideological basis

256 Al-Sulamī, *Ādāb al-ṣuḥbah* (Ṭanṭā: Dār al-Ṣaḥābah li-l-Turāth, 1990), 73.

> for a new social contract: it needed a faith that would make us understand the hollowness of material progress for the sake of progress alone—and nevertheless would give this life of this world its due; that would show us how to strike a balance between our spiritual and physical requirements—and thus save us from the disaster into which we were rushing headlong.[257]

Humanity, of course, requires both individual and collective salvation, and both are to be found within Islam. On the other hand, in secular modernity, religious beliefs have been deemed irrelevant to public reason and to the development of a moral society. The consequence of this view is a pervasive relativism where personal beliefs and values become totally meaningless. In 2001, a viral campaign encouraged people to record their religious belief as "Jedi" (in reference to the population science fiction franchise *Star Wars*), which was done by 70,000 Australians, 21,000 Canadians, and in the UK a whopping 390,127 people, making it the fourth largest religion in Britain, even surpassing Sikhism, Judaism, and Buddhism.[258] What this viral stunt illustrates is that technically speaking, in a secular society there is in fact no basis for distinguishing between someone who is a passionate Buddhist, Christian, or Jew from someone who is a passionate fan of Harry Potter or the Lord of the Rings, so long as a person claims something or other as his religious identity. All "religions" are deemed equally irrelevant to the public order, and all truth claims are subjective and relative. Moreover, modern culture emphasises the importance of being different and standing out from the crowd, and people seek to make a name for themselves on social media by courting controversy to

257 Muhammad Asad, *The Road to Mecca*, 305.

258 Tom de Castella, "Have Jedi Created a New 'Religion'?," BBC, October 25, 2014, https://www.bbc.com/news/magazine-29753530.

attract followers. Yet, one of the meanings of the "straight path" is sticking to the path of the mainstream Muslim community, that of the "vast majority."[259] God's guidance does not manifest in chasing eccentric views or "hot takes."

Why do we need religion to be good?

Four domains of morality

1 Moral truths

Do good and evil exist?
Without religion, we have no basis to affirm that there is even such a thing as objective morality. In fact, some atheists have called for abolishing morality.

2 Moral knowledge

How do I know what is good and what is evil?
Without proper guidance, people have no uniform point of reference to determine what actions are good and what actions are evil.

3 Moral development

How is one motivated to strive for good and avoid evil?
Without faith in God and the afterlife, there is no enduring motivation to strive against one's own personal interest or forgo worldly pleasures.

4 Moral society

How do people make a society that cares about promoting good and avoiding evil?
Without a foundation of sacred values, there is no way to organise society around shared ethical aims and objectives.

259 Al-Thaʿlabī, *al-Kashf wa-l-bayān*, 2:448. See also *Sunan Ibn Mājah*, no. 3950.

By dislocating human beings from their commitment to a singular ultimate truth, society has inadvertently diminished the value of truth altogether. But truth does matter, and it is worth pursuing earnestly and with sincere conviction. The COVID-19 pandemic showed that even a secular society may be required to arbitrate between two polarised groups with radically opposing beliefs; the problem is that it has lost the value structure and dialectical tools to do so effectively. The age of alternative facts, fake news, and post-truth politics has aptly illustrated the modern epistemic crisis. In Islam, truth and justice are inseparable and both are encompassed in the meaning of the Qur'anic term *ḥaqq* (truth). Imam Ibn Taymiyyah notes that *ḥaqq* is used to encompass both truths of existence (*ḥaqq mawjūd*) and truths of purpose (*ḥaqq maqṣūd*); the former is the basis of true knowledge and the latter is the basis of true action, in accordance with justice.[260] A society that undermines its commitment to the truth inevitably undermines its commitment to justice.

Returning to the verse "Guide us on the straight path," Ibn ʿAbbās explained it to mean "Enable us to realise Your true religion."[261] We acknowledge that there is a singular true path of guidance.[262] This verse dismisses the notion of perennialism, the notion that various religions all express the same fundamental truth. It also dismisses religious universalism, the idea that there are multiple truths of comparable value in differing religions.[263] For the perennialist, the choice between religions is deemed as inconsequential as choosing between different flavors of ice cream.

260 On the distinction between truths of essence and truths of purpose, see Ibn Taymiyyah, *Majmūʿ al-fatāwā*, 2:102 and 15:241. On truth being inclusive of justice, see Ibn Taymiyyah, *al-Radd ʿalā al-manṭiqiyyīn* (Beirut: Mu'assasat al-Rayyān, 2005), 480–81.

261 Al-Ṭayyār, *Mawsūʿat al-tafsīr al-ma'thūr*, 1:36. Arabic: *alhimnā dīnaka al-ḥaqq*. Similarly, al-Saʿdī explains, "Guidance to the straight path means adhering to the religion of Islam and forsaking all other religions." ʿAbd al-Raḥmān Nāṣir al-Saʿdī, *Tafseer as-Sa'di*, trans. Nasiruddin Khattab (Riyadh: IIPH, 2018), 1:29.

262 Zarabozo, *Al-Fātiḥah*, disc 18.

263 On these terms, see Mark Sedgwick, *Traditionalism: The Radical Project for Restoring Sacred Order* (New York: Oxford University Press, 2023), 31–32.

A society that undermines its commitment to the truth inevitably undermines its commitment to justice.

Shaykh Muḥammad al-Ghazālī writes:

> A straight line is the shortest distance between two points and is therefore unique. Whoever leads a straight and righteous life will be on the right path to God, for that is the one and only sure and direct way that leads to Him. God's religion is one religion, preached by all prophets and messengers at all stages of human history. It is founded on the oneness of God, who deserves total allegiance and full praise and on whom everyone and everything depend.[264]

Imam Ibn al-Qayyim notes that the wording of this verse specifically highlights the singularity of the straight path by using the definite article *al-* in *al-ṣirāṭ* (the path), thus indicating it to be the only true path of guidance.[265] Moreover, the next verse repeats the word *ṣirāṭ* (path) alongside an elaboration, as though specifically intended to respond to the objection that those opposed to the truth also presume to be following the straight path. Thus, the very next verse contains an apposition (*badal*): "Guide us on the straight path—the path of those whom You have favoured," thus making it clear that the path of true guidance is only that path traversed by the prophets and the righteous.[266] The linguistic eloquence (*balāghah*) in the precise phrasing of the verse emphasises the singularity of the straight path.

---

264 Muhammad al-Ghazali, *Thematic commentary,* 3. See also al-Rāzī, *Great Exegesis,* 1:402.

265 Ibn al-Qayyim, *Badāʾiʿ al-fawāʾid,* 412.

266 Ibn al-Qayyim, *Badāʾiʿ al-fawāʾid,* 410.

By dislocating humans from their commitment to a singular ultimate truth, society has inadvertently diminished the value of truth altogether. But truth does matter, and it is worth pursuing earnestly and with sincere conviction.

Relativism rejects the singularity of the straight path and thus undermines the concept and value of truth itself. Perennialism combines numerous contradictory paths into a nebulous shared path, rendering the path effectively meaningless and directionless. Tom Facchine notes that perennialism plays a role that is conducive to the goals of secularism:

> Perennialism makes a parallel move [to secularism], searching out the lowest common denominator of religious belief and practice, and in the process watering down and depoliticizing its notion of truth. This neutered vision, in turn, provides secularism with an important tool for neutralizing rival claimants to transcendent truth and alternative transcendent political imaginations. The perennialist project of lending theological legitimacy to other religions sits comfortably adjacent to liberal political values of tolerance, inclusion, and multiculturalism. Indeed, perennialism, in addition to universalism, postmodernism, and other ideologies that undermine alternate claims to ultimate truth, are actually key conscripts of secularism allowed to flourish in order to undermine its Others.[267]

Perennialism might seem like a good pluralistic solution to the problem of religious diversity: people simply find some basic truth shared by the different religions that everyone can agree upon and then dismiss religious differences as trivial. What this ends up doing, however, is incapacitating genuine truth-seeking, which requires wrestling with deep and irreconcilable theological, moral, and metaphysical disagreements in order to ascertain worthy objects of belief and worthy goals of action.

---

267 Tom Facchine, "Are All Religions the Same? Islam and the False Promise of Perennialism," Yaqeen Institute for Islamic Research, September 13, 2023, https://yaqeeninstitute.ca/read/paper/are-all-religions-the-same-islam-and-the-false-promise-of-perennialism.

Sūrah al-Fātiḥah provides us with an alternative and far more robust basis for approaching religious pluralism or diversity in a manner that does not undermine our singular commitment to the truth: the values of mercy, gratitude, and justice. Recognising that Allah is *al-Raḥmān* and that His mercy encompasses all creation cultivates within one the desire to extend compassion to all others and to share the truth with them out of an earnest desire to seek their betterment. Ahmad Zaki Hammad writes, "It is foreign to the nature and the logic of Islam that one should be passive in belief and not share it with others, for it is the inalienable right of every person to hear the words of the Lord of creation and have access to His guidance."[268]

Furthermore, cultivating one's gratitude towards Allah through the expression *alḥamdulillāh* also requires sharing one's appreciation towards others for the good they offer and the good that comes through them. A hadith states, "Wisdom is the lost property of the believer; wherever he finds it, he is most worthy of adopting it."[269] The Turkish sociologist Prof. Recep Şentürk argues that Islam acknowledges multiple layers ("multiplexity") of reality and discourse, affirming an ultimate truth while also acknowledging the diversity in perspectives of different communities. This allows him to conclude that "unity of Muslims and humanity can be achieved best by adopting a multiplex worldview, which allows pluralism without falling into the trap of relativism."[270] Moreover, Islam's approach to pluralism without relativism focuses on cooperating on goals of justice: "Cooperate in virtue and piety, but do not cooperate in sin or aggression" (Qur'an 5:2) and "Do not let others' hatred allow you to deviate from justice;

268 Hammad, *The Opening*, 27.

269 *Jāmiʿ al-Tirmidhī*, no. 2687. Though the authenticity of this hadith is weak, its meaning has been accepted by scholars as sound and attested by other evidence in the Qur'an and Sunnah.

270 Recep Şentürk, "Unity in Multiplexity: Islam as an Open Civilization," *Journal of the Interdisciplinary Study of Monotheistic Religions* (*JISMOR*) 7 (2011): 49–60.

be just—that is closer to piety" (Qur'an 5:8). Shaykh Muṣṭafā al-Sibāʿī writes, "Differences of religion should not make people fight one another or commit aggression against one another; rather, they should cooperate in doing good and warding off evil."[271] The common moral values embedded within human nature (*fiṭrah*) provide a solid basis for collaborative efforts to achieve justice and compassion and to alleviate human suffering.[272]

Recognising that Allah is *māliki yawm al-dīn* allows one to focus on ensuring that rights are fulfilled while relegating ultimate judgement of the moral standing of other individuals to God alone: "Your duty is but to deliver the message, and judgement is for Us" (Qur'an 13:40). While God has made clear to us that Islam is the sole path to salvation, He alone will judge as to whether someone sincerely sought to find His path or not and how far he moved in its direction and the direction of its lofty aims. Reiterating our commitment to seek out that straight path and seeking His support in traversing its ethical precepts are therefore the most noble of objectives.

---

271 Al-Sibāʿī, *Civilization of Faith*, 119.

272 On the *fiṭrah* and natural human ethics, see Muhammad al-Tahir Ibn Ashur, *Ibn Ashur: Treatise on Maqasid Al-Shari'ah*, trans. Mohamed El-Tahir El-Mesawi (Washington: The International Institute of Islamic Thought, 2006), 83–86.

“Differences of religion should not make people fight one another or commit aggression against one another; rather, they should cooperate in doing good and warding off evil.”

Shaykh Muṣṭafā al-Sibāʿī

صرط
الذين
أنعمت
عليهم

Ṣirāṭ alladhīna an'amta 'alayhim

The path of those whom You have favoured

Progressivism dismantled

After requesting that Allah guide us along the straight path, we realise the need for travel companions for the long journey that lies ahead.[273] *Sūrah al-Fātiḥah* further elaborates the path as "the path of those whom You have favoured." Shaykh Muḥammad 'Abdullāh Dirāz notes that the description of the path in this chapter describes both its intrinsic value (it is inherently correct, or *mustaqīm*) and its extrinsic value (it leads to our being blessed by God).[274] Building upon this, we can say that Islam motivates ethical action through both deontological (rule-based) and teleological (consequence-based) considerations while also indicating worthy ethical role models for us (an important basis for virtue ethics). What exists as conflicting ethical

Progressivism
The idea that humans today are morally enlightened and that people of the past were morally inferior and backwards.

273 See al-Khuwayyī, *Yanābī' al-'ulūm*, 318.

274 Muḥammad 'Abdullah Dirāz, "*Naẓarāt fī fātiḥat al-kitāb al-ḥakīm*," *al-Majallah* 7 (Dhū al-Ḥijjah 1376 AH), 97–107.

paradigms in the Western tradition are eloquently harmonised throughout Islamic discourse, including in this concise description of the straight path. Who are those whom Allah has favoured? Scholars often note that this is answered in the Qur'an itself:

> Whoever obeys Allah and the Messenger will be in the company of those whom Allah has favoured: the prophets, the *ṣiddīqīn* (people of truth), the martyrs, and the righteous—how fine are such companions! (Qur'an 4:69)[275]

In Western philosophy, ethics is typically divided into three approaches:

1. **Deontological ethics:** the morality of an action is determined by whether it adheres to a set of rules.
2. **Teleological ethics:** the morality of an action is based on its outcomes.
3. **Virtue ethics:** the morality of an action is determined by whether it is performed by a person of good character.

Islam provides a **balanced view** that harmonises the positive elements within these approaches while avoiding their extremes.

But why not mention those favoured directly in *al-Fātiḥah* itself? Why not say, "Guide us to the straight path, the path of the prophets and the righteous"? Ibn al-Qayyim explains that the actual phrasing of the verse ("the path of those whom You have favoured") makes it clear that the reason for which they received divine favor was on account of their guidance along the path to God. Moreover, the phrasing indicates our desire to be alongside them in also receiving divine favor.[276] The fact that this path has been traversed before is also an acknowledgement that it is something practicable rather

275 This was mentioned by Ibn Jarīr al-Ṭabarī, Ibn ʿAṭiyyah, Ibn Taymiyyah, Ibn Kathīr, and others. Note also that a very similar explanation was provided by Ibn ʿAbbās, who explained the verse to mean "the path of those you have favoured of the angels, the prophets, the people of truth, the martyrs, and the righteous, those who obey You and worship You." See al-Ṭayyār, *Mawsūʿat al-tafsīr al-maʾthūr*, 2:43–44.

276 Ibn al-Qayyim, *Badāʾiʿ al-fawāʾid*, 418–20.

than a matter of mere idealism, as the Sudanese scholar Professor Jaafar Sheikh Idris pointed out, "The straight path described in the Quran is not a theoretical path; it is an actual path that some people before us have taken."[277] This verse tells us that guidance is found in following the well-trodden path of these timeless ethical role models. This is in stark contrast to the notion of progressivism that tells us that we have become morally superior to people of the past and must abandon their guidance. A related notion, modernism, tells us that the ways of the past may have been valid for those times but are no longer morally relevant for our own times. This verse of *al-Fātiḥah* therefore directly addresses the fallacy underlying both progressivism and modernism.[278] Since both are closely connected and share the same error in reasoning, we will suffice with analysing the former in this discussion.

Before delving into some of the details related to how this verse addresses progressivism, there are a number of other basic concepts and important considerations to outline with respect to the verse. This verse connects our personal quest towards God with that of others, learning from those who have preceded us on the path towards God. One cannot take guidance only from the books without the tutelage of teachers and the examples set by role models.[279] For a person sincerely seeking to live a virtuous life according to the truth, the clearest compass he has is the example of those who have exemplified virtue in every aspect of their lives. This again underscores the collectivist element within human epistemology: we come to know the truth through the

277 Jaafar Sheikh Idris, "A Commentary on the First Chapter of the Quran," IslamReligion, November 1, 2010, https://www.islamreligion.com/articles/10190/first-chapter-of-quran.

278 Zarabozo, *al-Fātiḥah*, disc 19.

279 Muḥammad Shafī', *Ma'ārif al-Qur'ān*, 1:80–81.

moral example and the guidance of the people of truth.[280] This is particularly evident in much of the online social commentary around the genocide in Gaza. On the one hand, people witness the actions of the so-called "most moral army in the world": Israeli soldiers rifling through women's underwear, posing over the ruins of Palestinian homes, joking about killing children, laughing as they desecrate mosques, mocking Palestinians as they knock on the doors of demolished houses. On the other hand, people witness the resolute and serene faith of those being bombed and starved, standing firm despite losing their family members, prostrating to God amidst the rubble, giving preference to the needs of others over themselves. Any sound human conscience can distinguish between the moral standing of these two groups and will naturally find an affinity with the latter. Indeed, many people have embraced Islam during the Gaza genocide as a result of recognising the path of virtue exemplified in the faith of the Palestinians.

The righteous (*al-ṣāliḥūn*) are those who go above and beyond their required obligations and strive to fulfil voluntary acts of virtue in order to be closest to God.[281] Two special categories of the righteous have been singled out for mention in verse 4:69: those who live by the truth (*al-ṣiddīqūn*) and those who die for it (*al-shuhadā'*, or martyrs).[282]

280 At first glance, this principle may seem to conflict with the saying attributed to ʿAlī ibn Abī Ṭālib: "Verily, truth and falsehood are not recognised by the ranks of men. Know the truth and you will recognise its people; know falsehood and you will recognise the one who brings it." See al-Balādhurī, *Ansāb al-ashrāf* (Beirut: Dār al-Fikr, 1996), 3:64. However, ʿAlī's statement refers to declaring a particular opinion to be correct solely based on the name of someone who adopts the opinion, whereas the principle established in this verse is about recognising the path of guidance and moral virtue through the collective example of all those who lived righteously, first and foremost amongst them being the infallible prophets of God.

281 Muḥammad Shafīʿ, *Maʿārif al-Qurʾān*, 1:78.

282 The Prophet's Companion and first caliph Abū Bakr was the person most widely known as *al-Ṣiddīq*, given his consistent acceptance of the truth without hesitation including his acceptance of the Prophet's night journey to Jerusalem when the Quraysh reacted with skepticism. Abū Bakr said, "Verily, I believe in that which is even more astounding—that he receives news from heaven in the morning and evening." See al-Bayhaqī, *Dalāʾil al-nubuwwah*, (Beirut: DKI, 1988), 2:361. Given Abū Bakr's pre-eminence in carrying this title, al-Rāzī even includes the appointment of Abū Bakr al-Ṣiddīq as the first caliph as one of the allusions of "the path of those whom You have favoured." See al-Rāzī, *Great Exegesis*, 1:405.

Islam

God

The prophets and righteous exemplars

Pious role models in the past favoured by God are the epitome of a successful life.

Progressivism

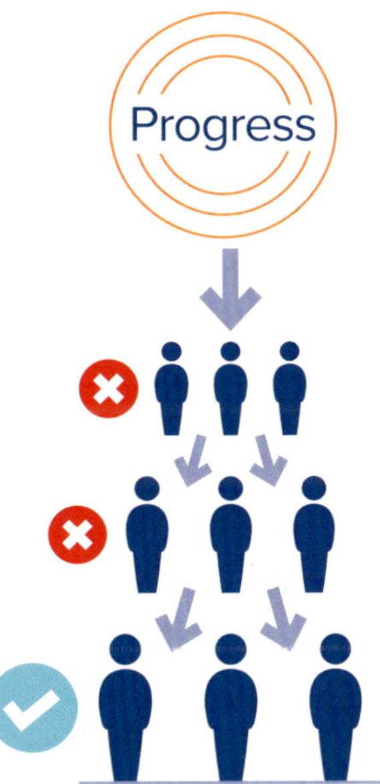

Previous generations are regarded as morally inferior, or irrelevant to our guidance. Our cumulative experience and technological success are equated with moral progress.

Those who are killed unjustly, including those killed for their faith or in defence of their homes or family, testify through their death to the demands of truth and justice. The Prophet Muhammad ﷺ said, "He who is killed while protecting his property is a martyr, and he who is killed while defending his family, his blood, or his religion is a martyr."[283] They have an honourable rank because they paid the ultimate sacrifice in the cause of Allah, and the community bears witness to the injustice by which a sacred life was taken from this world.[284]

283 *Sunan Abī Dāwūd*, no. 4772.

284 For a correction of some of the contemporary misapprehensions surrounding martyrdom, see Jonathan Brown, "Is Islam a Death Cult? Martyrdom and the American-Muslim Imagination," Yaqeen Institute for Islamic Research, September 12, 2017, https://yaqeeninstitute.org/read/paper/is-islam-a-death-cult-martyrdom-and-the-american-muslim-imagination

We belong to an unbroken tradition of worshippers of God who sacrificed everything in seeking the pinnacle of virtue, and the best hope we have for moral progress is in emulating their example.

Understanding that those who were killed unjustly are recompensed by Allah is a source of tremendous comfort for the grieving. Hala Abulebdeh is a Palestinian pharmacist from Gaza whose entire family of doctors, engineers, therapists, and teachers were killed by the Israeli army during the genocide in Gaza. In an interview, she described the horror of her family not being able to find the bodies of the deceased beneath the rubble, and when describing the intensity of the psychological trauma she has endured, she said, "At some point, I feel like even experts in psychology will never be able to help me, but I feel like my religion does because we have this belief that our families are still alive."[285]

Allah says concerning the fate of martyrs:

> And never think of those who have been killed in the cause of Allah as dead. Rather, they are alive with their Lord, receiving provision. Rejoicing in what Allah has bestowed upon them of

285 Hala Abulebdeh, "Israel Killed My Entire Family of Doctors, Engineers, Teachers and Therapists in Gaza," Interview with Ahmed Alnaouq, Palestine Deep Dive, YouTube video, April 11, 2024, https://www.youtube.com/watch?v=tuzcOPNTars.

> His bounty, and they receive good tidings about those [to be martyred] after them who have not yet joined them—that there will be no fear concerning them, nor will they grieve. They receive good tidings of favour from Allah and bounty and [of the fact] that Allah does not allow the reward of believers to be lost. (Qur'an 3:169–171)

Let us return to the subject of progressivism. In this verse, "the path of those whom You have favoured," we recall the historical memory of the righteous who have preceded us upon this path: prophets, martyrs, and all those who lived their lives according to the lofty ethical teachings of divine revelation. We belong to an unbroken tradition of worshippers of God who sacrificed everything in seeking the pinnacle of virtue, and the best hope we have for moral progress is in emulating their example. This directly negates one of the most enduring myths at the heart of Western civilisation, namely, the myth of moral progress or progressivism. Wael Hallaq calls this "theology of progress" one of the "most essential and potent tools of imperialism."[286] There is an imagined trajectory in history that supposedly leads from "primitive barbarism" to the rationally superior values of the European Enlightenment. Aníbal Quijano and Michael Ennis write:

> The fact that Western Europeans will imagine themselves to be the culmination of a civilizing trajectory from a state of nature leads them also to think of themselves as the moderns of humanity and its history, that is, as the new, and at the same time, most advanced of the species. But since they attribute the rest of the species to a category by nature inferior and consequently anterior, belonging to the past in

286 Hallaq, *Restating Orientalism*, 214.

> the progress of the species, the Europeans imagine themselves as the exclusive bearers, creators, and protagonists of that modernity.[287]

A common fallacy lies in mistaking technological progress for moral progress. Technological advancements have equipped the modern nation-state with the security and surveillance forces to replace certain forms of premodern violence and torture with forms of modern warfare and "enhanced interrogation techniques" that the state deems in its interests.[288] Innovations in medical science have significantly reduced the burden of a vast array of diseases, although the modern lifestyle has itself precipitated a plethora of new illnesses. At least a third of global deaths are caused by just four industries: tobacco, ultra-processed food, fossil fuel, and alcohol.[289]

Even if it were the case that statistical measures of violence and disease were uniformly reduced in the modern era, it would not logically follow that human beings have actually made moral progress in the sense that they are more inclined to think ethically and behave selflessly. Instead, they are merely compliant with modern social structures that regulate human behavior. In the face of true injustice, their lack of moral courage becomes readily apparent. Indeed, some of the most vocal proponents of the West's supposed moral progress

---

287 Aníbal Quijano and Michael Ennis, "Coloniality of Power, Eurocentrism, and Latin America," *Nepantla: Views from South* 1, no. 3 (2000): 533–80. Patrick Deneen points out another irony: "Those whose view of time is guided by such belief implicitly understand that their 'achievements' are destined for the dustbin of history, given that the future will regard us as backward and necessarily superseded." Patrick Deneen, *Why Liberalism Failed* (New Haven: Yale University Press, 2018), 74.

288 For a relevant discussion, see Talal Asad, *Formations of the Secular*, 100–124.

289 Anna Gilmore et al., "Defining and Conceptualising the Commercial Determinants of Health," *Lancet* 401, no. 10383 (2023): 1194–213.

brazenly decry people of the past as "morally retarded,"[290] although the same individuals appear to lack the rudimentary moral sensibility to condemn the mass murder of children in Gaza.[291] These vacuous ideologues epitomise the moral depravity of secular modernity as they continue to champion the project of Western imperialism which has visited some of the worst forms of carnage and tyranny upon the world.

While moral depravity certainly existed in the past in great abundance as well, the best exemplars of moral virtue for us to follow likewise lived in the past. In Islamic theology, the most moral human beings are the prophets chosen by God, the greatest of whom is the final messenger, the Prophet Muhammad ﷺ. Prophet Muhammad's companions are the next in line in piety, followed by the early generations of the Muslim community. They responded to God with the utmost sincerity, abandoning every worldly comfort and every personal convenience for the attainment of moral virtue. The Prophet Muhammad said, "The best people are those of my generation, then those who will come after them (the next generation), then those who will come after them."[292]

---

290 Steven Pinker, *The Better Angels of Our Nature: Why Violence Has Declined* (New York: Penguin Publishing Group, 2011), 795. See also Nick Spencer, "Are the Better Angels Really Winning?," Theos, January 17, 2024, https://www.theosthinktank.co.uk/comment/2024/01/17/are-the-better-angels-really-winning. Pinker's methodological failures in claiming that violence has declined in the modern era were noted by Pasquale Cirillo and Nassim Nicholas Taleb, "On the Statistical Properties and Tail Risk of Violent Conflicts," *Physica D: Nonlinear Phenomena* 452 (June 15, 2016): 29–45. Pinker also falls into the same tired Islamophobic tropes which have been used to legitimate violence against Muslims. See Steven Pinker, *Enlightenment Now: The Case for Reason, Science, Humanism, and Progress* (New York: Penguin Books, 2018), 439–40.

291 Steven Pinker referred to accusations of genocide against Israel as "blood libel". On the abundant evidence of genocide, see the report by UN Special Rapporteur Francesca Albanese, "Anatomy of a Genocide," February 26–April 5, 2024, https://www.un.org/unispal/document/anatomy-of-a-genocide-report-of-the-special-rapporteur-on-the-situation-of-human-rights-in-the-palestinian-territory-occupied-since-1967-to-human-rights-council-advance-unedited-version-a-hrc-55/.

292 *Ṣaḥīḥ al-Bukhārī*, no. 6429.

Can the world of secular modernity fathom the magnanimous forgiveness of the Prophet Muhammad towards those who tortured and persecuted him and his followers, including those who pelted him with stones in Ṭā'if?[293] Is there any modern leader who demonstrates the humility of such noble figures as Abū Bakr and ʿUmar? The forbearance of ʿUthmān? The courage of ʿAlī ibn Abī Ṭālib? The care and devotion of Khadījah or ʿĀ'ishah? The piety of Fāṭimah? The problem with progressivism is that it requires that we abandon the moral paradigm of such figures in exchange for that offered by secular ethics. We must rightfully object, "Would you take a lesser thing in exchange for what is better?" (Qur'an 2:61).

Modernist Muslims seduced by the allure of liberalism fall prey to the same fallacy in dismissing the scholars of the Islamic tradition and their collective works out of undue confidence in the West's putative moral superiority and progress. In truth, they uncritically adopt the assumptions of secularism and liberalism and fail to understand the intricate considerations behind rulings in the Islamic tradition (see author's previous article *Difference of Opinion: Where do we draw the line?*).[294] Shaykh Amjad Mohammed also observes that modernists advocating a move from the Islamic tradition to liberalism "tend not to be traditionally trained scholars and are therefore not versed in the dynamic nature of the traditional approach."[295] Due to lack of schooling in the Islamic sciences, modernists present a caricature of the tradition as stagnant and unresponsive to change, rendering it incapable of

---

293 See Mohammad Elshinawy and Omar Suleiman, "How Muhammad ﷺ Confronted Hate and Became the Most Influential Person in History," Yaqeen Institute for Islamic Research, January 2017, for a list of seventy such examples from his life: https://yaqeeninstitute.ca/read/paper/how-muhammad-confronted-hate-and-became-the-most-influential-person-in-history.

294 Nazir Khan, "Difference of Opinion: Where do we draw the line?," Yaqeen Institute for Islamic Research, December 10, 2019, https://yaqeeninstitute.org/read/paper/difference-of-opinion-where-do-we-draw-the-line.

295 Amjad Mohammed, *Muslims in Non-Muslim Lands: A Legal Study with Applications* (Cambridge: Islamic Texts Society, 2013), 33. See also 45–46.

The problem with progressivism is that it requires that we abandon the moral paradigm of the prophets and companions in exchange for that offered by secular ethics.

Sharīʿah
The unchanging Divine law; the guidance found in the sacred texts of the Qur'an and Hadith.

Fiqh
The human interpretation of the Divine law and its codification into rules for application in daily life.

Fatwā
A formal legal opinion provided by a qualified scholar to specific scenario or issue.

dealing with the diverse needs of modern society. The reality of the matter is that Islamic scholarship includes a vast discussion on the parameters and principles that govern how rulings are tailored to unique and changing circumstances. The scholars of Islam typically described the factors that could lead to a *fatwā* (legal edict) changing based on the changing of circumstances under the topic *taghayyur al-fatwā bi taghayyur al-zamān wa al-makān* (a *fatwā* changing due to the changing circumstances of time and place). The moral bedrock of Islam is constituted by the vast corpus of unchanging rulings and principles that form the foundation and upon this edifice, Muslim scholars elaborate an upper layer of elements subject to interpretation in application. Thus, Islamic law contains a dual-layer morality—an immutable scripturally enshrined set of precepts (*sharīʿah*), and the human derivation and application of those principles sensitive to changes of time and place (*fiqh*).[296]

296 Muṣṭafā al-Zarqā', *al-Madkhal al-fiqhī al-ʿām* (Damascus: Dar al-Qalam, 2004), 1:153.

Traditional scholars certainly can re-evaluate juridical opinions where warranted in light of scriptural evidence and the contemporary context. However, their scholarly activities operate with the value structure, hermeneutics, and theological principles indigenous to Islam rather than adopting Western cultural norms and liberal ethics as a universal yardstick for morality as progressives are wont to do. The reformist agenda of "progressive Islam" invariably seeks to transpose onto Islam the incoherent values of Western liberalism and secular humanism after eviscerating Islam of its own indigenous value system. If one is trying to manipulate the interpretation of sacred texts to conform to one's wishes, then one has not entered into true submission to Allah's guidance as it was taught by the Prophet, understood by his Companions, and explained by the righteous of this *ummah* for fourteen centuries.

Another important element to note in this verse of *al-Fātiḥah* is that the reason for following the moral exemplars of the past is that God blessed them with the gifts of divine guidance and piety. There are several important lessons here that solve much of the confusion arising from the contemporary 'gender wars' online. First of all, our understanding of masculinity and femininity should follow the examples of our Islamic role models. When we examine Prophetic masculinity, we find many important attributes that are absent from today's self-appointed digital purveyors of masculinity who thrive as hustle bros and pickup artists, teaching men money-making schemes and how to seduce women. In contrast, Prophetic masculinity emphasises one's responsibility to the *ummah*, one's duty towards one's family, and traits like mercy, humility, modesty, nobility and so forth.[297]

297 See also Yahya Ibrahim, "'Be a Man!' Constructing Prophetic Masculinity," Yaqeen Institute for Islamic Research, July 24, 2019, https://yaqeeninstitute.org/read/paper/be-a-man-constructing-prophetic-masculinity.

Secondly, when we examine this verse in *al-Fātiḥah,* we find another important lesson regarding those whom Allah favoured. It is virtue alone, rather than identity politics, that determines their worthiness to serve as our moral guides. The idea that someone's gender, for instance, may disqualify them from contributing on a particular subject is one of the corollaries of such identity politics. The very phrase *anʿamta alayhim* (those whom You have favoured) provides a sufficient answer to any radical feminist who might object that the messengers, being men, cannot serve as guides for women.[298] That God chose them as His messengers to humanity precludes any other consideration. Messengers aside, when it comes to the ranks of the righteous, there are undoubtedly many women whom God has favoured as moral exemplars for all humanity. This debunks sentiments exhibiting the opposite extreme found within the manosphere (online forums discussing male interests), including the idea of men disavowing women altogether, a movement sometimes called MGTOW ("men going their own way").

Indeed, a major ritual during pilgrimage commemorates the faith in Allah exemplified by Hājar, whose footsteps between Ṣafā and Marwah every pilgrim continues to retrace until today:

> What is truly remarkable about this ritual is the person we emulate. Through it we commemorate the faith in God held by Hājar—a woman, originally a slave girl from Egypt, possessing no status, fame, or wealth. And yet, her devotion to God was so beloved to Him that He established it as an eternal ritual to be followed by people all over the world.

298 Every messenger was a prophet but not every prophet was a messenger. Note that a minority view in the Islamic tradition affirms the existence of women who were prophets (but not messengers) based on the definition that receiving divine communication (*waḥy*) qualifies one as a prophet. See Ibn Ḥazm, *al-Fiṣal,* 5:13. This view was also adopted by al-Qurṭubī, *al-Jāmiʿ li-aḥkām al-Qurʾān,* 4:83 (Qur'an 3:46), and attributed to Abū al-Ḥasan al-Ashʿarī (d. 324 AH) by Ibn Fūrak (d. 406 AH). See Halim Calis, "Mary's Prophethood Reassessed: Overlooked Medieval Islamic Perspectives in Contemporary Scholarship," *Religions* 15, no. 4 (2024): 461.

> A righteous woman, in whose footsteps millions of men and women are commanded to walk.[299]

There is a longstanding tradition of female participation in Islamic scholarship, copiously documented in the recent 43-volume work *al-Wafāʾ bi-asmāʾ al-nisāʾ* by Shaykh Mohammad Akram Nadwi with over 10,000 examples.[300] ʿĀʾishah had 300 students, narrated 2210 hadith, served as the go-to expert for male Companions of the Prophet,[301] and was declared the leading expert in Islamic jurisprudence,[302] as well as the best-versed in Arabic poetry and literature.[303] A single scholar like Ibn al-Najjār (d. 643 AH) studied under 400 women, while Ibn ʿAsākir (d. 571 AH) is noted to have learned from eighty female scholars.[304]

What we don't find, however, are scholars looking to fill "gender quotas" in their *ijāzāt* (certifications) or considering whether a teacher's gender might preclude him from teaching a particular chapter of *fiqh*. Such performative concerns are championed by the shallow ideological feminism of the West that has been conspicuously silent as women are massacred alongside their children in Gaza, unable to nurse their infants due to

299 Ibrahim Hindy and Nazir Khan, "Living Abraham's Legacy of Hajj: Relevance of Rites and Rituals in the Modern Age," Yaqeen Institute for Islamic Research, August 13, 2018, https://yaqeeninstitute.org/read/paper/living-abrahams-legacy-relevance-of-rites-and-rituals-in-the-modern-age.

300 Akram Nadwi, *al-Wafāʾ bi-asmāʾ al-nisāʾ* (Jedda: Dar al-Minhāj, 2021).

301 Abū Mūsā al-Ashʿarī stated "There was never a time we found a religious matter confusing except that we would go and ask ʿĀʾishah, and always find that she was knowledgeable concerning it." See *Jāmiʿ al-Tirmidhī*, no. 3883. The famous scholar of the second-generation, Masrūq (d. 62 AH), was asked whether ʿĀʾishah excelled in inheritance law, whereupon he replied, "I swear by the One true God, verily I used to see the most senior of companions consulting her on matters of inheritance law." See *Muṣannaf ibn Abī Shaybah* (Riyadh: Dār Kunūz, 2015), 17:244, no. 33095.

302 ʿAṭāʾ ibn Abī Rabāḥ (d.114 AH) stated that ʿĀʾishah was the leading expert in jurisprudence and the most knowledgeable of people; see *Mustadrak al-Ḥākim*, no. 6748.

303 ʿUrwah ibn al-Zubayr narrated that ʿĀʾishah was also the most well-versed in Arabic literature and poetry. See al-Bayhaqī in *al-Zuhd*, 216.

304 Mohammad Akram Nadwi, *al-Muhaddithat: The Women Scholars in Islam* (Oxford: Interface Publications, 2007), 138, 257–58.

starvation, living in tents unable to address basic health or hygiene needs, undergoing Cesarean sections without anesthetic, and subjected to sexual abuse and torture by Israeli soldiers.[305] Meanwhile, they applaud "breaking the glass ceiling" of female representation in the Israeli army that bombs and massacres Palestinians.[306] "Not only is Gaza not a universal feminist touchstone, but it also barely seems to register at all for some of the world's most famous feminists," Fatima Bhutto writes. She observes, for instance, the hypocritical stance on the genocide in Gaza of popular "feminist" icons from Hillary Clinton to Brené Brown, in addition to fifty French actresses who cut their hair in solidarity with protests against hijab in Iran. Bhutto writes:

> But 9,671 dead women in Gaza and 15,370 slaughtered children have warranted no public acts of sisterhood from any of the public figures who made videos, wore T-shirts, posted, and bellowed the Iranian cry of Women, Life, Freedom during the Iranian protests against the veil… The hypocrisy of Western feminists is not a new discovery. Their shallow version of women's liberty only surfaces when the issue of women's rights aligns with Western political interests, wars, and agendas.[307]

---

305 Yasmine Akrimi, "What the War on Gaza Tells Us About Western Feminism," Business International Centre, April 9, 2024, https://www.bic-rhr.com/research/what-war-gaza-tells-us-about-western-feminism; Maryam Aldossari, "For Feminists, Silence on Gaza Is No Longer an Option," Al Jazeera, January 4, 2024, https://www.aljazeera.com/opinions/2024/1/4/for-feminists-silence-on-gaza-is-no-longer-an-option; Nimao Ali, "The Silent Betrayal of Palestinian Women by Global Feminism," *Toronto Star,* December 10, 2023, https://www.thestar.com/opinion/contributors/the-silent-betrayal-of-palestinian-women-by-global-feminism/article_79aec4e0-95de-11ee-8e8c-a775e9ab793c.html; Jacqueline Potvin and Mayme Lefurgey, "Canada's Inaction in Gaza Marks a Failure of Its Feminist Foreign Policy," The Conversation, March 12, 2024, https://theconversation.com/canadas-inaction-in-gaza-marks-a-failure-of-its-feminist-foreign-policy-225067.

306 Tal Shalev, "IDF Co-ed Battalion Makes History by Sending Women Troops to Gaza," *Jerusalem Post,* December 15, 2023, https://www.jpost.com/israel-hamas-war/article-778101#google_vignette.

307 Fatima Bhutto, "Gaza Has Exposed the Shameful Hypocrisy of Western Feminism," Zeteo News, April 18, 2024, https://open.substack.com/pub/zeteo/p/gaza-has-exposed-the-shameful-hypocrisy.

The guidance of Islam leads one back to the illustrious examples of those—be they male or female—whose moral convictions were substantive, whose piety was comprehensive, whose virtue was enduring, and whose love of God was paramount.

This is why it is important to carefully evaluate the ideas behind slogans rather than simplistically adopting labels. Do the ideas arise from the paradigms and thought structures of Western colonialism or are they truly indigenous to our value structure as Muslims? For instance, the term feminism has been defined in different ways by different groups.[308] It is important to clarify what a person means by the term to avoid unnecessary confusion. If the term is taken to mean advocating for the rights of women against injustice and mistreatment, then such an endeavor is an essential Islamic aim provided that it occurs according to the guidance of the Qur'an and Sunnah. If on the other hand, one takes feminism to entail the elimination of gender norms and differences, dismissing the guidance of the prophets because they were men, or regarding the Islamic scholarly tradition as a patriarchal institution, then such notions are indicative of European cultural imperialism and a colonised mindset.[309]

The guidance of Islam leads one back to the illustrious examples of those—be they male or female—whose moral convictions were substantive, whose piety was comprehensive, whose virtue was enduring, and whose love of God was paramount. Allah says in the Qur'an, "So their Lord responded to them: "I will never deny any of you—male or female—the reward of your deeds. Both are equal in reward" (Qur'an 3:195). *Sūrah al-Fātiḥah* highlights for us the importance of following the most worthy role models based on their ethical standing with God. Embedded within this prayer to follow in their path is an indication of our love for them and our desire to be in their company. It is such love that motivates true ethical transformation.

308 "American women not identifying as feminists is perhaps more indicative of a lack of common agreement or understanding about what the word means," according to Catherine Morris. "Less than a Third of American Women Identify as Feminists," Ipsos, November 25, 2019, https://www.ipsos.com/en-us/american-women-and-feminism.

309 See Nazir Khan, Safiah Chowdhury, and Tesneem Alkiek, "Women in Islamic Law: Examining Five Prevalent Myths," Yaqeen Institute for Islamic Research, July 2019, https://yaqeeninstitute.org/read/paper/women-in-islamic-law-examining-five-prevalent-myths.

Ghayri al-maghḍūbi ʿalayhim

Not (the path) of those who have incurred anger

Liberalism dismantled

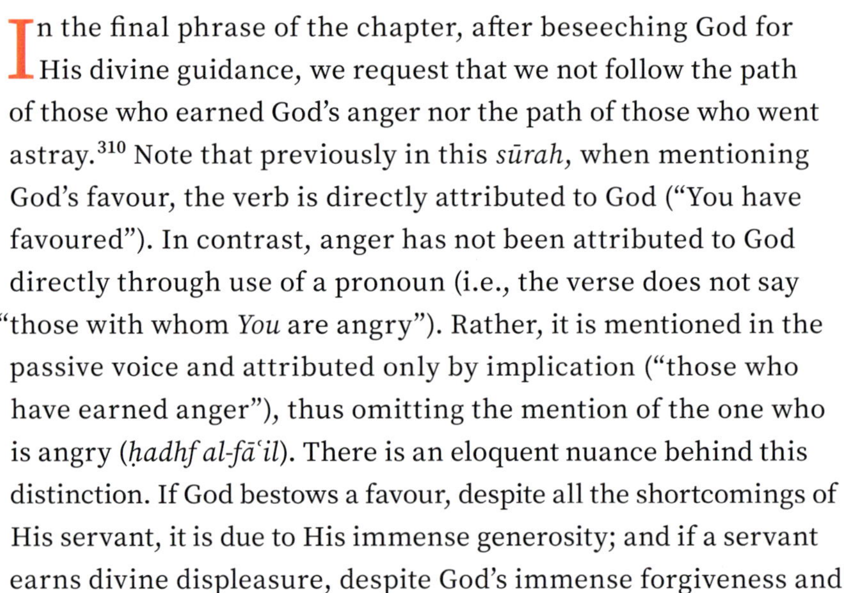

In the final phrase of the chapter, after beseeching God for His divine guidance, we request that we not follow the path of those who earned God's anger nor the path of those who went astray.[310] Note that previously in this *sūrah*, when mentioning God's favour, the verb is directly attributed to God ("You have favoured"). In contrast, anger has not been attributed to God directly through use of a pronoun (i.e., the verse does not say "those with whom *You* are angry"). Rather, it is mentioned in the passive voice and attributed only by implication ("those who have earned anger"), thus omitting the mention of the one who is angry (*ḥadhf al-fāʿil*). There is an eloquent nuance behind this distinction. If God bestows a favour, despite all the shortcomings of His servant, it is due to His immense generosity; and if a servant earns divine displeasure, despite God's immense forgiveness and

310 Aḥmad ibn al-Khalīl al-Khuwayyī mentions that while on the path we want to avoid two dangers: bandits and getting lost. The former are those who obstruct our path toward God and toward good, while the latter regards becoming obstacles to the path ourselves. See al-Khuwayyī, *Yanābīʿ al-ʿulūm*, 318.

patience, it is due to the servant's gross misdeeds.[311] Thus, God is mentioned in the former case, but not the latter. Moreover, the phrasing epitomises the Islamic ethics of attributing the source of everything positive to God, recognising that gratitude is due to Him and that He is the source of all bounties and blessings. Meanwhile, that which is negative is attributed to mankind, recognising that it occurs as a consequence of human choices. Furthermore, the fact that the one who is angry is not explicitly mentioned allows us to understand that God is not the only one who is angry with those who transgress.

Liberalism
A political and moral philosophy arising from the European enlightenment which emphasises individual freedom as the ultimate societal value.

311 See al-Khuwayyī, *Yanābīʿ al-ʿulūm*, 331–32. The Yemeni scholar ʿAbd al-Raḥmān al-Muʿallimī (d. 1966) also observes that the stylistic choice here is consistent with the *sūrah*'s emphasis on God's mercy, noting also that God has derived names for Himself based on the attribute of mercy but has not derived a name for Himself based upon the attribute of anger. See al-Muʿallimī, *Āthār ʿAbd al-Raḥmān ibn Yaḥyā al-Muʿallimī al-Yamānī* (Mecca: Dār ʿĀlam al-Fawāʾid, 1434 AH), 7:126.

Moral transgressions earn not only divine wrath but the wrath of creation as well. Finally, since transgression is a cause of distancing oneself from the Divine, the syntax of the verse mirrors this distancing through the absence of a direct pronoun connecting one to God, in contrast to the case of those receiving His divine favor.[312]

Avoiding God's displeasure and eschewing misguidance should be of tremendous concern to a sincere believer. In fact, this is something we can learn from the supplications the Prophet ﷺ used to make. We find examples in his supplications where he would specifically seek refuge in Allah from incurring His anger and from going astray.

> When the Prophet's uncle Abū Ṭālib died, he went to preach to the people of al-Ṭā'if. When he was rejected by them, he performed two units (*rakʿahs*) of prayer and then said, "O Allah, to You do I complain of my weakness, my lack of resources, and my insignificance before people. You are the most Merciful of those who show mercy! Unto whom will You entrust me? To an enemy who regards me with contempt? Or to a distant person whom you grant control over me? As long as You are not *angry* with me, I do not care, but Your protection is more desirable for me. I seek refuge in the light of Your face—by which darkness is dispelled and the affairs of this world and the next are rectified—from ever incurring Your *anger* or receiving Your displeasure. I desire your pleasure and satisfaction until You are pleased. There is no power and no might except with You."[313]

312 Ibn al-Qayyim, *Badāʾiʿ al-fawāʾid*, 2:420–23 and al-Suhaylī, *Natāʾij al-fikr fī al-naḥw* (Beirut: DKI, 1996), 237.

313 See al-Ṭabarānī, *al-Duʿāʾ* (Beirut: DKI, 1413), 315; Ibn Hishām, *al-Sīrah al-nabawiyyah* (Cairo: Maṭbaʿat Muṣṭafā al-Bābi al-Ḥalabī, 1955), 1:420.

> The Messenger of Allah ﷺ never went out of my house without raising his eye to the sky and saying, "O Allah! I seek refuge in You *lest I stray or be led astray,* slip or be made to slip, cause injustice or suffer injustice, do wrong or have wrong done unto me."[314]

Regarding the two paths of misguidance referred to in this verse of *al-Fātiḥah,* it is reported by ʿAdī ibn Ḥātim, a Christian convert to Islam, that the Prophet Muhammad identified the Jews and Christians, respectively, as the paradigmatic examples of these errors.[315] Known in Islam as the 'people of the Book' (*ahl al-kitāb*), these two religious communities acknowledge many of the same prophets described in Islam. In mentioning them, the Prophet illustrated how religious communities can be sent guidance, scriptures, and messengers from Allah and still become misguided. It is for this reason that the example of their error is particularly salient for Muslims and one from which Muslims are commanded to take heed. The Indian Muslim scholar Amīn Aḥsan Iṣlāḥī (d. 1997) observed that the two subsequent chapters, *Sūrah al-Baqarah* and *Sūrah Āl ʿImrān,* elaborate the lessons to be learned from the mistakes of these two communities respectively.[316] It should be noted, as scholars of Islam have pointed out, that the attributes of incurring divine anger or going astray are not exclusive to

314 *Sunan Abī Dāwūd,* no. 5094.

315 *Jāmiʿ al-Tirmidhī,* no. 2954. Similar reports have been transmitted by many of the early Muslim commentators. See al-Ṭayyār, *Mawsūʿat al-tafsīr al-maʾthūr,* 44–46. Al-Bayḍāwī notes that the Qur'anic descriptions in 5:60 and 5:77 also match the respective descriptions of the two communities. Al-Bayḍāwī, *Anwār al-tanzīl,* 1:31. An oft-cited parallel is with the Old Testament verse Judges 2:14: "So the anger of the Lord was kindled against Israel." Moreover, another narration that recounts the story of Zayd ibn ʿĀmir ibn Nufayl indicates this description was self-reported by the religious communities in Arabia before the Prophet's time. When Zayd asked to embrace Judaism, he was told, "You will not embrace our religion until you receive your share of Allah's anger," and when he asked to embrace Christianity, he was told, "You will not embrace our religion until you receive your share of Allah's curse." Eventually, Zayd chose neither and declared himself a truth seeker (*ḥanīf*) upon the path of Prophet Abraham. See *Ṣaḥīḥ al-Bukhārī,* no. 3827.

316 Amīn Aḥsan Iṣlāḥī, *Tadabbur-e-Qur'an: Pondering Over The Qur'an—Volume One: Tafsir of Surah al-Fatiha and Surah al-Baqarah,* trans. Mohammad Saleem Kayani (Petaling Jaya: Islamic Book Trust, 2016), 87.

these groups, as the Qur'anic usage indicates elsewhere (see, e.g., 16:106, 4:167).[317] Moreover, Ibn ʿĀshūr explained that these are not the only groups to which this description applies but simply the most prominent examples; in mentioning these religious communities the Prophet provided examples that were familiar to the early Muslim community in its encounter with other tribes.[318] ʿAbd al-Salām al-Majīdī explains that there is wisdom in the verse mentioning the attributes of misguidance rather than the names of particular groups so that Muslims would not exempt themselves from this warning:

> Thus, the warning about those who have incurred wrath and those who are astray is given with their attributes, not their identities, as you may commit actions that bring about wrath, or deeds that cause misguidance... Allah did not want Muslims to consider themselves above reproach or to think that merely affiliating with Islam suffices them from performing actions. Therefore, He described the wrongdoers not by their identity but by their attributes, saying "not the path of those who have incurred wrath or have gone astray" to warn Muslims against incurring divine wrath by doing what necessitates it, or falling into misguidance by doing what leads to it.[319]

The scholars, moreover, have explained that the moral failures alluded to in this verse relate to undermining either of the two foundations of faith, knowledge, and action, and their intended objectives, truth and justice. We do not follow the way of those who claim to pursue the truth but disregard justice, nor do we

---

317 Al-Nasafī, *al-Taysīr fī al-tafsīr,* 1:166. He also notes that the Qur'anic usage indicates that wrath is likewise used for the leaders and stubborn rejectors of truth, while misguidance is used for the followers. See al-Nasafī, 1:169. See also ʿAbd al-Qāhir al-Jurjānī (d. 471 AH), *Daraj al-durar fī tafsīr al-Āy wa al-Suwar* (Amman: Dār al-Fikr, 2009), 103.

318 Ibn ʿĀshūr, *al-Taḥrīr wa al-tanwīr,* 1:200.

319 Al-Majīdī, *al-Islām,* 272.

follow the way of those who claim to pursue justice but disregard truth. Ibn al-Qayyim writes:

> The one who incurs wrath is in error for lacking the guidance to practice his knowledge, and the one who is in error also incurs wrath for failing to acquire the knowledge that would lead to righteous action. Thus, both are in error and incur wrath. But the one who fails to act in accordance with the truth after having known it is more deserving of being associated with wrath.[320]

In other words, although both groups are misguided and incur wrath, the verse describes the predominant characteristic of each group. The group that is predominantly associated with earning divine anger is the group that fails to practice righteous action, while the group that is predominantly associated with going astray is the one that fails to acquire sound knowledge.[321]

Prophet Muhammad ﷺ prayed, "O Allah! I seek refuge in You *lest I stray or be led astray,* slip or be made to slip, cause injustice or suffer injustice, do wrong or have wrong done unto me."

---

320 Ibn al-Qayyim, *Ranks of the Divine Seekers*, 1:90. See also Ibn Taymiyyah, *al-Nubuwwāt* (Riyadh: Aḍwāʾ al-Salaf, 2000), 1:337.

321 Another perspective views the two categories as referring to those who were deficient in their religious obligations versus those who indulged in excesses, respectively. The former transgression includes killing the prophets (Qur'an 2:91), while the latter transgression entails deification of a prophet (Qur'an 4:171). See Muḥammad Shafīʿ, *Maʿārif al-Qurʾān*, 1:78–79. This interpretation also potentially applies to the failures of liberalism and postmodernism as the former privileges individual freedom over moral duties while the latter overzealously attempts to resist all hierarchy and authority, often adopting misguided approaches.

Ibn al-Qayyim further writes:

> As for the healing of hearts, [The Opening] includes it in the most perfect fashion, for all weaknesses and illnesses of hearts revolve around two axes, the corruption of knowledge and the corruption of intention. These two lead to two lethal ailments: error and wrath. Error is the result of the corruption of knowledge and wrath the result of the corruption of intention. These two are the source of all ailments of the heart. Guidance to the straight path, thus, includes healing from the ailment of error, which is why the plea for this guidance is the greatest of obligations upon every servant every day and night in every regular prayer, due to the utter need of the servant for the guidance that is required [to avert these ailments]. No other supplication may supplant it.[322]

While traditional religions like Judaism and Christianity have declined in the West, the accompanying psychoepistemic ailments have not, as these have simply been transposed to the new ideologies of the age. In particular, liberalism epitomises the corruption of intention, a fetishisation of knowledge at the expense of action. Liberalism, born out of the European Enlightenment, is an ideology that prides itself on its commitment to the values of freedom, reason, and science in the pursuit of truth. It loudly proclaims its commitment to knowledge but ultimately disregards the importance of moral duties and ethical action. Meanwhile, postmodernism, born out of the failures of Enlightenment reason, takes aim at the power structures that perpetuate injustices in the world. However, it entirely denies the existence of objective truth and disregards pursuit of it.

322 Ibn al-Qayyim, *Ranks of the Divine Seekers,* 1:168.

Liberalism has been at the helm longer in Western culture and has aggressively been marketed as part of the project of Western imperialism. Paul Kahn writes:

> Our contemporary missionaries preach democracy, free markets, and the rule of law—all institutions founded on our belief in the equality and liberty of every person. This dogged commitment to a universal community is a part of our Christian and Enlightenment traditions.[323]

Accepting the message of these "missionaries" of liberalism is not, in fact, optional, as Joseph Massad notes:

> Thus if Muslims refuse to convert willingly to liberalism or at least to forms of Islam that liberalism finds tolerable, then they must be forced to convert using military power, as their resistance threatens a core value of liberalism, namely its universality and the necessity of its universalization as globalization.[324]

Liberalism is predicated on the West's supremacist fantasy and has therefore been closely connected to colonialism and racial subjugation. Murzban Jal writes:

> What needs to be said is that the inherent relation between colonialism and liberalism has to be seen in order to expose its imperialist characteristics. It must be noted that both John Locke and Mill were not merely advocates of liberalism, but also of colonialism... One should say that colonialism's accumulation of capital by looting Asia, Africa and the

323 Paul Kahn, *Putting Liberalism in Its Place* (Princeton: Princeton University Press, 2005), 6–7.

324 Joseph Massad, *Islam in Liberalism* (Chicago: University of Chicago Press, 2015), 3.

> Americas projected this white Anglo-Saxon male as the ideal figure to be revered all over the world. This white Anglo-Saxon Christian male would civilize the entire world.[325]

Liberalism requires the construction of an imagined barbaric and savage 'other' in order to justify its civilising mission and continued violence against other populations. Indeed, as Joseph Kaminski notes, according to the architects of liberalism, "liberty is only for the Enlightened; until Enlightenment is reached, imperial domination is the savage's only hope."[326] These thought trajectories continue to define the behavior of liberal democracies today and their violent exploitation and domination of populations around the world. Joseph Massad comments:

> I am always perplexed when people question Israel's commitment to Western liberal values because they think Western liberal values are actually the propagandistic values that Western imperialist governments put out there. I believe Israel is sincere when it says it indeed abides by Western liberal values—one of which is genocide, one of which is settler colonialism, one of which is utter racism and racial contempt for its racial inferiors—all of that is part of western values and Israel I believe is correct and sincere in claiming that it upholds them and protects them in its War.[327]

325 Murzban Jal, "Who Wants Liberalism?" *Critique: Journal of Socialist Theory* 47, no. 3 (2019): 473–494, at 484.

326 Kaminski, *Islam, Liberalism, and Ontology*, 59.

327 Joseph Massad, "Why genocide is a 'Western value'", The Electronic Intifada podcast, YouTube, Oct 11, 2024. https://www.youtube.com/watch?v=ODUz0a2UzEE. Aria Nakissa writes, "Over the past 2 decades, scholarship on colonialism has challenged the widespread assumption that liberal ideology inherently opposes imperialism, authoritarianism, ethnocentrism, and racism. Instead, it is asserted that liberal ideology allows for, or even encourages, these things." See Aria Nakissa, "Liberalism's distinctive policy for governing Muslim populations: Human rights, religious reform, and counter-terrorism from the colonial era until the present", *History Compass,* 20 no. 9 (2022): e12748.

Even at a domestic level, the moral and philosophical failures of liberalism have become increasingly evident, and intellectuals argue that they can no longer be ignored. Patrick Deneen writes in *Why Liberalism Failed*:

> Currently we attempt to treat the numerous social, economic, and political symptoms of liberalism's liberty, but not the deeper sources of those symptoms, the underlying pathology of liberalism's philosophic commitments.[328]

Liberalism identifies individual freedom, or liberty, as the pinnacle of its value hierarchy. This is a negative conception of freedom, that is, freedom from external constraints or interference.[329] According to liberalism, with exceptions dictated by the state's interests, people should be free to think, act, and say whatever they want. But what *should* they want? The end goal of society amounts to following one's desires (*ittibāʿ al-hawā*), and those desires are relentlessly programmed by the marketing industries of the corporate engines of society. The mindless consumerism fuels violent extraction of resources around the world and labor exploitation. This is best seen in the example of the brutal exploitation of children mining for cobalt in Congo in order to produce rechargeable batteries to sustain consumer demands for the latest smartphones, computers and electric vehicles.[330]

---

328 Patrick Deneen, *Why Liberalism Failed*, 42.

329 Deneen writes, "Liberalism rejects the ancient conception of liberty as the learned capacity of human beings to conquer the slavish pursuit of base and hedonistic desires." Deneen, *Why Liberalism Failed*, 37.

330 Siddharth Kara, "Is Your Phone Tainted by the Misery of the 35,000 Children in Congo's Mines?" The Guardian, October 12, 2018, https://www.theguardian.com/global-development/2018/oct/12/phone-misery-children-congo-cobalt-mines-drc.

Islam

True freedom arises from knowing one's purpose in life, worshiping God alone and being free to develop spiritually, morally and intellectually.

Liberalism

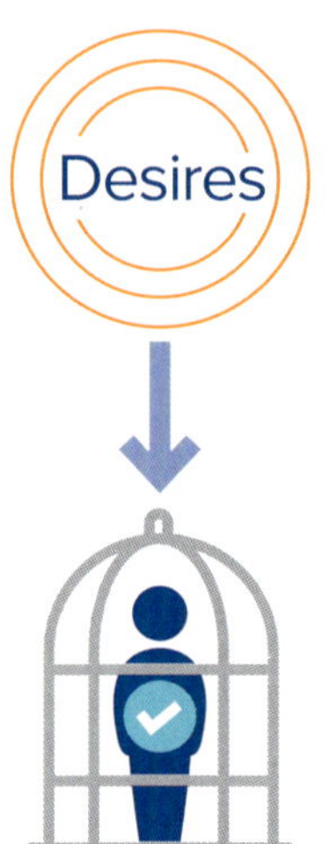

Individual freedom is the ultimate goal in society. Freedom to follow one's desires becomes enslavement to the marketing and entertainment industries, which programme one's desires. Individualism strips one of family and community, leaving one alone.

Moreover, the "liberated" individual is, ironically, increasingly controlled by the state and corporate interests.[331] Freedom to follow one's desires becomes the paramount virtue in modern culture, and those who service desires are accorded the greatest importance. Entertainers are worshiped as celebrities, while educators are devalued. Influencers replace experts, offering quick fixes to all of life's ills and shallow, feel-good motivational slogans. All of this content is, of course, punctuated with messages from sponsors and advertisements clamouring for the worship of one's wallet. This is what ends up determining how people think and act. In the end, their freedom is their slavery.

331 The decline of traditional relations was accompanied by an expansion of the role of the state. See Deneen, *Why Liberalism Failed*, 38, 46.

The Prophet ﷺ said, "Wretched is the slave of the dinar, wretched is the slave of the dirham, wretched is the slave of velvet and silk embroidery."[332] The worship of wealth and the free market is the defining feature of capitalism, a core pillar of liberalism.

When society has no overarching organising principle besides freedom to follow one's desires, its moral and structural deterioration becomes an inevitability. The great ethicist of Islamic law Imam Abū Isḥāq al-Shāṭibī (d. 790 AH) writes:

> Neither material nor spiritual benefits are achieved by submitting without hesitation to one's caprices and desires or by freely pursuing earthly aims. This is clear given what such a pursuit leads to by way of disorder, strife, and destruction, all of which are contrary to these very interests.[333]

With its obsessive individualism, liberalism speaks only of individual rights and freedoms but rarely of duties, responsibilities, or communal obligations as we see in Islam.[334] In liberal ethics, the very rationale of marriage and family itself is lost.

Liberalism epitomises the corruption of intention, a fetishisation of knowledge at the expense of action.

332 *Jāmiʿ al-Tirmidhī*, no. 2375; *Sunan Ibn Mājah*, no. 4136.

333 Al-Shāṭibī, *al-Muwāfaqāt*, ed. Mashhūr Ḥasan Āl Salmān (Cairo: Dār ʿAffān, 1997), 2:292, as translated in Gamal el-Din Attia, *Towards Realization of the Intents of Islamic Law*, trans. Nancy Roberts (London: IIIT, 2007), 8.

334 Refer to Yousef Wahb, "Fard Kifaya: The Principle of Communal responsibility in Islam," Yaqeen Institute for Islamic Research, June 10, 2021, https://yaqeeninstitute.org/read/paper/fard-kifayah-the-principle-of-communal-responsibility-in-islam.

Rather than the ethos of every man for himself, the Qur'an teaches that the poor and needy have an established right to one's wealth. Islam provides the human being with a true sense of belonging, situating one within a network of overlapping relationships in life.

Why sign up for lifelong marital commitments and why have kids?[335] Why restrict one's freedoms unnecessarily with such duties and obligations? For the liberal hedonist, who lives life simply to maximise pleasure, children represent nothing but a physical, financial, and emotional burden. Anti-natalists take liberalism to its logical conclusion, arguing that it is unethical even to have children since they do not consent to being born. From almost every angle, the notion of family falls apart in liberalism. Indeed, social isolation may be a structural feature of liberalism:

> Loneliness, we see, is not merely a sad state of mind. It is the cost of privileging individual rights and freedoms over community values and cohesion. When people are free to choose, they may choose so differently from one another that they recognize nothing of themselves in each other.[336]

Liberalism has stripped the human being of traditional sources of stability—faith, family, community, and tradition—leaving one helpless in the face of the tumultuous destabilising forces he encounters in life. It numbs the pain of emptiness with heavy doses of heedlessness afforded by the massive entertainment industry. Liberalism thus sowed the seeds for the widespread crisis of meaning that has erupted in modernity, accelerated by existential angst over the looming threat of large-scale disasters like another viral pandemic, nuclear warfare, or malevolent artificial general intelligence.

---

335 Deneen writes, "The norm of stable lifelong marriage is replaced by various arrangements that ensure the autonomy of the individuals, whether married or not. Children are increasingly viewed as a limitation upon individual freedom, which contributes to liberalism's commitment to abortion on demand, while overall birth rates decline across the developed world." Deneen, *Why Liberalism Failed*, 39.

336 Shannon Gormley, "Why Liberalism Itself Wants Us to Be Alone," *Ottawa Citizen*, January 19, 2018, https://ottawacitizen.com/opinion/columnists/gormley-why-liberalism-itself-wants-us-to-be-alone.

Liberalism fosters a society based on apathy toward the world and a lifelong pursuit of self-indulgence and the gratification of one's desires.

Islam instead provides the human being with a true sense of belonging, situating one within a network of overlapping relationships. As the Prophet ﷺ taught, "The best of you are the best to their family,"[337] "Whoever believes in Allah and the last day should treat his neighbour with excellence,"[338] "Whoever goes to sleep full while knowing his neighbour is hungry is not a true believer,"[339] "The believers in their mercy and compassion towards one another are like a single body,"[340] and "Donate in charity to people of all faiths (*adyān*)."[341] Rather than the ethos of every man for himself, the Qur'an teaches that the poor and needy have an established right to one's wealth: "And those within whose wealth is a known right, for the beggar and the destitute" (Qur'an 70:24–25). Indeed, "*zakāt* was one of the most important instruments of social justice"[342] in Islam and is built into the five pillars of faith. Liberalism fosters a society based on apathy toward the world and a lifelong pursuit of self-indulgence and gratification of one's desires.

---

337 *Jāmiʿ at-Tirmidhī,* no. 3895; *Sunan Ibn Mājah,* no. 1977.

338 *Ṣaḥīḥ Muslim,* no. 47c.

339 Al-Ṭabarānī, *al-Muʿjam al-kabīr,* no. 751.

340 *Ṣaḥīḥ Bukhārī,* no. 6011; *Ṣaḥīḥ Muslim,* no. 2586a.

341 *Muṣannaf Ibn Abī Shaybah,* no. 1194. See also, Abū ʿUbayd al-Qāsim ibn Sallām, *Kitāb al-amwāl* (Cairo: Dār al-Shurūq, 1989), 727–28.

342 Wael Hallaq, *Impossible State,* 123.

Manufactured consent is a concept that refers to the process by which public opinion is shaped and controlled by powerful institutions, often through the manipulation of information, media, and propaganda.

Moreover, even the individualism promoted within liberalism is an impoverished individualism that neglects the importance of individual moral and spiritual development, individual access to the truth, and the individual as an agent of establishing justice on earth. Under capitalism, the individual is ultimately reduced to nothing more than a consumer and individuals without financial means are treated like second-class citizens. The freedom offered is also shallow and closely connected to the capitalist system of values.[343] In many cases, the freedom offered turns out to be a mirage and the instruments appointed to enable freedom are used to undermine it. Freedom of speech has become freedom to spread misinformation, dehumanizing political narratives, and fake news. Meanwhile those who speak truths that do not align with the interests of the political elite are shadow banned, censored, stigmatised, deplatformed, or canceled. Freedom of thought is undermined by the state's **manufacturing of consent** and its manipulation of the media to ensure that its subjects do not think in ways that threaten its secular project. These measures were intended to bring human beings towards the truth, but they have led to profound moral failures instead. On the other hand, Islam offers a notion of true freedom that liberates the human soul from the shackles of subjugation to worldly powers and desires. This is evident from a cursory examination of the five pillars of Islam.

343 Hallaq writes, "The modern constitution of moral value rests on a posited metaphysic of individual freedom and rationality that in turn inheres in an enveloping political and capitalist system of value that shapes the qualities, and therefore specific types, of freedom and rationality—all this being a process formative of the self but one that was kept distinct from that (unacknowledged) metaphysic." Hallaq, *Restating Orientalism*, 235–36.

The *shahādah* (testimony of faith) entails intellectual freedom by affirming one's true purpose in life, recognising that there is none worthy of our worship and devotion except Allah. The *ṣalāh* exemplifies spiritual freedom, allowing us to take a moment from our busy lives to reflect on our relationship with God and ensuring that we are not consumed and controlled by a world of distractions. The *zakāt* affords freedom from attachment to wealth and materialistic possessions, *ṣīyām* (fasting) affords freedom from bodily desires, and *ḥajj* entails freedom from all that which divides us as human beings from our commitment to God and from each other.

Furthermore, the form of rationalism championed by liberalism's "Enlightenment reason" is one that suffers from many significant limitations. The concept of rationality in the modern West is effectively divorced from the concept of morality. This is entirely foreign to the Islamic concept of the *ʿaql* (intellect), which linguistically carries the connotation of moral self-restraint, related to *ʿiqāl* (the rope that binds the camel).[344] The goal of intelligent thought is to lead one to think ethically and pursue moral self-development. This is also how the intellect has been understood in the Islamic tradition. The learned scholar of hadith Imam Ibn Ḥibbān (d. 354 AH) compiled a work on the intellect collecting fifty traits of the intelligent entitled *Rawḍat al-ʿuqalāʾ* (Gardens of the intelligent), which revolves around spiritual and moral virtues. The hadith that begins the work is the Prophet's saying, "Indeed, Allah loves the noble traits of moral character (*makārim al-akhlāq*) and dislikes the traits of wickedness."[345] This is the essence of the *ʿaql*, Ibn Ḥibbān explains. Islam teaches that the intellect is concerned with moral action, not mere abstract argumentation.

344 Ibn Manẓūr, *Lisān al-ʿArab* (Beirut: Dār Ṣādir, 1414 AH), 11:458–59.

345 Ibn Ḥibbān, *Rawḍat al-ʿuqalāʾ* (Beirut: DKI, 2022), 16.

Islam offers a notion of true freedom that liberates the human soul from the shackles of subjugation to worldly powers and desires.

The dysfunctional conception of the intellect that emerged from the European Enlightenment is a key factor in the modern moral failures of Western civilisation. How else do we account for the fact that seemingly well-educated and cognitively intact individuals are incapable of recognising the basic moral truth that the mass slaughter of innocent men, women and children in Gaza is evil? The dysfunctional rationality of liberalism is further compounded by the hedonistic character of liberalism with its focus on desires and distractions. The opportunity for ethical reflection does not even arise when the mind is constantly bombarded by the forces of heedlessness in the entertainment industry and throughout popular culture.

This is the path we seek to avoid in supplicating to God that He enables us to avoid the misguidance of those who earn His displeasure by claiming to uphold knowledge but disregarding moral action.

Wa-lā al-ḍāllīn

Nor (the path) of those who have gone astray

Postmodernism dismantled

In the concluding verse of *al-Fātiḥah,* we learn that there is more than one path of error. The word used in this verse to indicate the second path of error is *al-ḍāllīn,* which refers to those who are lost and have gone astray. *Ḍalāl* (misguidance) refers to "pursuing a path other than the one intended, leading to destruction, confusion, and heedlessness."[346] Scholars observe that the word is mentioned in the active participle form (*al-ḍāllīn:* those who *have gone* astray) rather than the passive form (*al-muḍallīn:* those who *have been sent* astray) to clarify that misguidance is earned by the deliberate choices of those who devalue the truth.[347] The furthest one may stray from the path of truth is by engaging in *shirk*: "those who ascribe divinity to others beside God have indeed gone far astray" (Qur'an 4:116).

Postmodernism

A late 20th-century movement in philosophy and the arts that rejects belief in an objective truth or grand narratives.

346 Al-Kāfījī, *al-Ghurrah,* 209.

347 Ibn al-Qayyim, *Badāʾiʿ al-fawāʾid,* 2:442 and al-Suhaylī, *Natāʾij al-fikr fī al-naḥw,* 239.

Tawḥīd is the ultimate truth and the very bedrock of reality. The archetypal example of straying from the straight path is the abandonment of the pure monotheism taught by all prophets. Trinitarian theology and the attribution of divinity to Jesus are key manifestations of this departure exemplified by Christianity. However, Imam Abū Isḥāq al-Shāṭibī provides an important reminder regarding the generality of the warning in this verse:

> And included among those who are astray are the polytheists who associated other gods with Allah, as indicated in the Qur'an, and because the Qur'anic wording in the verse "nor those who have gone astray" (*wa-lā al-ḍāllīn*) encompasses them and others. Therefore, anyone who deviates from the straight path is included in this. It is also not far-fetched to say that "those who have gone astray" includes anyone who has deviated from the straight path, whether they belong to this *ummah* (community) or not, as mentioned in the previous verses before this.[348]

348 Al-Shāṭibī, *al-Iʿtiṣām* (Dammam: Dār ibn al-Jawzī, 2008), 1:242.

The straight path entails both knowledge and action. The goal of knowledge is truth and the goal of action is justice. The path of *ḍalāl* is of those who fetishise action without knowledge.[349] They make claims concerning justice but without regard for truth. The ideology that best epitomises this in contemporary society is postmodernism. According to postmodernism, there is no universal truth.[350] This movement emerged within Western culture as a "reaction against the suffocating embrace of modernity" and "a rebellion against the Enlightenment" and the excesses of liberalism.[351] Philosopher Stephen Hicks explains that postmodernists "deconstruct reason, truth, and reality because they believe that in the name of reason, truth, and reality Western civilization has wrought dominance, oppression, and destruction... Postmodernism then becomes an activist strategy against the coalition of reason and power."[352] Postmodernism adopts relativism (discussed earlier) when it comes to beliefs ("everyone has their own truth") but adopts objectivism when it comes to actions ("you must follow this path to justice").

Postmodernism is liberalism's chickens coming home to roost. In constructing an apparatus of radical skepticism to undermine the truths of religion, liberalism eventually succumbed to the same apparatus, leading to the anarchy of values in postmodernism. The radical distrust of authority initiated by liberalism is further extended and expanded under postmodernism, undermining the very notion of truth itself. Doubt is the "perpetual and perennial condition of postmodernism."[353] Muslim scholars centuries earlier

349 Ibn Taymiyyah, *Jāmiʿ al-masāʾil* (Beirut: Dar Ibn Ḥazm 2019), 4:50.

350 Ziauddin Sardar, *Postmodernism and the other: the new imperialism of Western culture* (London: Pluto Press, 1998), 4.

351 Sardar, *Postmodernism and the other*, 6.

352 Stephen Hicks, *Explaining Postmodernism: Skepticism and Socialism from Rousseau to Foucault* (Tempe, AZ: Scholarly Publishing, 2004), 3.

353 Sardar, *Postmodernism and the other*, 10.

analysed this phenomenon of radical skepticism, or *safsaṭah* or *sūfisṭāʾiyyah* as it was known in Arabic, because it traced back to the attitudes of the ancient Greek Sophists. The heresiologist ʿAbd al-Qāhir al-Baghdādī (d. 429 AH) explains that *sūfisṭāʾiyyah* entails denying knowledge or denying the reality of all things: some of them doubt the existence of independent realities (*shakkū fī wujūd al-ḥaqāʾiq*), while others believe that realities are contingent upon one's beliefs about them and that all beliefs are correct despite being mutually contradictory.[354] This is the very skepticism that underlies postmodernism today. Stephen Hicks writes:

> Metaphysically, postmodernism is anti-realist, holding that it is impossible to speak meaningfully about an independently existing reality. Postmodernism substitutes instead a social-linguistic, constructionist account of reality. Epistemologically, having rejected the notion of an independently existing reality, postmodernism denies that reason or any other method is a means of acquiring objective knowledge of that reality.[355]

British-Pakistani philosopher Ziauddin Sardar observes:

> When Truth and Reason are dead, what becomes of knowledge? Postmodernism considers all types, as well as all sources, of knowledge with equal skepticism. There is hardly any difference between science and magic, as Feyerabend took such pains to demonstrate. For postmodernists, knowledge is acquired not through inquiry but by imagination. As such, fiction rather than philosophy, and narrative rather than theory, provide a better perspective on human behavior.[356]

354 ʿAbd al-Qāhir al-Baghdādī, *al-Farq bayna al-firaq* (Cairo: Maktabat Ibn Sīnā, 1988), 280.

355 Hicks, *Explaining Postmodernism*, 6. He also writes: "The postmodernists, by contrast, are anti-realists, holding that it is meaningless to speak of truths out there or of a language that could capture them" (p. 66).

356 Sardar, *Postmodernism and the other*, 8–9.

Postmodernism is liberalism's chickens coming home to roost. The radical distrust of authority initiated by liberalism is further extended and expanded under postmodernism, undermining the very notion of truth itself.

All truth claims are meaningless according to postmodernism. There is no "correct" interpretation of a text nor any intended meaning residing therein: the author is metaphorically 'dead' and their intent holds no authority over the meaning of the text.[357] Likewise, there is no objective way to understand reality, the postmodernist claims.[358] There are only the ideas and narratives that legitimate the dominant power structures of society[359] and ethical resistance to those power structures.[360]

A major feature of postmodernism is resistance against so-called grand narratives about reality (i.e., worldviews). Postmodernism entails that all metanarratives are to be met with incredulity, as indicated by the words of the French philosopher Jean-François

357 Roland Barthes, *The Death of the Author,* trans. S. Heath (London: Fontana, 1977), 142–48.

358 It is interesting that postmodernism combines a skeptical attitude in interpreting texts with a skeptical attitude towards interpreting reality. These very same two phenomena were linked by Ibn Taymiyyah (*safsaṭah fī al-ʿaqlīyāt, qarmaṭah fī al-samʿīyāt*). See Khan, "Atheism and Radical skepticism."

359 Michel Foucault, *Discipline and Punish: The Birth of the Prison* (New York: Vintage Books, 1995), 27. He also states, "Power produces; it produces reality; it produces domains of objects and rituals of truth" (p. 194).

360 Michel Foucault, *Ethics: Subjectivity and Truth* (New York: The New Press, 1997), 167–68, 292. Foucault viewed sadomasochism and homosexuality as forms of resistance. He was himself addicted to extreme forms of sadomasochistic torture. See Roger Kimball, "The Perversions of Michel Foucault," *The New Criterion,* March 1993.

Lyotard.[361] The Qur'an, however, provides us with the ultimate metanarrative that explains our very purpose in life: Allah says, "I did not create jinn and humans except to worship Me" (Qur'an 51:56). The skeptical response to narratives is not new; it is, in fact, addressed in the Qur'an itself:

> When Our verses are recited to him, he says, "Legends of the peoples of old!" (*asāṭīr al-awalīn*). (Qur'an 68:15, 83:13)

> And whenever Our messages were conveyed to them, they would say, "We have heard [all this] before; if we wanted, we could certainly compose sayings like these [ourselves]: they are nothing but fables of ancient times!" (Qur'an 8:31)

In each of these examples, the Qur'an proceeds to remind the human being of his own personal accountability before God for the way he chooses to live. The trouble for the postmodernist is that, like any radical skeptic, sooner or later he must confront the incoherence and inconsistencies of his choices. Every human being must make sense of the big questions of life through a set of answers, that is, a "narrative." The questions can be summarised as follows:

> The big questions of life tend to aggregate into three clusters—intellectual, moral, and spiritual. No matter what culture or ideology one is raised in, one seeks to answer questions such as 'What makes my life worth living?' (*spiritual*), 'How do I live a good life?' (*moral*), and 'What is worth knowing?' (*intellectual*). Pursuing truth means to search for the answers that serve a purpose in making sense of these fundamental questions. Every human being intuitively prefers a system of belief and value that is able to yield meaningful answers to questions in these

361 Jean-François Lyotard, *The Postmodern Condition: A Report on Knowledge*, trans. Geoff Bennington and Brian Massumi (Minneapolis: University of Minnesota Press, 1984), xxiv: "Simplifying to the extreme, I define postmodern as incredulity toward metanarratives."

> three domains rather than answers that are incoherent and meaningless. Ultimately, the human being is confronted with a basic choice, between meaningfulness or meaninglessness.[362]

One must inevitably come to terms with the answers (a narrative) that animates one's choices in life, and those answers can either be coherent and well-substantiated or they may be incoherent and groundless. The majority of people follow the latter: "They follow nothing but conjecture and their own fanciful desires, even though true guidance has come to them from their Lord" (Qur'an 53:23). Unlike human narratives constructed to serve worldly interests or to pacify the mind with idle fantasies, the Qur'anic narrative speaks directly to the spiritual, intellectual, and moral needs of human beings, providing them with all-encompassing truth from the Divine. The Qur'an provides a simple challenge: "Say: Produce a revelation from God that would offer better guidance than either of these two [i.e., the *Tawrāt* and the Qur'an] and I shall follow it, if indeed you speak the truth!" (Qur'an 28:49). The greatest sign of truth is in the answers it provides and the guidance it offers. In the chaos of incoherent ideologies, vacillating norms, cultural shifts, and fluctuating values, the ethical worldview of the Qur'an provides one with clear truth and the only firm anchor: "Let there be no compulsion in religion, for the truth stands out clearly from falsehood. So whoever renounces false gods and believes in Allah has certainly grasped the firmest, most unfailing handhold. And Allah is All-Hearing, All-Knowing" (Qur'an 2:256).

Postmodernism offers nothing substantive beyond a skeptical critique of modernity and liberalism. Skepticism cannot get one very far without having a meaningful alternative, which postmodernism fails to offer: "postmodern philosophy is to be defined as an updated version of skepticism, more concerned with destabilizing

362 Nazir Khan, "Atheism and Radical Skepticism."

other theories and their pretensions to truth than setting up a positive theory of its own."[363] Postmodernism cannot recuperate what liberalism has destroyed. Dismantling all hierarchies of value and meaning leads not only to contradictions but also to nihilism. Ziauddin Sardar writes:

> Deconstruction—the methodology of discursive analysis—is the norm of postmodernism. Everything has to be deconstructed. But once deconstruction has reached its conclusion, we are left with a grand void: there is nothing, but nothing, that can remotely provide us with meaning, with a sense of direction, with a scale to distinguish good and evil.[364]

The flawed moral compass of postmodernism does not provide an accurate appraisal of the true sources of evil. There is a tendency to externalise evil onto a set of circumstances or power hierarchies outside of one's own agency, without confronting the reality of the psychological motivations within the human being. In contrast, Islam consistently emphasises both internal and external sources of evil. Every Friday sermon typically begins with the *khuṭbat al-ḥājah* (sermon of need), an opening speech taught by the Prophet that includes the phrase "We seek refuge in Allah from the evils of ourselves and our foul deeds."[365] The Islamic framework provides the individual with the necessary tools to pursue spiritual and moral purification by recognising his internal inclinations towards evil and combatting them. This struggle against one's lower desires (*nafs*) is necessary for achieving moral discipline, as the Prophet confirmed when he said, "The *mujāhid* is one who strives against his own *nafs*."[366]

---

363 Stuart Sim, "Postmodernism and Philosophy," in *The Routledge Companion to Postmodern Philosophy*, ed. Stuart Sim (London: Routledge, 2001), 13.

364 Sardar, *Postmodernism and the other*, 10.

365 *Sunan Abī Dāwūd*, no. 1097; *Sunan al-Nasāʾī*, no. 1404; *Sunan Ibn Mājah*, no. 1892; *Jāmiʿ al-Tirmidhī*, no. 1105.

366 *Jāmiʿ al-Tirmidhī*, no. 1621.

Unlike human narratives constructed to serve worldly interests or to pacify the mind with idle fantasies, the Qur'anic narrative speaks directly to the spiritual, intellectual, and moral needs of human beings, providing them with all-encompassing truth from the Divine.

> ***Wokeism***
> A movement of social justice activism inspired by the ideas of postmodernism.

In spite of its failure to provide any meaningful answers of its own, postmodernist ideas have come to dominate contemporary social discourse in media, academia, and activism, within a relatively short period of time. "Slowly but surely, postmodernism is taking over the world we inhabit, the thoughts we think, the things we do…", writes Sardar.[367] In popular culture, traditional stories of heroes in the contest between good and evil have been replaced with morally ambiguous anti-heroes defying labels of "good" or "bad," a reflection of our own accelerating moral confusion as a society. Postmodernist thought in social justice activism has given rise to a movement sometimes referred to as "wokeism." Philosopher Hans-Georg Moeller writes:

> Wokeism shares numerous similarities with religions and particularly with Christianity. It is highly dogmatic by focusing on a few "absolute" moral values related to social justice which can only be affirmed but not denied. In this way, it does not invite argumentation or debate but, instead, fosters moral sentiment and feelings of righteousness. It promises a secular absolution from inherited wickedness and "cancels" heretics. What is more, it operates performatively with a strong emphasis on public display including demonstrations, public gestures (kneeling, etc.), memes, or signs (such as the "one love" armband which caused controversy at the 2022 soccer world cup) and, importantly, speech acts (e.g., "diversity statements," pledges, corporate values), typically proliferated on (social) media.[368]

367 Sardar, *Postmodernism and the other*, 6.

368 Hans-Georg Miller, "Wokeism: A Global Civil Religion in the 'Age of Profilicity'?," *Meridian* 4 (March 2023): 4–5.

Islam

Islam is the ultimate truth. God provides us with guidance on how to achieve true justice in our lives and in the world. Our moral worth is determined by God on the basis of our deeds.

Postmodernism

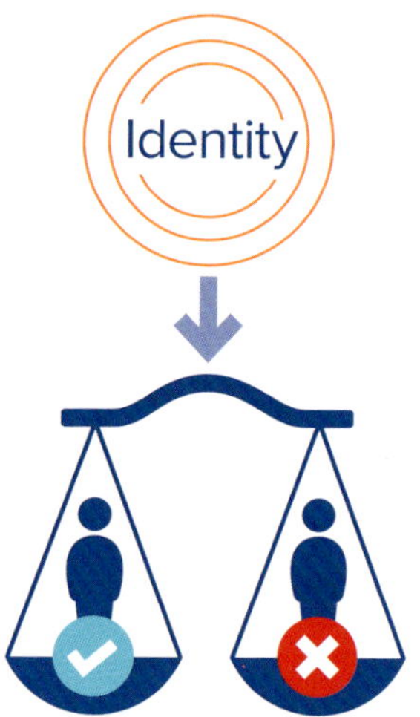

There is no ultimate truth. Our moral worth is determined by identity politics. People are inherently good or irredeemably evil. There is no concept of spiritual purification or moral self-discipline.

As aptly illustrated, the "justice" offered by wokeism and postmodernism is rarely substantive but often amounts only to superficial performative gestures and virtue signaling. People recite land acknowledgements without any calls for accountability or action to redress the dispossession,[369] and while conveniently ignoring their government's support for the ongoing violent dispossession of Palestinian land. Moral evaluation is based not on actions but on identitarian considerations. A presidential candidate from an administration that has enabled the genocide in Gaza is celebrated because she is a woman of colour.[370] Wokeism considers individuals

369 Michael C. Lambert, Elisa J. Sobo, and Valerie L. Lambert, "Rethinking Land Acknowledgments," *Anthropology News*, December 20, 2021, https://www.anthropology-news.org/articles/rethinking-land-acknowledgments.

370 Norman Solomon, "Harris Refuses to Change Course on US Complicity With Israel's Genocide in Gaza," *Common Dreams*, August 30, 2024, https://www.commondreams.org/opinion/harris-refuses-to-change-course-on-us-complicity-with-israel-s-genocide-in-gaza; Dorothy Tucker, "For women at the DNC, nomination of Kamala Harris is deeply personal," *CBS News*, August 22, 2024, https://www.cbsnews.com/chicago/news/women-dnc-nomination-kamala-harris-deeply-personal/

to be irremediably evil or irremediably good based on where their identity lies within a matrix of power structures. Identity itself becomes the greatest object of worship. The chief concern of postmodernists becomes who is talking rather than what they are saying and what they are doing.

Many perceive postmodernism as a useful tool for identifying the injustices of modernity. In its skepticism towards liberalism and modernism, postmodernist thought has formed the basis of decolonial scholarship. Indeed, many of those critiques echo points made above and therefore may be useful to Muslims confronting Western colonialism. However, Ziauddin Sardar observes that "far from being a new theory of liberation, postmodernism...is simply a new wave of domination riding on the crest of colonialism and modernity."[371] He writes:

> While postmodernism is a legitimate protest against the excesses of suffocating modernity, instrumental rationality, and authoritarian traditionalism, it has itself become a universal ideology that kills everything that gives meaning and depth to the life of non-western individuals and societies. ...If postmodernism had a slogan it would be 'anything goes'; but when 'anything goes,' everything stays and expediency guides thought and action. Postmodernism preserves—indeed enhances—all the classical and modern structures of oppression and domination. ...Seen from this perspective, postmodernism emerges as a worldview conjured from the pathological necessity of the west to define reality and truth as its reality and truth. Now that the west itself doubts the validity of its own reality and truth it seeks to maintain the status quo and continue unchecked on its trajectory of expansion and domination by undermining all criteria of

371 Sardar, *Postmodernism and the other*, 13.

> reality and truth. Western oppression of Other cultures seems to move in endless spirals, each ushered in with the promise of infinite freedom and expansion of civilisation. Postmodernism is the latest of these spirals, taking over from modernity, which itself is a product of colonialism.[372]

Muslims seeking to advocate for their rights will thus find themselves pressured by wokeism to abandon their indigenous Islamic values and adopt the "enlightened" values of Western cultures. For example, Western cultural imperialism and postmodern colonialism takes the shape of subjugating traditional Muslim values to new Western notions of sexual identity and orientation.[373] Muslim scripture is assigned new meanings to accord with whatever suits the latest fancy of secular morality. There is no truth preserved in the fourteen centuries of Islamic scholarship that cannot be waved away by the postmodernist wand of reinterpretation.

Postmodernism degrades and disrespects traditional sources of authority including classically-trained Muslim scholars. Power is given instead to the online influencer who commands an army of keyboard warriors. In order to legitimise their own authority, the influencer builds a platform by launching tabloid refutations against popular scholars drawing on the utility of 'cancel culture' as a popular tool of wokeism. They fail to recognise that such methods do not compensate for their own lack of scholarly learning and only serve to sow distrust towards all scholars of Islam among the general public. The online *daʿwah* scene becomes more consumed with refutations of popular speakers

372 Sardar, *Postmodernism and the other,* 14–15.

373 Yaqeen Institute, "Islam and the LGBT Question: Reframing the Narrative," Yaqeen Institute for Islamic Research, October 7, 2022, https://yaqeeninstitute.org/read/paper/islam-and-the-lgbt-question-reframing-the-narrative (summarised from a July 2022 presentation by Carl Sharif El-Tobgui).

and teachers than with actually guiding people towards Allah and towards good deeds. Even when criticism of an individual is valid it must be done according to sound Islamic principles rather than the digital vigilantism of postmodernism. Imam al-Biqāʿī (d. 885 AH) writes on the subject of criticism in the introduction to his work *Maṣāʾid al-naẓar fī maqāṣid al-suwar*:

> The way of the sincere critics—if their criticism was based upon insight and offered sincerely for the sake of God with the goal of *naṣīḥah* (sincere advice), was to come to me in person or send me a message, in order to see whether I could inform them of the correct meaning of my words regarding the substance of their criticism, or in order that I might recognize my mistake. Thus, if I corrected the error, then we would have been of those who cooperate in *birr* (righteousness) and *taqwā* (piety), and if I let it remain in my work (disregarding their feedback), then criticism would be required according to the degree warranted by the erroneous meaning. However, if they did not take such steps, then their refutation of me was due to either one of two reasons. It was either due to ignorance, because the one who is ignorant of something opposes it (how many have faulted a true concept when their failure was due to a misunderstanding?) or it was due to envy towards one who should not be envied. Their work was thus the work of one who wishes only to smear a Muslim.[374]

Much of the online refutation culture amounts to nothing more than smear campaigns to humiliate and disparage fellow believers. There is a world of difference between supporting a person of knowledge through valuable feedback and trying

374 Al-Biqāʿī, *Maṣāʾid al-naẓar fī maqāṣid al-suwar* (Riyadh: *Maktabah al-Maʿārif*, 1987) 1:105.

to publicly discredit him. This phenomenon arises from the postmodernist emphasis on disparaging traditional authority and the focus on public judgement of people rather than the moral evaluation of statements and actions.

In its rejection of an ultimate narrative and a fixed reality, postmodernism has no objective standard for guidance. As a result, much of the resistance, criticism, and skepticism that postmodernism marshals invariably fall upon generational fault lines in Western culture. The young reject the ways of thinking of the old, and so too will they be rejected by future generations. Embodying ethical virtue becomes an unattainable fantasy, never realised. As Syed Naquib al-Attas aptly illustrates:

> Western civilization is constantly changing and 'becoming' without ever achieving 'being', except that its 'being' is and always has been a 'becoming'. This is and has been so by virtue of the fact that it acknowledges no single, established Reality to fix its vision on; no single, valid Scripture to confirm and affirm in life; no single human Guide whose words and deeds and actions and entire mode of life can serve as a model to emulate in life, but that each and every individual must find for himself and herself each one's identity and meaning of life and destiny. Western civilization affirms the evanescent (*fanā'*) aspect of reality, and its values pertain to the secular, material and physical realities of existence.[375]

Al-Attas proceeds to explain that in Western society, a generational divide exists among the youth, the middle-aged, and the elderly. Each generation embarks on its own quest for identity, often rejecting the values of the previous generation. This perpetual

375 Al-Attas, *Prolegomena*, 81.

search for identity and meaning across generations, combined with dissatisfaction with self-derived values, creates a cycle of perpetual unfulfilment. As al-Attas writes:

> The three generations that in such wise comprise Western society are forever engaged in the search for identity and meaning of life...And this condition, we maintain, is what we mean by injustice (*ẓulm*). This condition is further aggravated by the fact that in Western society there exists also a crisis of identity between the sexes, in that women are engaged, as women, in the search for their own, separate identity.[376]

An identity crisis can be located in every arena of Western culture, fueled by the polarizing approach of postmodernism which pits identities against one another. Postmodernism does not allow for true moral growth or rectification. Islam, by contrast, recognises the dynamic moral status of the human being in accordance with their deeds, efforts, and intentions in seeking God. Thus, Islam offers a tangible path to combat internal and external forms of evil in order to achieve guidance and avoid the paths that lead one astray. In order to achieve real justice in the world, one must not lose sight of the truth. Although postmodernism has rapidly achieved a wide range of influence throughout popular culture and academia and has challenged colonialism on many fronts, it does not provide a successful strategy for true moral development. The Qur'anic worldview provides the ethical framework vital for such an endeavour.

---

376 Al-Attas, *Prolegomena*, 83.

Conclusion

Sūrah al-Fātiḥah is a prayer for guidance, and the Prophet ﷺ instructed us upon reaching its conclusion to say *āmīn* (amen).[377] This is a confirmation of our prayer and a request for God to accept it.[378] Having undertaken the journey of examining the dominant ideologies of our time, it becomes evident that the guidance contained in *Sūrah al-Fātiḥah* is incredibly comprehensive and direly needed. The elevated principles embedded in *Sūrah al-Fātiḥah* provide the human being with a clear understanding of the moral purpose for which God placed humanity on this earth. It highlights the moral and philosophical failures of atheism, materialism, secularism, polytheism, naturalism, relativism, progressivism, liberalism, and postmodernism. It calls upon us to engage in the ethical restoration of our world and ourselves, to reclaim our humanity by recovering the value structure indigenous to the human natural constitution (*fiṭrah*). It offers a complete worldview that is consonant with our natural inclination to know our Creator, thank Him, love Him, worship Him, and strive to serve Him by caring for His creation. It establishes the importance of both knowledge and action, as well as truth and justice. It provides a curriculum for our spiritual, moral, and intellectual cultivation.

This message is one that should resonate with every human being as every soul is beckoned to the pursuit of justice, truth and wisdom. Muslims have a unique responsibility to act as ambassadors of the Qur'an by living its ideals and inviting others to work together towards its goals: "cooperate in righteousness and piety, and do not cooperate in sin and aggression" (Qur'an 5:2). The ethical aims of Islam are to be internalised and actualised

377 *Ṣāḥīḥ al-Bukhārī*, no. 782.

378 Al-Thaʿlabī, *Kashf al-bayān ʿan tafsīr al-Qurʾān*, 2:471–87.

by every believer. There is wisdom in the regular recitation of this chapter in every unit of prayer as it continues to affirm our covenant anew and develop our moral sensibilities. Shaykh Muḥammad al-Ghazālī writes:

> We recite these blessed words of supplication and praise for the benefit of our own souls, just as washing regularly is necessary for the health of our bodies. The benefits we reap justify the regularity and repetition of the recitation. A body would not remain clean by washing it only now and then; it needs to be washed regularly all through one's life.
>
> Likewise, human temperament and behavior are never put right by a short prayer, casually repeated but soon forgotten. One has to stand before God as frequently as possible, because human recklessness and imprudence, as well as Satan's insinuations, never cease nor know any bounds. Prayer, supplication, and submission to God have to be observed and performed as a matter of habit.[379]

Despite its brevity, *Sūrah al-Fātiḥah* is incredibly comprehensive.[380] The subtle nuances of its linguistic eloquence are inexhaustible.[381] It contains the subcategories of *tawḥīd,* as well as an affirmation of prophethood, the Day of Judgement, the divine decree and free will, and the importance of sincerity (*ikhlāṣ*) in worship.[382] It contains both incentivizing the right path and disincentivizing the wrong path (*targhīb wa al-tarhīb*), providing spiritual motivation through hope in divine mercy and fear of divine

379 Muhammad al-Ghazali, *Thematic Commentary,* 5.

380 Abū Ḥafṣ al-Nasafī provides a very detailed discussion of the various categories of knowledge that are subsumed within this chapter while discussing the fact that the chapter is called *Umm al-Kitāb* (Mother of the Book). See al-Nasafī, *al-Taysīr fī al-tafsīr,* 1:72, 76–86.

381 Ibn al-Qayyim discusses twenty issues in the concluding verses alone. See Ibn al-Qayyim, *Badāʾiʿ al-fawāʾid,* 406–53.

382 Al-Saʿdī, *Tafseer,* 1:29–30. See also Saʿīd Ḥawwā, *Asās fī al-tafsīr,* 1:40.

punishment.[383] It contains the foundations of faith, the methods of worship, the cultivation of virtue (*akhlāq*), and the lessons from past nations.[384] It corrects misapprehensions about fate and free will, affirming our freely chosen actions in *iyyāka naʿbudu* (You alone do we worship) but also reminding us when we say *ihdinā* (guide us) that guidance occurs ultimately by God's divine will.[385] Allah makes it clear that He will guide those who sincerely turn to Him, striving to come closer to Him (Qur'an 29:69) and seeking His guidance (Qur'an 13:27, 42:13).

Moreover, there is a profound connection between *Sūrah al-Fātiḥah* as a supplication for guidance and the opening of the subsequent chapter, *Sūrah al-Baqarah,* which declares that the Qur'an provides guidance for those with *taqwā*.[386] The opening chapter of the Qur'an is articulated from our perspective and voice, expressed as our collective address to God, while the remainder of the Qur'an is expressed as the divine address to humanity; *al-Fātiḥah* poses a question, and the rest of the Qur'an provides the answer.[387] The entire Qur'an speaks to its audience on the basis of this prerequisite, namely, that we have already made the choice to exist as ethical beings and to fulfil our purpose in life, and that we have willingly sought out divine guidance and are spiritually prepared to meet its demands with acceptance and responsiveness. Having implored God by His *raḥmah* (mercy) and His sovereignty over *al-ʿālamīn* (the worlds), He provided the perfect response to our request in sending us Prophet Muhammad, "a mercy to all the worlds" (*raḥmatun li al-ʿālamīn*) (Qur'an 21:107).

383 Riḍā, *Tafsīr al-Manār,* 1:47.

384 Al-Qūnawī and Ibn al-Tamjīd, *Ḥāshiyat al-Qūnawī ʿalā tafsīr al-Bayḍāwī wa maʿahu ḥāshiyat Ibn al-Tamjīd,* 1:56.

385 Al-Qurṭubī, *al-Jāmiʿ li-aḥkām al-Qurʾān,* 1:149; al-Zahrānī, *"Aḍwāʾ ʿalā al-iʿjāz al-balāghī fī Sūrat al-Fātiḥah,"* 129.

386 Saʿīd Ḥawwā, *Asās fī al-tafsīr,* 1:50.

387 Dirāz, *Naẓarāt,* 105.

Scholars have also noted the intricate structure that runs through *Sūrah al-Fātiḥah*. Imam Fakhr al-Dīn al-Rāzī noted that the *sūrah* mentions five divine names (Allāh, *al-Rabb, al-Raḥmān, al-Raḥīm,* and *al-Mālik*) and five human goals (worship, seeking help, seeking guidance, seeking steadfastness, and seeking favor), and the two lists correspond to each other in the exact same sequence.

It is as though one were to say, "We worship You alone because You are Allah, we seek Your help because You are the *Rabb,* we seek Your guidance because You are *al-Raḥmān,* we ask You to grant us steadfastness in following it because You are *al-Raḥīm,* and we ask You to make us among those who will receive Your favor and not to make us among the misguided because You are the *Mālik/Malik* (sovereign) who will judge us all on the Day of Recompense."[388]

One may also identify within *al-Fātiḥah* a message that comes full circle, with the first half mirroring the second half. We can construct one potential representation of this mirroring relationship with the concentric "ring structures"[389] in the diagram below. We can observe how the two groups mentioned at the end of *al-Fātiḥah* are linked with the Divine names mentioned at the beginning. The name 'Allah' signifies *ilāhiyyah* (Divinity) and the name *'al-Rabb'* signifies *rubūbiyyah* (Lordship). Those who disregarded the moral and legislative authority of God are in defiance of His Lordship,[390] and those who misconstrue the Divine nature or disregard ultimate truth are in defiance of His Divinity.

388 See al-Rāzī, *Great Exegesis,* 1:444; al-Zahrānī, *"Aḍwā' ʿalā al-iʿjāz al-balāghī fī Sūrat al-Fātiḥah,"* 140. Al-Nasafī enumerates six human actions in the *sūrah;* however, the correspondence structure remains the same. See al-Nasafī, *al-Taysīr fī al-tafsīr,* 1:75–76.

389 See also another approach to identifying concentric ring structures in the *sūrah* by Munir Eltal, "Structural Cohesion in the Qur'an: Surah al-Fatihah," Muslim Matters, May 19, 2023, https://muslimmatters.org/2023/05/19/structural-cohesion-in-the-quran-a-series-surah-al-fatihah/.

390 ʿAdī ibn Ḥātim heard the Prophet reciting "They took their rabbis and monks as lords besides Allah" (Qur'an 9:31). The Prophet explained this by saying, "Although they did not worship them, when they made something lawful for them, they considered it lawful, and when they made something unlawful for them, they considered it unlawful." See *Jāmiʿ at-Tirmidhī,* no. 3095. Another connection between this verse and the corresponding verse indicated in the concentric structure is that these groups all fall under *al-ʿālamīn*.

The ring structure of *Sūrah al-Fātiḥah*

In the name of Allah, the All-Merciful, the Ever-Merciful.

God's Divinity and Perfection
"All praise belongs to Allah..."

God's Lordship
"Lord of the Worlds."

God's Mercy
"The All-Merciful, the Ever-Merciful."

All will be judged by God
"Sovereign of the Day of Judgement."

Our covenant
"You alone do we worship,
and You alone do we ask for help."

We will be judged as to whether we followed God's path
"Guide us on the straight path."

Those who receive His mercy
"The path of those whom You have favoured."

Those who do not act in accordance with His Lordship and cause injustice among the creation
"Not (the path) of those who have incurred anger..."

Those who misunderstand His Divinity and disregard the truth
"nor (the path) of those who have gone astray."

Sūrah al-Fātiḥah ultimately represents a conversation with the Divine, one that reflects our continued commitment to renew our moral covenant with Allah in order to fulfil our purpose in this world. In a famous *ḥadīth qudsī*, the Prophet ﷺ told us that Allah has said:

> I have divided the prayer into two halves between Me and My servant, and My servant will receive what he asks for.
>
> When the servant says: Praise be to Allah, Lord of the universe, Allah Most High says: My servant has praised Me (*ḥamidanī ʿabdī*).
>
> And when the servant says: The Most Compassionate, the Merciful, Allah Most High says: My servant has lauded Me (*athnā ʿalayya ʿabdī*).
>
> And when the servant says: Master of the Day of Judgement, Allah says: My servant has glorified Me (*majjadanī ʿabdī*).[391]
>
> And when the servant says: You alone do we worship and You alone do we ask for help, Allah says: This is between Me and My servant, and My servant will receive what he asks for.
>
> Then, when the servant says: Guide us along the straight path, the path of those whom You have favoured, not of those who have incurred Your anger, nor of those who have gone astray, Allah says: This is for My servant, and My servant will receive what he asks for.[392]

---

391 In one narration we also read, "My servant has entrusted his affairs to Me." See *Ṣaḥīḥ Muslim*, no. 395.

392 *Ṣaḥīḥ Muslim*, no. 395; *Sunan Abī Dāwūd*, no. 821; *Sunan al-Nasāʾī*, no. 909; *Jāmiʿ al-Tirmidhī*, no. 2953; *Sunan Ibn Mājah*, no. 3784.

As this powerful hadith illustrates, the recitation of *Sūrah al-Fātiḥah* in prayer is a deeply intimate conversation with the Divine, one that is guaranteed a response by Allah when made with sincerity. The emotional dimension and spiritual connection are actually integral to internalising the meanings of this chapter and realising the fruits of this knowledge within our souls. When we recite this chapter, we are engaged in an emotional conversation with our Creator, clinging to hope in His divine guidance. This is a supplication to God, and in order to receive a response, one's heart must be engaged and attentive. The Prophet said, "Invoke Allah while being certain of [His] response, and know that Allah does not respond to a prayer from a heart that is heedless and distracted."[393] In another narration, the special status of *Sūrah al-Fātiḥah* is further emphasised along with its guaranteed response:

> Abdullāh ibn ʿAbbās reported that while Angel Jibrīl was sitting with the Messenger of Allah ﷺ, he heard a sound above him. He lifted his head, and said, "This is a gate which has been opened in heaven today. It was never opened before." Then an angel descended through it and Jibrīl said, "This is an angel who has come down to earth, having never descended before today." He conveyed the greetings of peace and said, "Rejoice with two lights given to you. Such lights were not given to any Prophet before you. These lights are the opening of the book (*Sūrah al-Fātiḥah*), and the concluding verses of *Sūrah al-Baqarah*. You will never recite a word from them without being granted (your supplication)."[394]

The Qur'an is not a text of mere abstract information; it is meant to connect us directly with Allah in order to transform our souls and lead us to spiritual purification. Our knowledge of God is

393 *Jāmiʿ al-Tirmidhī*, no. 3479.

394 *Ṣaḥīḥ Muslim*, no. 806.

grounded through direct participation in the relationship of *ʿubūdiyyah* (servitude to God), as exemplified in our prayers, supplications, and worship. In other words, all the lessons described in the previous pages need to be internalised through the practice of worship and love for the Divine. Every prostration to God is an expression of absolute love and reverence and, simultaneously, a refusal to surrender to the false idols of our age. It is our deeply held conviction that through renewing and rectifying our relationship with Allah, we can effect a true transformation of our situation as individuals and as a collective.

Every transformation unfolds according to a sequence of events orchestrated by Allah's divine wisdom. Allah prepares the world according to His will, providing us with opportunities to rise up and answer His call. No human being could have imagined the chain of events that would lead us to where we are today. The COVID-19 pandemic ushered in an era of greater reliance on social media for news and connection, which in turn facilitated social justice movements through hashtags and viral posts, most notably in the case of the Black Lives Matter protests.[395] Western support for Ukraine during Russia's invasion highlighted the moral inconsistency in the attitudes of these same nations towards the suffering of the Palestinians under Israeli occupation.[396] All these events were beyond human prediction and imagination, yet they set the stage for the global solidarity movement for Gaza that we are witnessing today. Understanding Allah's divine decree (*qadar*) allows us to recognise the wisdom in the cascade of events that have brought us to this point and humbly to acknowledge that only Allah knows what the future holds.

395 H. H. Chang, A. Richardson, and E. Ferrara, "#JusticeforGeorgeFloyd: How Instagram Facilitated the 2020 Black Lives Matter Protests," *PLoS One* 17, no. 12 (2022): e0277864.

396 Andreas Motzfeldt Kravik, "We Must Avoid Double Standards in Foreign Policy," Al Jazeera, April 18, 2024, https://www.aljazeera.com/opinions/2024/4/18/we-must-avoid-double-standards-in-foreign-policy.

This teaches us the profound lesson of focusing our efforts on fulfilling the moral responsibilities entrusted to us by Allah and placing our trust in His divine promise. As Allah says:

> Or do you think that you will enter Paradise without facing the trials of those who came before you? They were afflicted with poverty and hardship and were so severely shaken that even the Messenger and the believers with him cried out, "When will the help of Allah come?" Indeed, the help of Allah is always near. (Qur'an 2:214)

The genocide in Gaza has undoubtedly caused indescribable pain and grief. But it has also awoken us to the failures of the existing thought structures and ideologies of the modern secular world. It has awoken us to the immeasurable value of the Qur'anic worldview. And it has awoken within us an undying resolve to turn back to Allah and renew our covenant with Him, remaining steadfast in our faith and standing firm for justice for all humanity. It is a pillar of the Islamic faith to believe in Allah's divine decree (*qadar*) and to recognise that there is always wisdom in His decree. Even difficult tribulations and calamitous events can be a source of glad-tidings for those who patiently persevere (Qur'an 2:155). Viewed from this perspective, Allah has blessed the people of Gaza with tremendous patience and granted them an indescribable honour in becoming the means by which light has overcome darkness. They have made the greatest sacrifice, and in the afterlife, their reward and solace will be with God. In this life, it is through them that Allah has enabled thousands to see reality for what it is, to seek the truth, and to stand up against oppression. Through the indomitable faith that permeates their flesh, blood, and bones, the cries for truth and justice have emerged more intensified than ever before. It is through their steadfastness that Allah has inspired countless hearts to turn towards truth, turn towards justice, and turn towards Him and embrace His divine message. And it is through their courageous example that hope has been rekindled anew for a free Palestine and freedom for all peoples suffering under tyranny and oppression.

Our faith is our greatest source of strength and resilience and our most trusted guide through the hardest times. In the face of overwhelming darkness, *Sūrah al-Fātiḥah* reminds us that Allah's mercy is always near and that He is the final and ultimate Judge before whom all will be summoned for reckoning. Reflecting upon the meaning of these short but profound verses is the beginning of a project to rebuild the moral order that our souls and the world desperately need.

May Allah, the Most Compassionate and Most Just, guide us in fulfilling this aim, and help us to walk upon the straight path, *āmīn*.

Glossary

Authoritarianism
An autocratic form of leadership that does not care about the views or opinions of others.

Atheism
The ideology that rejects belief in the existence of God.

Capitalism
An economic system defined by private ownership of capital goods and free market competition. Society becomes increasingly controlled by the interests of wealthy corporations and moral values are superseded by the goal of maximising profit.

Colonialism
The practice of seizing political control over a territory from its indigenous population in order to establish settlements or for economic exploitation.

Communism
An economic system defined by communal ownership of wealth and property. Communism, like capitalism, is a manifestation of materialism and has historically involved significant human rights abuses and suppression of religious beliefs.

Consumerism
Consumerism is a psychological and cultural form of materialism that focuses entirely on acquiring worldly possessions.

Deism
Belief in a God who created the world but is not involved in it and does not send guidance or answer prayers.

Feminism
A movement aiming to establish social and political equality between genders by eliminating gender differences in society, traditional gender roles, and male-dominated institutions (NB: this term is often given diverse definitions, and therefore it is important to clarify what one means by the term before it may be evaluated).

Individualism
A social theory that emphasises the personal preferences, freedoms, and desires of the individual rather than their social responsibilities and role within the community.

Liberalism
A political and moral philosophy arising from the European enlightenment which emphasises individual freedom as the ultimate societal value.

Materialism
A philosophical stance positing that nothing exists except physical matter.

Modernism
The belief that the teachings of the past may have been valid and appropriate in those times but are no longer morally relevant for our times.

Naturalism
The philosophical belief that everything can be explained through the properties and forces of nature without the need to invoke Divine intervention or supernatural explanations.

Nihilism
A philosophical belief that life is without objective meaning, purpose, or intrinsic value.

Perennialism
The idea that all of the world's religious traditions share a common metaphysical truth.

Pluralism
The peaceful coexistence of diverse groups of people with different beliefs, cultures, and values within a society.

Polytheism
The belief in, or worship of, more than one god.

Postmodernism
A late 20th-century movement in philosophy and the arts that rejects belief in an objective truth or grand narratives.

Progressivism
The idea that humans today are morally enlightened and that people of the past were morally inferior and backwards.

Racism
Prejudice, discrimination, or antagonism directed against someone of a different race based on the belief that one's own race is superior.

Radical Skepticism
A philosophical mode of thinking that emphasises doubt, suspicion, and distrust of claims to knowledge.

Relativism
The doctrine that moral values and truth claims differ between cultures and peoples, and there is no absolute correct answer.

Religious universalism
The doctrine that all religions ultimately lead to salvation even if they each express different beliefs and truths.

Scientific Anti-Realism
The view that the aim of science is not to find true theories or descriptions of the world, but to find theories that are empirically adequate or useful.

Scientific Realism
The view that the aim of science is to provide true descriptions of the nature of reality, including both observable and unobservable elements.

Scientism
The idea that science alone provides us with knowledge of the truth.

Secularism
The ideology that seeks to remove religion from the public domain and confine it to the private affairs of the individual.

Totalitarianism
A system of government that is dictatorial and requires complete subservience to the state, ruling through fear, repression, and subjugation.

Western Imperialism
The political, economic, and cultural domination of Western nations over other countries, often through colonisation, military force, or other means of coercion.

Wokeism
A movement of social justice activism inspired by the ideas of postmodernism.

Bibliography

Classical Islamic works (in chronological order)

Ibn Jarīr al-Ṭabarī, Muḥammad ibn Jarīr (d. 310/923). *Jāmiʿ al-bayān*. Cairo: Dār Hajr, 2001.

Ibn Jarīr al-Ṭabarī, Muḥammad ibn Jarīr (d. 310/923). *The Comprehensive Exposition of the Interpretation of the Verses of the Qur'an*. Translated by Scott Lucas. Cambridge: The Royal Aal al-Bayt Institute for Islamic Thought and the Islamic Texts Society, 2017.

Al-Māturīdī, Abū Manṣūr Muḥammad ibn Muḥammad (d. 333/944). *Ta'wīlāt Ahl al-Sunnah*. Beirut: DKI, 2005.

Al-Naḥḥās, Abū Jaʿfar (d. 338/950). *Maʿānī al-Qurʾān*. Mecca: Umm al-Qurāʾ University, 1988.

Al-Samarqandī, Abū al-Layth Naṣr ibn Muḥammad (d. 373/983). *Baḥr al-ʿulūm*. Beirut: DKI, 1993.

Al-Thaʿlabī, Abū Isḥāq Aḥmad ibn Muḥammad (d. 427/1035). *Kashf al-bayān ʿan tafsīr al-Qurʾān*. Jeddah: Dār al-Tafsīr, 2015.

Al-Baghdādī, Abū Manṣūr ʿAbd al-Qāhir (d. 429/1037). *Al-Farq bayna al-firaq*. Cairo: Maktabat Ibn Sīnā, 1988.

Al-Rāghib al-Iṣfahānī, Abū al-Qāsim al-Ḥusayn ibn Muḥammad (d. 431/1040). *al-Dharīʿah ilā makārim al-Sharīʿah*. Beirut: DKI, 1980.

Al-Rāghib al-Iṣfahānī, Abū al-Qāsim al-Ḥusayn ibn Muḥammad (d. 431/1040). *Al-Mufradāt fī gharīb al-Qurʾān*. Damascus: Dār al-Qalam, 1412/1991.

Al-Rāghib al-Iṣfahānī, Abū al-Qāsim al-Ḥusayn ibn Muḥammad (d. 431/1040). *Tafsīr al-Rāghib al-Iṣfahānī*. Tanta: University of Ṭanṭā, 1999.

Al-Qaysī, Abū Muḥammad Makkī ibn Abī Ṭālib (d. 437/1045). *Al-Hidāyah ilā bulūgh al-nihāyah*. Sharjah: University of Sharjah, 2008.

Al-Māwardī, Abū al-Ḥasan ʿAlī ibn Muḥammad (d. 450/1058). *Al-Nukat wa-l-ʿuyūn*. Beirut: Dār al-Kutub al-ʿIlmiyah, 2012.

Al-Bayhaqī, Aḥmad ibn Ḥusayn (d. 458/1066). *Shuʿab al-īmān*. Riyadh: Maktabat al-Rushd, 2003.

Ibn Ḥazm, Abū Muḥammad ʿAlī ibn Aḥmad (d. 456/1064). *Al-Iḥkām fī uṣūl al-aḥkām*. Beirut: Dār al-Āfāq al-Jadīdah.

Ibn Ḥazm, Abū Muḥammad ʿAlī ibn Aḥmad (d. 456/1064). *al-Fiṣal fī al-milal wa-l-ahwāʾ wa-l-niḥal*. Cairo: Maktabat al-Khānjī, 1903.

Al-Bayhaqī, Abū Bakr Aḥmad ibn Ḥusayn (d. 458/1066). *Shuʿab al-īmān*. Riyadh: Maktabat al-Rushd, 2003.

Ibn ʿAbd al-Barr, Abū ʿUmar Yūsuf ibn ʿAbd Allāh (d. 463/1071). *Al-Istidhkār*. Beirut: DKI, 2000.

Ibn ʿAbd al-Barr, Abū ʿUmar Yūsuf ibn ʿAbd Allāh (d. 463/1071). *Al-Tamhīd limā fī al-Muwaṭṭā min al-maʿānī wa-l-asānīd*. London: Furqan Institute, 2017.

Al-Jurjānī, Abū Bakr ʿAbd al-Qāhir ibn ʿAbd ar-Raḥmān (d. 471/1078), *Daraj al-durar fī Tafsīr al-Āy wa al-Suwar*. Amman: Dār al-Fikr, 2009.

Al-Juwaynī, Abū al-Maʿālī ʿAbd al-Malik ibn Yusuf (d. 478/1085). *Al-Burhān fī uṣūl al-fiqh*. Beirut: DKI, 1997.

Al-Ghazālī, Abū Ḥāmid Muḥammad ibn Muḥammad (d. 505/1111). *Jawāhir al-Qurʾān*. Beirut: Dār Iḥyāʾ al-ʿUlūm, 1986.

Al-Ghazālī, Abū Ḥāmid Muḥammad ibn Muḥammad (d. 505/1111). *Al-Mankhūl min taʿlīqāt al-uṣūl*. Beirut: Dār al-Fikr, 1998.

Al-Ghazālī, Abū Ḥāmid Muḥammad ibn Muḥammad (d. 505/1111). *Al-Maqṣad al-Asnā*. Beirut: Dār Ibn Ḥazm, 2003.

Al-Kalwadhānī, Abū al-Khaṭṭāb Maḥfūẓ ibn Aḥmad (d. 510/1116). *Al-Tamhīd fī uṣūl al-fiqh*. Mecca: Umm al-Qurā, 1985.

Al-Baghawī, al-Ḥusayn ibn Masʿūd (d. 516/1122). *Maʿālim al-tanzīl fī Tafsīr al-Qurʾān*. Beirut: Dār Iḥyāʾ Turāth al-ʿArabī, 1420 AH.

Al-Nasafī, Abu Ḥafṣ Umar bin Muḥammad (d. 537/1142). *Al-Taysīr fī al-tafsīr*. Istanbul: Dār al-Lubāb, 2019.

Ibn ʿAṭiyyah, Abū Muḥammad ʿAbd al-Ḥaqq ibn Ghālib (d. 541/1147). *Al-Muḥarrar al-wajīz*. Beirut: DKI, 2001.

Al-Shahrastānī, Muḥammad b. ʿAbd al-Karīm (d. 548/1153). *Nihāyat al-iqdām fī ʿilm al-kalām*. Cairo: Maktabat al-Thaqāfah al-Dīniyyah, 2009.

Al-Suhaylī, Abū al-Qāsim ʿAbd al-Raḥmān ibn ʿAbdullah (d. 581/1185). *Natāʾij al-fikr fī al-Nahw*. Beirut: DKI, 1996.

Ibn al-Jawzī, Abū al-Faraj ʿAbd al-Raḥmān ibn ʿAlī (d. 597/1201). *Zād al-masīr fī ʿilm al-tafsīr*. Beirut: Dār Ibn Ḥazm, 2002.

Al-Rāzī, Fakhr al-Dīn Muḥammad ibn ʿUmar (d. 606/1210). *The Great Exegesis*. Translated by Sohaib Saeed. Cambridge: The Royal Aal al-Bayt Institute for Islamic Thought and Islamic Texts Society, 2018.

Al-Rāzī, Fakhr al-Dīn Muḥammad ibn ʿUmar (d. 606/1210). *Al-Maḥṣūl fī ʿilm uṣūl al-fiqh*. N.p.: Muʾassasat al-Risālah, 1997.

Al-Āmidī, Sayf al-Dīn ʿAlī ibn Muḥammad (d. 631/1233). *Al-Iḥkām fī uṣūl al-aḥkām*. Beirut: al-Maktab al-Islamī, 1986.

Al-Khuwayyī, Shams al-Dīn Aḥmad ibn al-Khalīl ibn Saʿādah (d. 637/1240). *Yanābīʿ al-ʿulūm*. In ʿAbd al-Hādī ʿAlī Muḥammad al-Qarnī, "*Yanābīʿ al-ʿulūm (aqālīm al-taʿālīm) li-Shams al-Dīn qāḍī al-quḍāh bi-l-Shām Aḥmad ibn al-Khalīl ibn Saʿādah ibn Jaʿfar ibn ʿĪsā al-Muhallabī 583–637 A.H. dirāsah wa-taḥqīq*," *al-Majallah al-ʿIlmiyyah li-Kullīyat Uṣūl al-Dīn wa-l-Daʿwah bi-l-Zaqāzīq* 33, no. 2 (2021): 285–356.

Al-Qurṭubī, Abū ʿAbd Allāh Muḥammad ibn Aḥmad (d. 671/1273). *Al-Jāmiʿ li-aḥkām al-Qurʾān*. Cairo: Dar al-Kutub al-Misriyya, 1964.

Al-Bayḍāwī, Nāṣir al-Dīn Abū Saʿīd ʿAbd Allāh ibn ʿUmar (d. 685/1286). *Anwār al-tanzīl wa asrār al-taʾwīl*. Beirut: Dār Iḥyāʾ al-Turāth al-ʿArabī, n.d.

Ibn Taymiyyah, Taqī al-Dīn Abū al-ʿAbbās Aḥmad ibn ʿAbd al-Ḥalīm (d. 728/1328). *Darʾ taʿāruḍ al-ʿaql wa al-naql*. Edited by Muḥammad Rashād Sālim. Riyadh: Jāmiʿat al-Imām Muḥammad b. Saʿūd al-Islāmiyyah, 1411/1991.

Ibn Taymiyyah, Taqī al-Dīn Abū al-ʿAbbās Aḥmad ibn ʿAbd al-Ḥalīm (d. 728/1328). *Al-Istiqāmah*. Riyadh: Jāmiʿat al-Īmām, 1403 AH.

Ibn Taymiyyah, Taqī al-Dīn Abū al-ʿAbbās Aḥmad ibn ʿAbd al-Ḥalīm (d. 728/1328). *Al-Jawāb al-ṣaḥīḥ li-man baddala dīn al-Masīḥ*. Riyadh: Dār al-ʿĀṣima, 1999.

Ibn Taymiyyah, Taqī al-Dīn Abū al-ʿAbbās Aḥmad ibn ʿAbd al-Ḥalīm (d. 728/1328). *Al-Nubuwwāt*. Riyadh: Aḍwāʾ al-Salaf, 2000.

Ibn Taymiyyah, Taqī al-Dīn Abū al-ʿAbbās Aḥmad ibn ʿAbd al-Ḥalīm (d. 728/1328). *Al-Radd ʿalā al-manṭiqiyyīn*. Beirut: Muʾassasat al-Rayyān, 2005.

Ibn Taymiyyah, Taqī al-Dīn Abū al-ʿAbbās Aḥmad ibn ʿAbd al-Ḥalīm (d. 728/1328). *Al-ʿUbūdiyyah*. Beirut: al-Maktaba al-Islāmiyya, 2005.

Ibn Taymiyyah, Taqī al-Dīn Abū al-ʿAbbās Aḥmad ibn ʿAbd al-Ḥalīm (d. 728/1328). *Jāmiʿ al-masāʾil*. Beirut: Dar Ibn Ḥazm 2019.

Ibn Taymiyyah, Taqī al-Dīn Abū al-ʿAbbās Aḥmad ibn ʿAbd al-Ḥalīm (d. 728/1328). *Minhāj al-sunnah al-nabawiyyah*. Riyadh: Jāmiʿat al-Īmām, 1986.

Ibn Taymiyyah, Taqī al-Dīn Abū al-ʿAbbās Aḥmad ibn ʿAbd al-Ḥalīm (d. 728/1328). *Majmūʿ al-fatāwā*. Mansoura: Dār al-Wafāʾ li-l-Ṭibāʿa wa-l-Nashr, 1998.

Ibn Taymiyyah, Taqī al-Dīn Abū al-ʿAbbās Aḥmad ibn ʿAbd al-Ḥalīm (d. 728/1328). *Qāʿida fī al-maḥabba*. Cairo: Maktabat al-Turāth al-Islāmī, 1987.

Ibn Juzayy, Abū al-Qāsim Muḥammad ibn Aḥmad (d. 741/1340). *Al-Tashīl li-ʿulūm al-tanzīl*. Beirut: Dār al-Arqam, 1416 AH.

Al-Ṭībī, al-Ḥusayn ibn ʿAbd Allah (d. 743/1342). *Futūḥ al-ghayb fī al-kashf ʿan qināʿ al-rayb*. Dubai: DIHQA, 2013.

Abū Ḥayyān Muḥammad ibn Yūsuf al-Gharnāṭī (d. 745/1344). *Al-Baḥr al-muḥīṭ*. Beirut: Dār al-Fikr, 2010.

Ibn al-Qayyim, Shams al-Dīn Abū ʿAbd Allāh Muḥammad ibn Abū Bakr (d. 751/1350). *Badāʾiʿ al-fawāʾid*. Beirut: Dār Ibn Ḥazm, 2019.

Ibn al-Qayyim, Shams al-Dīn Abū ʿAbd Allāh Muḥammad ibn Abū Bakr (d. 751/1350). *Iʿlām al-muwaqqiʿīn*. Dammam: Dār Ibn al-Jawzī, 2002.

Ibn al-Qayyim, Shams al-Dīn Abū ʿAbd Allāh Muḥammad ibn Abū Bakr (d. 751/1350). *Ibn Qayyim Al-Jawzīya on the Invocation of God : Al-Wabil al-Sayyib*. Translated by M. Youssef Slitine and M. Abdurrahman Fitzgerald. Cambridge: Islamic Texts Society, 2000.

Ibn al-Qayyim, Shams al-Dīn Abū ʿAbd Allāh Muḥammad ibn Abū Bakr (d. 751/1350). *Miftāḥ Dār al-Saʿādah*. Beirut: Dār Ibn Ḥazm, 2019.

Ibn al-Qayyim, Shams al-Dīn Abū ʿAbd Allāh Muḥammad ibn Abū Bakr (d. 751/1350). *Madārij al-sālikīn*. Beirut: Dār Ibn Ḥazm, 2019.

Ibn al-Qayyim, Shams al-Dīn Abū ʿAbd Allāh Muḥammad ibn Abū Bakr (d. 751/1350). *Ranks of the Divine Seekers*. Translated by Ovamir Anjum. Leiden: Brill, 2020.

Ibn al-Qayyim, Shams al-Dīn Abū ʿAbd Allāh Muḥammad ibn Abū Bakr (d. 751/1350). *Ṭarīq al-hijratayn*. Beirut: Dār Ibn Ḥazm, 2019.

Ibn al-Qayyim, Shams al-Dīn Abū ʿAbd Allāh Muḥammad ibn Abū Bakr (d. 751/1350). *ʿUddat al-ṣābirīn*. Beirut: Dār Ibn Ḥazm, 2019.

Ibn al-Qayyim, Shams al-Dīn Abū ʿAbd Allāh Muḥammad ibn Abū Bakr (d. 751/1350). *Al-Wābil al-ṣayyib*. Beirut: Dār Ibn Ḥazm, 2019.

Ibn Kathīr, Abū al-Fidāʾ Ismāʿīl ibn ʿUmar (d. 773/1373). *Al-Bidāya wa al-nihāya*. Cairo: Dār Hajr, 1998.

Ibn Kathīr, Abū al-Fidāʾ Ismāʿīl ibn ʿUmar (d. 773/1373). *Tafsīr al-Qurʾān al-ʿAẓīm*. Riyadh: Dār al-Ṭaybah, 1999.

Al-Shāṭibī, Abū Isḥāq Ibrāhīm ibn Mūsā (d. 790/1388). *Al-Iʿtiṣām*. Dammam: Dār ibn al-Jawzī, 2008.

Al-Shāṭibī, Abū Isḥāq Ibrāhīm ibn Mūsā (d. 790/1388). *al-Muwāfaqāt*, ed. Mashhūr Ḥasan Āl Salmān. Cairo: Dār ʿAffān, 1997.

Ibn Khaldūn, Abū Zayd ʿAbd al-Raḥmān ibn Muḥammad (d. 808/1406). *Al-ʿIbar wa dīwān al-mubtadaʾ wa al-khabar fī tārīkh al-ʿArab wa al-Barbar wa man ʿāṣarahum min dhawī al-shaʾn al-akbar*. Edited by A. Khalīl Shihāda, revised by Dr. Suhayl Zakkār. Beirut: Dār al-Fikr, 1401/1981.

Al-Fīrūzābādī, Abū al-Ṭāhir Muḥammad ibn Yaʿqūb (d. 817/1414). *Baṣāʾir dhawī at-tamyīz fī laṭāʾif al-Kitāb al-ʿAzīz*. Cairo: al-Majlis al-Aʿlā li-Shuʾūn al-Islāmiyya, Lajnat Iḥyāʾ at-Turāth al-Islāmī, 1416/1996.

Al-Biqāʿī, Burhān al-Dīn Ibrāhīm ibn ʿUmar (d. 885/1480). *Maṣāʾid al-naẓar fī maqāṣid al-suwar*. Riyadh: Maktabah al-Maʿārif, 1987.

Al-Kāfījī, Muḥammad ibn Sulaymān (d. 879/1474). *Al-Ghurrah al-Wāḍiḥah fī tafsīr Sūrat al-Fātiḥah*. In Marzūq ʿAlī Ibrāhīm, "*al-Ghurrah al-Wāḍiḥah fī tafsīr Sūrat al-Fātiḥah li-Shaykh al-Islām Muḥammad ibn Sulaymān ibn Saʿd al-Kāfījī (788-879 AH): taḥqīq wa dirāsah*," *Majallah al-Buḥūth al-Dirāsāt al-Qurʾāniyyah*, 10, no. 16: 161–259.

Al-Sanūsī, Muḥammad ibn Yūsuf (d. 895/1490). *Tafsīr Sūrat al-Fātiḥah*. Tunis: Dār al-Imām Ibn ʿArafah, 2023.

Al-Suyūṭī, Jalāl al-Dīn ʿAbd al-Raḥmān ibn Abū Bakr (d. 911/1505). *Nawāhid al-abkār wa shawārid al-afkār*. Mecca: Umm al-Qurā, 2005.

Al-Ālūsī, Shihāb al-Dīn Maḥmūd ibn ʿAbd Allāh (d. 1270/1854). *Rūḥ al-maʿānī fī tafsīr al-Qurʾān al-ʿaẓīm wa-l-sabʿ al-mathānī*. Beirut: Dār al-Kutub al-ʿIlmiyyah, 1995.

Other references (in alphabetical order)

Abdul-Rahman, Zohair. "Why Is Shirk the Greatest Sin?" Yaqeen Institute for Islamic Research, July 25, 2022. https://yaqeeninstitute.org/read/paper/why-is-shirk-the-greatest-sin-of-all.

Abdul-Rahman, Zohair and Jinan Yousef. "Mercy and Might on Judgment Day: Allah's Name Maliki Yawm al-Din." Yaqeen Institute for Islamic Research, March 29, 2022. https://yaqeeninstitute.org/read/paper/mercy-and-might-on-judgment-day-allahs-name-maliki-yawn-al-din.

Abdul-Rahman, Zohair and Nazir Khan. "Souls Assorted: An Islamic Theory of Spiritual Personality." Yaqeen Institute for Islamic Research, October 18, 2018. https://yaqeeninstitute.org/read/paper/souls-assorted-an-islamic-theory-of-spiritual-personality.

Abdul-Rahman, Zohair and Nazir Khan. "Proving God's Existence | In Pursuit of Conviction II." Yaqeen Institute for Islamic Research, October 11, 2019. https://yaqeeninstitute.ca/read/paper/in-pursuit-of-conviction-ii-proving-gods-existence.

Abulebdeh, Hala. "Israel Killed My Entire Family of Doctors, Engineers, Teachers and Therapists in Gaza." Interview with Ahmed Alnaouq, Palestine Deep Dive, YouTube video, April 11, 2024. https://www.youtube.com/watch?v=tuzcOPNTars.

Abu Rumaysah. *The Spiritual Cure: An Explanation to Surah al-Fātiḥah*. Birmingham: Daar us-Sunnah Publishers, 2006.

Adamson, Peter. "Ibn Khaldūn's Method of History and Aristotelian Natural Philosophy." *Journal of the History of Philosophy* 62, no. 2 (2024): 195–210.

Akrimi, Yasmine. "What the War on Gaza Tells Us About Western Feminism." Business International Centre, April 9, 2024. https://www.bic-rhr.com/research/what-war-gaza-tells-us-about-western-feminism.

Al-Attas, Syed Muhammad Naquib. *Islam and Secularism*. Kuala Lumpur: ISTAC, 1993.

Al-Attas, Syed Muhammad Naquib. *Prolegomena to the Metaphysics of Islam: An Exposition of the Fundamental Elements of the Worldview of Islam*. Kuala Lumpur: ISTAC, 1995.

Al-Azami, Usaama. "Locating Ḥākimiyya in Global History: The Concept of Sovereignty in Premodern Islam and Its Reception after Mawdūdī and Quṭb." *Journal of the Royal Asiatic Society* 32, no. 2 (2022): 355–76.

Al-Badr, ʿAbd al-Razzāq. *Sharḥ al-durūs al-muhimmah li-ʿāmmat al-ummah*. Kuwait City: Maktab al-Shuʾūn al-Fanniyyah, 2016.

Albanese, Francesca. "Anatomy of a Genocide." February26–April 5, 2024. https://www.un.org/unispal/document/anatomy-of-a-genocide-report-of-the-special-rapporteur-on-the-situation-of-human-rights-in-the-palestinian-territory-occupied-since-1967-to-human-rights-council-advance-unedited-version-a-hrc-55/.

Al-Dawsirī, Munīrah. *Asmāʾ suwar al-Qurʾān wa faḍāʾiluhā*. Dammam: Dār Ibn Jawzī, 1426 AH.

Aldossari, Maryam. "For Feminists, Silence on Gaza Is No Longer an Option." Al Jazeera, January 4, 2024. https://www.aljazeera.com/opinions/2024/1/4/for-feminists-silence-on-gaza-is-no-longer-an-option.

Al-Ghazālī, Muḥammad (d. 1996). *A Thematic Commentary on the Qur'an*. Translated by Ashur Shamis, edited by Zaynab Alawiye. Herndon: IIIT, 2000.

Al-Hararī, Muḥammad Amīn ibn ʿUmar (d. 1418/1997). *Tafsīr ḥadāʾiq ar-rūḥ wa al-rayḥān fī rawābī ʿulūm al-Qurʾān*. Beirut: Dār Ṭawq an-Najāt 1421/2001.

Ali, Nimao. "The Silent Betrayal of Palestinian Women by Global Feminism." *Toronto Star*, December 10, 2023. https://www.thestar.com/opinion/contributors/the-silent-betrayal-of-palestinian-women-by-global-feminism/article_79aec4e0-95de-11ee-8e8c-a775e9ab793c.html.

Al-Lāḥim, Sulaymān. *Al-Lubāb fī tafsīr al-istiʿādhah wa al-basmalah wa Fātiḥat al-kitāb*. Riyadh: Dār al-Muslim li an-Nashr wa al-Tawzīʿ, 1420/1999.

Al-Majīdī, ʿAbd al-Salām. *Al-Islām fī sabʿ āyāt*. Istanbul: Dār al-Uṣūl, 2021.

Al-Mawdūdī. *Four Basic Qur'anic Terms*. Translated by Abū Asad. Lahore: Islamic Publications, 1979.

Al-Maydānī, ʿAbd al-Raḥmān Ḥasan Ḥabannakah (d. 2004). *Al-ʿAqīdah al-Islāmiyyah wa Ususuhā*. Damascus: Dār al-Qalam, 2009.

Al-Nadwī, Abū al-Ḥasan ʿAlī. *Appreciation and Interpretation of Religion in the Modern Age*. Lucknow, 1982.

[Al-]Nadwī, Abū al-Ḥasan ʿAlī. *Islam and the World: The Rise and Decline of Muslims and Its Effect on Mankind*. Translated by Muhammad Asif Kidwai. Leicester: UK Islamic Academy, 2005.

Al-Saʿdī, ʿAbd al-Raḥmān Nāṣir (d. 1957). *Tafseer as-Sa'di*. Translated by Nasiruddin Khattab. Riyadh: IIPH, 2018.

Al-Shanqīṭī, Muḥammad al-Amīn ibn Muḥammad al-Mukhtār (d. 1973). *Aḍwāʾ al-bayān fī īḍāḥ al-Qurʾān bi-l-Qurʾān*. Cairo: Dār al-Ḥadīth, 2006.

Al-Sibāʿī, Muṣṭafā (d. 1964). *Civilization of Faith: A Journey through Islamic History*. Translated by Nasiruddin al-Khattab. Riyadh: IIPH, 2005.

Al-Ṭayyār, Muṣāʿid. *Al-Muḥarrar fī ʿulūm al-Qurʾān*. Jeddah: Maʿhad al-Imām al-Shāṭibī, 2008.

Al-Ṭayyār, Muṣāʿid. *Mawsūʿat al-tafsīr al-maʾthūr*. Beirut: Dar Ibn Ḥazm, 2017.

Al-ʿUmrānī, Aḥmad. *Mawsūʿat madrasat Makkah fī al-tafsīr*. Cairo: Dār al-Salām, 2010.

Al-Zahrānī. "*Aḍwāʾ ʿalā al-iʿjāz al-balāghī fī Sūrat al-Fātiḥah.*" *Majallat al-Buḥūth wa al-Dirāsāt al-Qurʾāniyyah* 4, no. 2: 117–81.

Al-Zarqāʾ, Muṣṭafā (d. 1999). *Al-Madkhal al-fiqhī al-ʿām*. Damascus: Dar al-Qalam, 2004.

Al-Zuḥaylī, Wahbah (d. 2015). *Al-Tafsīr al-munīr fī al-ʿaqīdah wa al-sharīʿah wa al-manhaj*. Beirut: Dār al-Fikr al-Muʿāṣir, 1411/1991.

Anjum, Ovamir. "Being a 'Good Person' is Not Enough: Why Ethics Need Islam." Yaqeen Institute for Islamic Research, January 27, 2022. https://yaqeeninstitute.ca/read/paper/being-a-good-person-is-not-enough-why-ethics-need-islam.

Asad, Muhammad (d. 1992). *Islam at the Crossroads*. Gibraltar: Dar al-Andalus, 1982.

Asad, Muhammad (d. 1992). *The Road to Mecca*. Louisville: Fons Vitae 2005.

Atkins, Peter. "Naturalism and Materialism." *Think* 19, no. 56 (2020): 121–32.

Attia, Gamal el-Din, *Towards Realization of the Intents of Islamic Law*. Translated by Nancy Roberts. London: IIIT, 2007.

Barthes, Roland. *The Death of the Author*. Translated by S. Heath. London: Fontana, 1977.

Bhutto, Fatima. "Gaza Has Exposed the Shameful Hypocrisy of Western Feminism." Zeteo News, April 18, 2024. https://open.substack.com/pub/zeteo/p/gaza-has-exposed-the-shameful-hypocrisy.

Brown, Jonathan. "Blind Spots: The Origins of the Western Method of Critiquing Hadith," Yaqeen Institute for Islamic Research, January 31, 2019. https://yaqeeninstitute.ca/read/paper/blind-spots-the-origins-of-the-western-method-of-critiquing-hadith.

Brown, Jonathan. "Is Islam a Death Cult? Martyrdom and the American-Muslim Imagination," Yaqeen Institute for Islamic Research, September 12, 2017, https://yaqeeninstitute.org/read/paper/is-islam-a-death-cult-martyrdom-and-the-american-muslim-imagination

Calis, Halim. "Mary's Prophethood Reassessed: Overlooked Medieval Islamic Perspectives in Contemporary Scholarship." *Religions* 15, no. 4 (2024): 461.

Chamorro-Premuzic, Tomas. "Are You a Digital Narcissist?" *Harvard Business Review,* April 10, 2023. https://hbr.org/2023/04/are-you-a-digital-narcissist.

Chang, H. H., A. Richardson, and E. Ferrara. "#JusticeforGeorgeFloyd: How Instagram Facilitated the 2020 Black Lives Matter Protests." *PLoS One* 17, no. 12 (2022): e0277864.

Chaudhuri, B. B., Shubhra Chakrabarti, and Utsa Patnaik. *Agrarian and Other Histories: Essays for Binay Bhushan Chaudhuri.* New Delhi: Tulika Books, 2017.

Chomsky, Noam. "Science, Mind, and Limits of Understanding." The Science and Faith Foundation (STOQ), The Vatican, January 2014. https://chomsky.info/201401__/.

Cirillo, Pasquale Cirillo, and Nassim Nicholas Taleb. "On the Statistical Properties and Tail Risk of Violent Conflicts." *Physica D: Nonlinear Phenomena* 452 (June 15, 2016): 29–45

"Conference of Zionists; Elect Delegates at Their Meeting in Baltimore. Will Colonize Palestine Rabbis Gottheil and Wise Were Chosen Members of the International Executive Committee." *New York Times,* June 20, 1899. https://www.nytimes.com/1899/06/20/archives/conference-of-zionists-elect-delegates-at-their-meeting-in.html.

Cunningham, Conor. *Genealogy of Nihilism*. London and New York: Routledgc, 2005.

Dagli, Caner K. "Dignity Is for the Heart, Not the Ego." *Renovatio* 7, no. 1 (2023). https://renovatio.zaytuna.edu/article/dignity-is-for-the-heart-not-the-ego.

Dirāz, Muḥammad ʿAbdullah (d. 1958). "*Naẓarāt fī fātiḥat al-kitāb al-ḥakīm*." *Al-Majallah* 7, Dhū al-Ḥijjah 1376 AH.

Davies, Paul. "Taking Science on Faith." *New York Times,* November 24, 2007. https://www.nytimes.com/2007/11/24/opinion/24davies.html.cx.

Davis, Angela. "Palestine Is a Moral Litmus Test for the World." Al Jazeera, October 27, 2023. https://www.aljazeera.com/program/upfront/2023/10/27/angela-davis-palestine-is-a-moral-litmus-test-for-the-world.

Dawkins, Richard. *River Out of Eden: A Darwinian View of Life.* London: Weidenfeld and Nicolson, 1995.

Dawkins, Richard. *The Selfish Gene*. Oxford: Oxford University Press, 2006.

Deneen, Patrick. *Why Liberalism Failed*. New Haven: Yale University Press, 2018.

De Castella, Tom. "Have Jedi Created a New 'Religion'?" BBC, October 25, 2014. https://www.bbc.com/news/magazine-29753530.

Dostoyevsky, Fyodor. *The Grand Inquisitor*. Translated by H. P. Blavatsky. Project Gutenberg, 2010. https://www.gutenberg.org/files/8578/8578-h/8578-h.htm.

Draz, M. A. (Muḥammad ʿAbdullāh Dirāz). *The Moral World of the Qur'an*. London: I. B. Tauris, 2008.

Elshinawy, Mohammed. "Why Do People Suffer? God's Existence and the Problem of Evil." Yaqeen Institute for Islamic Research, July 2, 2018. https://yaqeeninstitute.ca/read/paper/why-do-people-suffer-gods-existence-the-problem-of-evil.

Elshinawy, Mohammad. "Why Does God Ask People to Worship Him?" Yaqeen Institute for Islamic Research, December 26, 2017. https://yaqeeninstitute.ca/read/paper/why-does-god-ask-people-to-worship-him.

Elshinawy, Mohammad, and Omar Suleiman. "How Muhammad ﷺ Confronted Hate and Became the Most Influential Person in History." Yaqeen Institute for Islamic Research, January 2017. https://yaqeeninstitute.ca/read/paper/how-muhammad-confronted-hate-and-became-the-most-influential-person-in-history.

Eltal, Munir. "Structural Cohesion in the Qur'an: Surah al-Fatihah." Muslim Matters, May 19, 2023. https://muslimmatters.org/2023/05/19/structural-cohesion-in-the-quran-a-series-surah-al-fatihah/.

Ericson, Edward E. "Solzhenitsyn: Voice from the Gulag." *Eternity*, October 1985.

Facchine, Tom. "Are All Religions the Same? Islam and the False Promise of Perennialism." Yaqeen Institute for Islamic Research, September 13, 2023. https://yaqeeninstitute.ca/read/paper/are-all-religions-the-same-islam-and-the-false-promise-of-perennialism.

Foucault, Michel. *Discipline and Punish: The Birth of the Prison*. New York: Vintage Books, 1995.

Foucault, Michel. *Ethics: Subjectivity and Truth*. New York: The New Press, 1997.

Garner, Richard. "Morality: The Final Delusion?" *Philosophy Now* 82, 2011.

Gilmore, Anna, et al. "Defining and Conceptualising the Commercial Determinants of Health." *Lancet* 401, no. 10383 (2023): 1194–213.

Gormley, Shannon. "Why Liberalism Itself Wants Us to Be Alone." *Ottawa Citizen*, January 19, 2018. https://ottawacitizen.com/opinion/columnists/gormley-why-liberalism-itself-wants-us-to-be-alone.

Hallaq, Wael B. *Restating Orientalism*. New York: Columbia University Press, 2018.

Hallaq, Wael B. *The Impossible State*. New York: Columbia University Press, 2012.

Hammad, Ahmad Zaki. *The Opening to the Qur'an*. Bridgeview: Qur'anic Literary Institute, 1996.

Hani, Suleiman. "The Problem of Evil: A Multifaceted Islamic Solution." Yaqeen Institute for Islamic Research, April 20, 2020. https://yaqeeninstitute.ca/read/paper/the-problem-of-evil-a-multifaceted-islamic-solution.

Hao, Karen. "Artificial Intelligence Is Creating a New Colonial World Order." MIT Technology Review, April 19, 2022. https://www.technologyreview.com/2022/04/19/1049592/artificial-intelligence-colonialism/.

Harrington, Anne. "A Science of Compassion or a Compassionate Science? What Do We Expect from a Cross-Cultural Dialogue with Buddhism?" In *Visions of Compassion: Western Scientists and Tibetan Buddhists Examine Human Nature*. Edited by Richard J. Davidson and Anne Harrington. New York: Oxford Academic, 2002.

Ḥawwā, Saʿīd (d. 1989). *Al-Asās fī al-tafsīr*. Cairo: Dār al-Salām, 1985.

Hedges, Chris. *Empire of Illusion: The End of Literacy and the Triumph of Spectacle*. Toronto: Vintage Canada, 2010.

Hedges, Chris. "Israel's Willing Executioners." Consortium News, May 14, 2024. https://consortiumnews.com/2024/05/14/chris-hedges-israels-willing-executioners/.

Hicks, Stephen. *Explaining Postmodernism: Skepticism and Socialism from Rousseau to Foucault*. Tempe, AZ: Scholarly Publishing, 2004.

Hindy, Ibrahim and Nazir Khan. "Living Abraham's Legacy of Hajj: Relevance of Rites and Rituals in the Modern Age." Yaqeen Institute for Islamic Research, August 13, 2018. https://yaqeeninstitute.ca/read/paper/living-abrahams-legacy-relevance-of-rites-and-rituals-in-the-modern-age.

Ibn ʿĀshūr, Muḥammad al-Ṭāhir (d. 1973). *Al-Taḥrīr wa al-tanwīr.* Tunis: Dār al-Tunīsiyya, 1984.

Ibn ʿĀshūr, Muḥammad al-Ṭāhir (d. 1973). *Ibn Ashur: Treatise on Maqasid Al-Shari'ah*. Translated by Mohamed El-Tahir El-Mesawi. Washington: The International Institute of Islamic Thought, 2006.

Ibn ʿAṭāʾ Allāh. *Sufi Aphorisms (Kitāb al-ḥikam)*. Translated by Victor Danner. Leiden: Brill, 1973.

Ibn Fūdī, ʿUthmān ibn Muḥammad (d. 1817). *Ḍiyāʾ al-taʾwīl fī maʿānī al-tanzīl*. Sokoto: Al-Hajj Muhammad Ali Agha, n.d.

Ibn ʿUthaymīn, Muḥammad ibn Ṣāliḥ (d. 2001). *Tafsīr al-Fātiḥah wa al-Baqarah*. Riyadh: Dār Ibn al-Jawzī, 1423 AH.

Ibrahim, Yahya. "'Be a Man!' Constructing Prophetic Masculinity." Yaqeen Institute for Islamic Research, July 24, 2019. https://yaqeeninstitute.org/read/paper/be-a-man-constructing-prophetic-masculinity.

Ibrahim, Yuval. "'Lavender': The AI machine directing Israel's bombing spree in Gaza." +972 Magazine, April 3, 2024. https://www.972mag.com/lavender-ai-israeli-army-gaza/.

Idris, Jaafar Sheikh. "A Commentary on the First Chapter of the Quran." IslamReligion, November 1, 2010. https://www.islamreligion.com/articles/10190/first-chapter-of-quran.

Iṣlāḥī, Amīn Aḥsan (d. 1997). *Tadabbur-e-Qur'an: Pondering Over The Qur'an—Volume One: Tafsir of Surah al-Fatiha and Surah al-Baqarah*. Translated by Mohammad Saleem Kayani. Petaling Jaya: Islamic Book Trust, 2016.

"Israeli Apartheid: The Legacy of the Ongoing Nakba at 75." ReliefWeb, May 15, 2023. https://reliefweb.int/report/occupied-palestinian-territory/israeli-apartheid-legacy-ongoing-nakba-75-enar.

Izetbegović, Alija. *Islam between East and West*. Indianapolis: American Trust Publications, 1989.

Kahn, Paul. *Putting Liberalism in Its Place*. Princeton: Princeton University Press, 2005.

Kaminski, Joseph. *Islam, Liberalism, and Ontology*. London and New York: Routledge, 2021.

Kara, Siddharth. "Is Your Phone Tainted by the Misery of the 35,000 Children in Congo's Mines?" *The Guardian*, October 12, 2018. https://www.theguardian.com/global-development/2018/oct/12/phone-misery-children-congo-cobalt-mines-drc.

Kennedy, Emmet. *Secularism and Its Opponents from Augustine to Solzhenitsyn*. New York: Palgrave Macmillan, 2006.

Kent, Lauren. "European Colonizers Killed So Many Native Americans That It Changed the Global Climate, Researchers Say." CNN, February 2, 2019. https://www.cnn.com/2019/02/01/world/european-colonization-climate-change-trnd/index.html.

Khan, Nazir. "A Sacred Duty: Islam and Social Justice." Yaqeen Institute for Islamic Research, February 4, 2020. https://yaqeeninstitute.org/read/paper/a-sacred-duty-islam-and-social-justice.

Khan, Nazir. "Atheism and Radical Skepticism: Ibn Taymiyyah's Epistemic Critique." Yaqeen Institute for Islamic Research, July 7, 2020. https://yaqeeninstitute.org/read/paper/atheism-and-radical-skepticism-ibn-taymiyyahs-epistemic-critique.

Khan, Nazir. "Difference of Opinion: Where do we draw the line?" Yaqeen Institute for Islamic Research, December 10, 2019. https://yaqeeninstitute.org/read/paper/difference-of-opinion-where-do-we-draw-the-line.

Khan, Nazir. "Is Islam a Violent Religion? Debunking the Myth." Yaqeen Institute for Islamic Research, November 16, 2016. https://yaqeeninstitute.org/read/paper/is-islam-a-violent-religion-debunking-the-myth.

Khan, Nazir. "Shades of Structural Realism in Post-Classical Islamic Thought." *Theology and Science* 21, no. 3 (2023): 376–89.

Khan, Nazir, Safiah Chowdhury, and Tesneem Alkiek. "Women in Islamic Law: Examining Five Prevalent Myths." Yaqeen Institute for Islamic Research, July 2019. https://yaqeeninstitute.org/read/paper/women-in-islamic-law-examining-five-prevalent-myths.

Khan, Nazir and Yasir Qadhi. "Human Origins—Part 1: Theological Conclusions and Empirical Limitations." Yaqeen Institute for Islamic Research, August 31, 2018. https://yaqeeninstitute.org/read/paper/human-origins-part-1-theological-conclusions-and-empirical-limitations.

Kim, Jaegwon. *Mind in a Physical World*. Cambridge, MA: MIT Press, 1998.

Kimball, Roger. "The Perversions of Michel Foucault." *The New Criterion*, March 1993.

Kravik, Andreas Motzfeldt. "We Must Avoid Double Standards in Foreign Policy." Al Jazeera, April 18, 2024. https://www.aljazeera.com/opinions/2024/4/18/we-must-avoid-double-standards-in-foreign-policy.

Lambert, Michael C., Elisa J. Sobo, and Valerie L. Lambert. "Rethinking Land Acknowledgments." *Anthropology News*, December 20, 2021. https://www.anthropology-news.org/articles/rethinking-land-acknowledgments.

Law, David. *The Historical-Critical Method: A Guide for the Perplexed*. New York: Continuum, 2012.

Lee, Alfred McClung, and Elizabeth Briant Lee. *The Fine Art of Propaganda*. New York: Octagon Books, 1972.

Lumbard, Joseph. "Islam and the Challenge of Epistemic Sovereignty." *Religions* 15, no. 4 (2024).

Lyotard, Jean-François. *The Postmodern Condition: A Report on Knowledge*. Translated by Geoff Bennington and Brian Massumi. Minneapolis: University of Minnesota Press, 1984.

Machiavelli, Niccolo. *The Prince*. Translated by Peter Constantine. New York: Random House, 2007.

Malcolm X (d. 1965). *The Autobiography of Malcolm X: As Told to Alex Haley*. New York: Grove Press, 1964.

Masalha, Nur. *Expulsion of the Palestinians*. Washington, DC: Institute for Palestine Studies, 1992.

Massad, Joseph. *Islam in Liberalism*. Chicago: University of Chicago Press, 2015.

Masse, Eli. "Ilan Pappe: Israel Is the Last Remaining, Active Settler-Colonialist Project." In These Times, May 5, 2016. https://inthesetimes.com/article/ilan-pappe-bernie-sanders-noam-chomsky-bds-israel-palestine.

Miller, Hans-Georg. "Wokeism: A Global Civil Religion in the 'Age of Profilicity'?" *Meridian* 4 (March 2023).

Moad, Edward Omar. "Tying Your Camel: An Islamic Perspective on Methodological Naturalism." Yaqeen Institute for Islamic Research, March 28, 2018. https://yaqeeninstitute.org/read/paper/tying-your-camel-an-islamic-perspective-on-methodological-naturalism.

Mohammed, Amjad. *Muslims in Non-Muslim Lands: A Legal Study with Applications*. Cambridge: Islamic Texts Society, 2013.

Morris, Catherine. "Less than a Third of American Women Identify as Feminists." Ipsos, November 25, 2019. https://www.ipsos.com/en-us/american-women-and-feminism.

Nadwi, Mohammad Akram. *Al-Muhaddithat: The Women Scholars in Islam*. Oxford: Interface Publications, 2007.

Nadwi, Mohammed Akram. *Al-Wafāʾ bi-asmāʾ al-nisāʾ*. Jedda: Dar al-Minhāj, 2021.

Nagel, Thomas. *Mind and Cosmos: Why the Materialist Neo-Darwinian Conception of Nature Is Almost Certainly False*. New York: Oxford University Press, 2012.

Nakissa, Aria. "Liberalism's distinctive policy for governing Muslim populations: Human rights, religious reform, and counter-terrorism from the colonial era until the present", *History Compass*, 20 no. 9 (2022): e12748.

Nayed, Aref Ali. "Does Moral Action Depend on Reasoning? No, It Does Not!" In *Does Moral Action Depend on Reasoning? Thirteen Views on the Question*. Templeton Foundation, 2010.

Nursi, Bediuzzaman Said. *The Flashes*. Translated by Sukran Vahide. Istanbul: Sozler Publications, 2009.

Oborne, Peter. "Israel's Slaughter of Aid Workers Is a Tragedy. But It Is Also a Story of Western Racism." Middle East Eye, April 3, 2024. https://www.middleeasteye.net/opinion/israel-slaughter-aid-workers-tragedy-western-racism.

Pappé, Ilan. "Zionism as Colonialism: A Comparative View of Diluted Colonialism in Asia and Africa." *South Atlantic Quarterly* 107, no. 4 (October 1, 2008): 611–33.

Pilkington, Ed. "Top UN Official in New York Steps Down Citing 'Genocide' of Palestinian Civilians." *Guardian* (US), October 31, 2023. https://www.theguardian.com/world/2023/oct/31/un-official-resigns-israel-hamas-war-palestine-new-york.

Pinker, Steven. *Enlightenment Now: The Case for Reason, Science, Humanism, and Progress*. New York: Penguin Books, 2018.

Pinker, Steven. *The Better Angels of Our Nature: Why Violence Has Declined*. New York: Penguin Publishing Group, 2011.

Postman, Neil. *Amusing Ourselves to Death*. London: Penguin Books, 1985.

Potvin, Jacqueline, and Mayme Lefurgey. "Canada's Inaction in Gaza Marks a Failure of Its Feminist Foreign Policy." The Conversation, March 12, 2024. https://theconversation.com/canadas-inaction-in-gaza-marks-a-failure-of-its-feminist-foreign-policy-225067.

Prinz, Jesse. *The Emotional Construction of Morals*. Oxford: Oxford University Press, 2008.

Quijano, Aníbal. "Coloniality And Modernity/Rationality." *Cultural Studies* 21, no. 2 (2007): 168–78.

Quijano, Aníbal, and Michael Ennis. "Coloniality of Power, Eurocentrism, and Latin America." *Nepantla: Views from South* 1, no. 3 (2000): 533–80.

Quṭb, Sayyid. *In the Shade of the Qur'an*. Translated by Adil Salahi. Leicester: The Islamic Foundation, 2007.

Raïssouni, Ahmed. *Fiqh al-thawrah: Murājaʿāt fī al-fiqh al-siyāsī al-Islāmī*. Cairo: Dār al-Kalimah, 2013.

Rectenwald, Michael. "Mid-Nineteenth-Century Secularism as Modern Secularity." In *Organized Secularism in the United States: New Directions in Research*. Edited by Ryan T. Cragun, Christel Manning, and Lori L. Fazzino, pp. 31–56. Berlin: De Gruyter, 2017.

Riḍā, Muḥammad Rashīd (d. 1935). *Tafsīr al-manār*. Cairo: al-Hayʾa al-Miṣriyyah al-ʿĀmmah li-l-Kitāb, 1990.

"'Robodogs' Part of Israel's 'Army of Robots' in Gaza War." The New Arab, March 6, 2024. https://www.newarab.com/news/robodogs-part-israels-army-robots-gaza-war.

Rosenberg, Alex. *The Atheist's Guide to Reality: Enjoying Life Without Illusions*. NY: WW Norton, 2011.

Ross, Samuel. "What Were the Most Popular Tafsīrs in Islamic History? Part 1: An Assessment of the Manuscript Record and the State of Tafsīr Studies." *Journal of Qur'anic Studies* 25, no. 3 (2023): 1–54.

Rummel, R. J. *Death by Government*. Rutgers, NJ: Transaction Publishers, 1994.

Sardar, Ziauddin. *Postmodernism and the other: the new imperialism of Western culture*. London: Pluto Press, 1998.

Sedgwick, Mark. *Traditionalism: The Radical Project for Restoring Sacred Order*. New York: Oxford University Press, 2023.

Şentürk, Recep. "Unity in Multiplexity: Islam as an Open Civilization." *Journal of the Interdisciplinary Study of Monotheistic Religions (JISMOR)* 7 (2011): 49–60.

Shafīʿ, Muḥammad (d. 1976). *Maʿārif al-Qurʾān*. Translated by M. Hasan Askari and M. Shamim. Karachi: Maktaba-e Darul Uloom, 1996.

Shalev, Tal. "IDF Co-ed Battalion Makes History by Sending Women Troops to Gaza." *Jerusalem Post*, December 15, 2023. https://www.jpost.com/israel-hamas-war/article-778101#google_vignette.

Sim, Stuart. "Postmodernism and Philosophy." In *The Routledge Companion to Postmodern Philosophy*. Edited by Stuart Sim. London: Routledge, 2001.

Solomon, Norman. "Harris Refuses to Change Course on US Complicity With Israel's Genocide in Gaza." *Common Dreams*, August 30, 2024. https://www.commondreams.org/opinion/harris-refuses-to-change-course-on-us-complicity-with-israel-s-genocide-in-gaza.

Soomro, Taha, and Sharif Randhawa. "The Qur'an's Engagement with Christian and Jewish Literature." Yaqeen Institute for Islamic Research, February 28, 2023. https://yaqeeninstitute.ca/read/paper/the-qurans-engagement-with-christian-and-jewish-literature.

Spenser, Nick. "Are the Better Angels Really Winning?" *Theos*, January 17, 2024. https://www.theosthinktank.co.uk/comment/2024/01/17/are-the-better-angels-really-winning.

Stern, Adam Y. "On Zionism and the Concept of Deferral." *Critical Times* 5, no. 1 (April 1, 2022): 20–49.

Sullivan, Dylan, and Jason Hickel, "Capitalism and Extreme Poverty: A Global Analysis of Real Wages, Human Height, and Mortality Since the Long 16th Century." *World Development* 161 (2023): 106026.

Sullivan, Dylan, and Jason Hickel. "How British Colonialism Killed 100 Million Indians in 40 Years." Al Jazeera, December 22, 2022. https://www.aljazeera.com/opinions/2022/12/2/how-british-colonial-policy-killed-100-million-indians.

Ṭaha, ʿĀbidīn. *Al-Jāmiʿ fī hidāyāt al-Qurʾān: Sūrat al-Fātiḥah.* Mecca: Muʾassasat al-Nabaʾ al-ʿAẓīm, 2020.

Tucker, Dorothy. "For women at the DNC, nomination of Kamala Harris is deeply personal." *CBS News*, August 22, 2024. https://www.cbsnews.com/chicago/news/women-dnc-nomination-kamala-harris-deeply-personal.

Twenge, Jean, et al. "Egos Deflating with the Great Recession: A Cross-Temporal Meta-Analysis and Within-Campus Analysis of the Narcissistic Personality Inventory, 1982–2016." *Personality and Individual Differences* 179 (2021): 110947.

Vosoughi, Soroush, et al., "The Spread of True and False News Online." *Science* 359, no. 6380 (2018): 1146–51. https://doi.org/10.1126/science.aap9559.

Wahb, Yousef. "Fard Kifaya: The Principle of Communal responsibility in Islam," Yaqeen Institute for Islamic Research, June 10, 2021, https://yaqeeninstitute.org/read/paper/fard-kifayah-the-principle-of-communal-responsibility-in-islam.

Walid, Dawud. "How to Deal With Racism: Lessons From West African Scholars' Tafsīr of Sūrah al-Ḥujurāt." Yaqeen Institute for Islamic Research, June 23, 2023. https://yaqeeninstitute.ca/read/paper/how-to-overcome-racism-lessons-from-west-african-scholars-tafsir-of-surat-al-hujurat.

Watson, Peter. *The Age of Atheists: How We Have Sought to Live Since the Death of God*. New York: Simon and Schuster, 2014.

Yaqeen Institute. "Islam and the LGBT Question: Reframing the Narrative." Yaqeen Institute for Islamic Research, October 7, 2022, https://yaqeeninstitute.org/read/paper/islam-and-the-lgbt-question-reframing-the-narrative.

Yousef, Jinan. "Understanding the Qur'an Through the Names and Attributes of Allah." Yaqeen Institute for Islamic Research, March 30, 2023. https://yaqeeninstitute.org/read/paper/approaching-the-quran-through-the-names-of-allah.

Zarabozo, Jamaal. *Al-Fatihah: An In-Depth Study of Surah al Fatiha*. 28 Audio CD set. Boulder, CO: SoundKnowledge Audio Publishers, 2006.

Zeni, Tallal. *Revival of Piety through an Islamic Theodicy*. Seattle: KDP, 2020.

Zeni, Tallal. "The Divine Wisdom in Allowing Evil to Exist: Perspectives from Ibn al-Qayyim." Yaqeen Institute for Islamic Research, December 6, 2018. https://yaqeeninstitute.ca/read/paper/the-divine-wisdom-in-allowing-evil-to-exist-perspectives-from-ibn-al-qayyim.

Zinner, Samuel. "The Qur'ān's Detailed Knowledge of the Bible: The Explanatory Inadequacy of the 'Conversational' or 'Christian Missionaries' Models." *Interdisciplinary Studies of Quran and Hadith* 1, no. 2 (2023): 109–26.

Notes

Notes